LONDON ASSOCIATION OF CLASSICAL TEACHERS

LACTOR 4

INSCRIPTIONS OF ROMAN BRITAIN

Third Edition

EDITED BY
Valerie A. Maxfield
and
Brian Dobson

INSCRIPTIONS OF ROMAN BRITAIN

First edition   – July 1969
   (entitled Some Inscriptions from Roman Britain)
Second edition   – February 1972
Third edition   – May 1995

© The London Association of Classical Teachers, 1969, 1995

ISBN: 0 903625 23 7

TABLE OF CONTENTS

4

ILLUSTRATIONS

PREFACE TO THE THIRD EDITION

Exactly a quarter of a century has elapsed since the first appearance of LACTOR 4, and a continuing demand for the volume has led to the production of this 3rd. edition. In the last twenty-five years, even an epigraphically impoverished province such as Britain has produced a significant number of new inscriptions. Particularly notable among the new finds are three major collections of texts written in cursive Latin on lead and wood – two sets of curses, from the temple sites at Bath and Uley, and a remarkable assemblage of wooden writing tablets from the early timber forts at Chesterholm-Vindolanda. A small selection of these has been included in this volume, plus the most significant of the stone inscriptions found since 1969. The opportunity has also been taken to revise and update the entries, expanding the notes and incorporating the results of recent research.

The integration of new material has inevitably resulted in some renumbering of the entries, and the opportunity has therefore been taken at the same time to make minor adjustments to the ordering of some of the existing entries, for example, putting some into a more strictly chronological order (e.g. Hadrian's Wall milecastle inscription before the fort inscriptions). One completely new section has been added, that on Writing Tablets (Part IX), and a new category (curses) added within the religion section (Part VIII(d)). To lessen the inconvenience this may cause to those who will be using the old and new editions side by side, a concordance has been provided (inside front cover) and the individual entry numbers from the old editions retained (in brackets) beside the new numbers. A few more texts relating to, though found outside of, Roman Britain have been added; this adds further weight to a point made in a review of the first edition, and the title of the volume now reflects this – *Inscriptions of Roman Britain*.

Other changes include the use of a small number of line drawings to show the way in which inscriptions are laid out, the inclusion of a glossary of Latin terms, and the splitting up of Index 5 (Place and Tribe-Names) into two separate indices: one (Index 6) of the geographical names mentioned within the texts of the inscriptions, the other (Index 7) of the places where the inscriptions were found. A new Index 5 lists buildings and monuments mentioned in inscriptions.

Exeter   V. A. Maxfield
Durham   B. Dobson
July 1994

ACKNOWLEDGEMENTS

The production of this revised and expanded edition has been assisted in a variety of ways by numerous people. We are most grateful to Dr. C. Haselgrove for providing a note on the British coinage and individual notes on nos. 1–6, to Mr. P. J. Casey for commenting on the Roman coin entries, and to Professors M. Crawford, S. S. Frere and J. C. Mann for updating their notes on Coinage, on The Source Value of Inscriptions and on Religion respectively. The contribution by the late Professor A. L. F. Rivet on Roman Epigraphy has had very minor updating by the editors [whose comments have been added between square brackets].

Thanks are due to Oxford University Press for permitting us once again to take the majority of our entries from *The Roman Inscriptions of Britain* Vol. I; and to the following: Alan Sutton Publishing, Ltd., for the Haverfield Bequest (*RIB* Vol. II); Dr. A. K. Bowman, Dr. J. D. Thomas, and British Museum Press (excerpts from *The Vindolanda Writing Tablets (Tabulae Vindolandenses II)*); and the Society for the Promotion of Roman Studies (texts from the *Journal of Roman Studies* and *Britannia*).

Thanks are due also to Dr. R. S. O. Tomlin for permitting reproduction of the drawing which appears as Fig. 9, and to the Museum of Antiquities of the University and Society of Antiquaries of Newcastle upon Tyne, per Miss L. Allason-Jones, for providing the photograph on which Fig. 4 is based. The map and the line-drawings of the inscriptions are the work of Sue Rouillard from the Drawing Office of the Department of History and Archaeology at Exeter University.

Finally we should like to thank most warmly Mr. Malcolm Young for the very great care and attention to accuracy of detail that he has given to every stage of this revision.

FROM THE PREFACE TO THE FIRST EDITION

This selection is intended to present much of the inscriptional evidence underlying S. S. Frere's *Britannia*, for the convenience of both those with and those without a working knowledge of Latin. It arose out of the need for those studying the JACT "A" level syllabus to have Romano-British epigraphic evidence in front of them; it is hoped that other students and teachers may find the collection of interest.

Our primary debt is to Professor S. S. Frere for his thoroughly generous assistance, not only in supplying the basis of the collection but also in checking and correcting, and adding many valuable notes; also for his Foreword. We are grateful to Mr. A. L. F. Rivet of Keele University for his article and much information and advice besides; to Mr. A. R. Burn, late of Glasgow University; and to Mr. Michael Crawford of Christ's College, Cambridge for his work on the coinage sections of the collection.

We gratefully record the substantial financial help given by the Cambridge Faculty of Classics and by JACT Council; also the permission of Oxford University Press to take the majority of our entries from *The Roman Inscriptions of Britain* Vol. I, by R. G. Collingwood and R. P. Wright.

Harrow School   M. C. Greenstock
July 1969

FROM THE PREFACE TO THE SECOND EDITION

We are much indebted to Dr. J. C. Mann for his generous help with this edition, and also for his article on Religion.

October 1971   M. C. Greenstock

THE SOURCE-VALUE OF INSCRIPTIONS

In a Roman province such as Britain, which received only sporadic and often brief mention in the works of contemporary historians, the inscriptions erected by the inhabitants or by the garrison offer an invaluable independent source of information to the modern student. They are contemporary factual records, uncoloured by the conscious or unconscious bias of the ancient writer of history, and they provide a wide variety of information not found in other written sources and unlikely to be obtainable by purely archaeological investigation.

Official building records often date more or less closely the erection or repair of the buildings to which they relate, thus filling in the outline chronology, e.g. of frontier history, which is obtainable from historical sources. By careful isolation of contemporary material found in excavation of such structures a firm chronology can be extended to remains such as pottery, which thus acquire validity as independent means of dating. Such inscriptions, too, often give the names of governors, officers or officials whose careers so attested are of interest to the student of government, and of military units whose distribution and movements throw light on the history and organisation of the Roman army. In addition they sometimes give clues to the status of towns or to the organisation of local affairs in Britain.

Tombstones are often of use for the same ends, besides providing a wealth of information about the composition, thoughts or expectation of life of the ancient population. Dedications illustrate the workings of polytheism, the balance between official cults and those of major or minor Celtic deities, or the spread of novel religions from the oriental parts of the Empire.

Even *graffiti*, cut for instance on tiles or pottery vessels, can yield useful information on the names of manufacturers, the status of owners and the types and frequency of personal names used in Roman Britain, as well as on such subjects as the units of weight and capacity in common use.

In all these ways epigraphy, the study of inscriptions, broadens our knowledge of Roman Britain and its place in the Roman Empire, and provides depth of focus to our study of the remains revealed by excavation.

Many inscriptions are broken, battered or fragmentary when found. A study of the selection offered in this book, mainly of the better-preserved pieces, will show that certain word-orders and formulae tend to recur, and that a number of widely-used abbreviations can be recognised. Experience shows that a knowledge of these, together with a consideration of the space available for missing letters, will often enable a reasonably certain restoration to be made. Naturally, this involves a study of the stone itself or an accurate drawing of it. Reference should be made to R. G. Collingwood and R. P. Wright, *The Roman Inscriptions of Britain*, the source of the greater part of this selection, where facsimiles of all stones will be found.

New discoveries of inscribed material are potentially important, however fragmentary, and should be communicated to Dr R. S. O. Tomlin, Wolfson College, Oxford OX2 6UD (for northern Britain) or to Mr. M. W. C. Hassall, Institute of Archaeology, University College London, 31–34 Gordon Square, London WC1H 0PY (for southern Britain), who are responsible for the report on discoveries published annually in *Britannia* by the Society for the Promotion of Roman Studies. (Prior to 1969 these reports appeared in the *Journal of Roman Studies*.)

Oxford 1969 and 1994. S. S. Frere

NOTES ON ROMAN EPIGRAPHY

(References are to the numbers of the inscriptions in the text)

1. Modern Conventions

In printing inscriptions, the following conventions are in general use:

[...]   Square brackets enclose letters which are thought to have been originally engraved but which have been lost through the breaking or defacement of the stone. [In this volume, three dots have been used to indicate missing matter; no attempt has been made to show the estimated length of the omission.]

(...)   Round brackets enclose letters which have been added by the epigraphist to complete an abbreviated word; or, less commonly, which have been substituted by him to correct a blunder.

< >   Angular brackets enclose letters which the epigraphist believes were included in error.

| A vertical bar indicates the beginning of a fresh line on the stone.

P͡R P̄R   Ligatures (defined in 2(b) below), are indicated by a bar, straight or curved, over the letters which are joined. [There are several examples in Fig. 5, but they are not used in the text of this volume.]

A̤   A dot placed under a letter indicates that it is not fully legible (through decay or erasure). [This convention is not used in this volume.]

Various other conventions are sometimes employed, and in using a work it is always worth while to look for a "list of critical signs".

2. Techniques

(a) Materials. The normal material for monumental inscriptions is stone, but wood and bronze were also used, and sometimes bronze letters were fixed to wood or stone. Military diplomas (see 3(g) below) are engraved on bronze. Pottery and tiles carry impressions of stamps, and the stamps themselves might be of clay, wood or metal. Metal ingots are cast in moulds with embossed letters, but may have additions incised. Cursive graffiti (266) may be scratched on metal, clay or plaster, or written in ink on wood. Paint was also used.

(b) Lettering is always in capitals, but may be "monumental", which is deliberately formal, or "cursive", which is produced by the rapid use of a stylus or brush. The latter increasingly influenced the former, especially when the mason was working from letters chalked for him on stone. In good monumental work the strokes of the letters are cut with a chisel to a V-section, but in rough work a punch or mason's pick might be used; the guide-lines used by the mason to keep the lettering straight can occasionally be seen. In monumental inscriptions the letters were usually picked out with cinnabar (*minium*); traces of it are occasionally found (29, 195, 202), and some museums restore inscriptions to their original appearance by painting the lettering red (51).

Words are commonly abbreviated by docking their ends, and plurals are expressed by doubling, trebling or even quadrupling the last letter (thus AVGG = two Augusti, AVGGG three Augusti, etc.). Ligatures, or combined letters, become increasingly common after the first century AD (thus VETVSTATE may become VƎVSTAᴱ, or TIB ᵗB). Greek letters are less uniformly capital (126, 261). In letters, V is the normal form of U, and K often supplants C (e.g. KANOVIO, 166). In numerals, note that the forms IIII and VIIII may be used instead of IV and IX. Words are usually divided by stops, which may be simple or decorative and which are placed opposite the middle of the letter (i.e. not at its foot like a full stop). Words may be broken at any point to fit the lines; and stops are occasionally introduced in mid-word (51, 152, 171).

(c) *Erasures* were sometimes made deliberately as the result of a *damnatio memoriae* passed by the Senate on a deceased Emperor. Over 30 Emperors were condemned after death in this way, including Geta (e.g. 83) and Gordian III (see on 100).

3. Types of Inscription and Formulae

(a) *Religious Dedications*, usually of altars but sometimes of statues or whole temples (137). These normally begin with the name of the deity or deities (in the dative), followed by the name and status of the dedicator (in the nominative) and a verb or formula, usually abbreviated (e.g. P = *posuit*, REST = *restituit*, or, most common of all, V.S.L.M. = *votum solvit libens merito*) though this may be omitted (196). The reason for the dedication is sometimes stated (49, 72).

(b) *Honorific inscriptions*, often cut on the base of a statue (46). These give the name and rank, and often the career, of the man who is being honoured (in the dative), followed by a statement of the dedicator, usually corporate (in the nominative), with or without a verb (139).

(c) *Commemorative plaques* recording perhaps a victory or a vow of allegiance (127n., 136).

(d) *Building inscriptions* recording the erection or repair of buildings. These vary from lengthy accounts to a bald statement of the man or body responsible (29, 138). The longer examples may include:

(i) *The name and titles of the reigning Emperor* – in the nominative if he is the builder, in the dative if it is in his honour, in the ablative if it is intended merely to record the date; this is expressed in terms of his consulship and tribunician power (see below).

(ii) *The name and status of the builder*, if other than (i); this may be either an individual or a military unit, with or without the name of its commander (64).

(iii) *The nature of the building* – PORTAM, HORREVM, PRINCIPIA etc.

(iv) *If it is reconstruction*, its previous condition may be noticed – VETVSTATE CONLAPSVM (83), VI IGNIS EXVSTVM etc. (see esp. 149). If it is a complete reconstruction or a new building, it may be described in a form such as A SOLO RESTITVIT etc.

(v) The name of the man in charge of the work, who may be the provincial governor (65) or the commander of the unit (84). A very important class of building inscriptions are the stones from Hadrian's Wall and the Antonine Wall which record the lengths constructed by different units (e.g. 56).

(e) Milestones were set up when a road was first constructed or when it was repaired. They consisted of stone pillars bearing an inscription which gave, first, the name and titles of the reigning Emperor (in the nominative or ablative), secondly, his consulate and tribunician power, and finally the mileage from a stated town (the Roman mile, of 1,000 *passus*, measured 1618 yards = 1480 metres). Later, in the third and fourth centuries, new stones seem to have been erected purely for propaganda purposes and only the Emperor's name and titles are inscribed, but it is possible that the mileage figure was added in paint. (See 141 and 166–168 for examples of milestones).

(f) Tombstones are very numerous and the form of words varies a great deal. The commonest beginning is D M or DIS MANIBVS ("To the spirits of the Departed") followed by the name in the dative or nominative (or genitive, 24). But we also have MEMORIAE ("to the memory of ...") followed by the genitive, or the name may come first, either in the nominative or (with "the tomb of" implied) in the genitive. The name may be given in full, with that of the deceased's father, his voting-tribe (if he is a Roman citizen) and his place of origin. The careers of soldiers and prominent men are often recorded; soldiers' tombs give the length of their service, and a statement of age is normal. The heir, relative or friend who erects the stone is commonly added (128, 186). Common last lines are HSE (*hic situs est*) and STTL (*sit tibi terra levis*). But many other phrases occur, sometimes poignantly personal (185, 227). The pagan formula D M curiously persists even on some Christian tombstones, but here the age is often given as PLVS MINVS LX ("more or less sixty"), possibly to express unconcern over length of life in this world (270).

(g) Military diplomas were the certificates issued to auxiliary soldiers on completion of 25 years' service or on discharge, confirming the grant of Roman citizenship on themselves and their children and legitimising their children. Each diploma consisted of two linked bronze plates, to be folded together and sealed, and was a copy of an edict posted up in Rome. Hence it included the name and titles of the Emperor, the units to which the edict referred, the province in which they were serving and the name of its governor, followed by the date, the name of the individual soldier, and the names of seven witnesses to the accuracy of the copy (33). [All of the military diplomas from Roman Britain have been republished together in *RIB* 2.1. 2401, with general introductory comments by M. M. Roxan. A further four (or possibly five) diplomas relating to Britain appear in *RMD* III.]

(h) Other inscriptions include the stamps on tiles and ingots of metal (23, 25), seals, potters' stamps, votive plaques (often bronze) (228), curses (265, 266, 268), oculists' stamps (for impressing on ointment) and graffiti – words and sentences scratched on various objects (142). The latter particularly may reflect spoken Latin, though this is evidenced also in more formal inscriptions [as for example nos. 8 and 159].

(4) The Dating of Inscriptions

Under the Empire official Roman dating continued to be by reference to the *consules ordinarii* who took office at the beginning of the year, but consular dates are rare on inscriptions, especially in Britain. Much more useful are the statements of the Emperor's powers and titles, and especially his tenure of *tribunicia potestas*, for this provides the equivalent of regnal years. Down to the end of the third century, every Emperor assumed this power at or soon after his accession, and from Nerva onwards the normal pattern is that while his TRIB POT I may begin at any date, his TRIB POT II begins on 10 December. So Hadrian, for example, who succeeded Trajan in August AD 117, dates his TRIB POT I from 11 August 117, his TRIB POT II from 10 December 117, his TRIB POT III from 10 December 118, and so on.

Another indication of date is provided by the number of consulships held by an Emperor. When Hadrian succeeded he had already been consul once, in 108; he held his second consulship in 118 and his third and last in 119. So from January 119 until his death in 138 he may be described as COS III. Inscriptions may also record the number of times an Emperor has been saluted as IMPERATOR, and other offices and titles he holds. Hadrian was saluted as IMPERATOR for the first time in 117, for the second (IMP II) in 135; he became PONTIFEX MAXIMVS (P.M.) in 117 and PATER PATRIAE (P.P.) in 128 [though on nos. 141 and 166 it is incorrectly ascribed to him prior to this date]. Finally there are titles derived from victories. These are often useful in identifying an Emperor whose actual name is missing from the surviving fragments of an inscription, but they are especially valuable for dating when a title was assumed during his reign: Trajan, for example, became DACICVS in 102, PARTHICVS in 116.

Because of local differences in style and variations in the skill of the engravers, it is extremely difficult to date inscriptions, even approximately, by the form of the letters; this can be attempted only by a very experienced epigraphist.

Keele University 1969   A. L. F. Rivet
[with minor editorial comment added 1994]

Note

A full list of the Emperors from Augustus to Constantine III, with the dates of their tribunician power and consulships, will be found in Collingwood and Richmond 1969, Appendix, 326–333.

A NOTE ON BRITISH COINAGE

The inhabitants of southern Britain began to use coinage in the 100 years preceding Julius Caesar's invasions in 55–54 BC. The earliest issues were uninscribed, and it was not until the later 1st. century BC that short legends began to be added to the different coin types. These inscriptions are normally in the Roman alphabet, and their appearance belongs to the period when Roman influence was beginning to make itself felt in south-east England, most probably due to several British rulers having established treaties of friendship with the Roman emperor Augustus. The earliest coin types were of gold and cast bronze, with silver and struck bronze issues coming into widespread usage only after Caesar's invasions.

In the absence of written British history and the relative silence of Roman authors about the situation in Britain between Caesar's and Claudius's invasions, inscribed British coins provide a valuable, if sketchy, source of information about political developments in the island. From the coins themselves, we learn the personal names of the rulers under whose authority they were issued, while the circulation pattern of their coinages gives us a broad idea of the areas under their control. Some individuals evidently succeeded in uniting two or more peoples under their sole rule, while others evidently ruled over only part of the territories later formalised by the Roman authorities as separate administrative cantons. The overall picture is one of relative instability, with few of these kingdoms surviving long after the eclipse of their founder.

In addition to the issuer's name, coin legends sometimes make reference to his lineage and status, using Latin words such as *filius* (son) and *rex* (king) to do so. It is often suggested that the latter title denotes British rulers who had been formally recognised as Roman client kings, but this is not necessarily the case. A few coin types bear the name of the place where they were minted, usually in abbreviated form. Where the details given on the coinage can be checked against the passing references to Britain by the classical authors, they appear substantially accurate. Cunobelinus, for example, whose abundant coinage is found throughout south-east England, is described by Suetonius as "king of the Britons", while Cassius Dio refers to Camulodunum – which appears in abbreviated form on several of his types – as the "seat of his kingship". Together with the copying of dated Roman coins, such incidental details also help us to establish the approximate periods when different rulers reigned. By the time of Augustus's death in AD 14, two British rulers, Dumnobellaunus and Tim-..., the latter almost certainly the individual whom we know from his coinage as Tincommius, had sought refuge with the Roman emperor, while Cunobelinus was evidently not long dead when Claudius's armies invaded southern England in AD 43.

Further Reading

The reference numbers used in Part I refer to R. D. Van Arsdell's catalogue, *Celtic Coinage of Britain*, published by Spink and Son, London, in 1989. This contains photographs and descriptions of most known British coin types. Note, however, that few other scholars accept the very precise dating scheme put forward by Van Arsdell.

For a brief introduction to pre-Roman coinage in Britain, see D. Nash, *Coinage in the Celtic World*, B. A. Seaby, London, 1987, and D. F. Allen, *An Introduction to Celtic Coinage*, British Museum, London, 1976. A compendium of known legends on British Iron Age coins, with accompanying commentary, is given by M. Mays, Inscriptions on British Celtic coins, *Numismatic Chronicle* 1992, 57–82.

Durham 1994   Colin Haselgrove

A NOTE ON ROMAN COINAGE

The legends and types on ancient coins can do two things: indicate the author-ity responsible for the coins, and convey a message put out by that authority. The first of these is essential for a coin to be a coin at all; the second is an optional extra.

The Greeks, who took over the Lydian invention of coinage and spread it through the Greek world, on the whole only concerned themselves with the first possibility. The important coinages of Classical Greece, those of Athens, Corinth and Aegina, bore a more or less constant type which was the badge of the city. Thus the silver tetradrachms of Athens bore the head of Athena on one side and the owl of Athena (the mark also used to brand prisoners in the Samian War) on the other. With the advent of the Hellenistic monarchs the same approach to coin types was given a new twist – the coins bore their own portraits, as their badge and the symbol of their sovereignty, together with their titles, e.g. "PTOLEMAIOU BASILEOS" ("Of King Ptolemy") etc. The coinage of pre-Roman Britain is a distant barbarian derivation from the coinage of the Hellenistic world.

When the Roman Republic took over the notion of coinage in the early third century BC it entrusted production to a junior magistracy, holders of which were regularly chosen from the ranks of the aristocracy. These men naturally enough came to place their own distinguishing marks on the coins they produced, e.g. an allusion to a famous ancestor or to his great deeds. With the beginning of the Civil Wars, the heads of Caesar, Antony, Brutus etc. appeared on the coinage, in imitation of the coins of the Hellenistic monarchs. Augustus, the victor in the Civil Wars, made the coinage the property of himself and his family: the Emperor's head became the normal obverse type, and an allusion to various aspects of his position or a commemoration of important events the normal reverse type. Neither evidence nor probability suggests that coin types were a matter of Imperial policy. We should rather envisage the artists in the Mint, whose patron was the Emperor, mingling on the coinage standard items (such as the Emperor's head and his principal virtues) with their own portrayals of the more striking events in the Imperial calendar. The precise significance of S(ENATVS) C(ONSVLTO) on the bronze coinage is disputed (its apparent absence on no. 95 is probably due to the poor preservation of all recorded spec-imens). It is not now believed that the Senate had any effective control over the bronze coinage.

The standard equivalents are as follows:

    1 aureus = 25 denarii
    1 denarius = 16 asses
    1 sestertius = 4 asses
    1 dupondius = 2 asses
    1 antoninianus = 2 denarii

The gold coinage of the Roman Empire was reformed by Diocletian,whose gold unit, slightly modified, became the solidus of Constantine.

The radiate crown is a symbol of autocracy and divinity: it does not occur on the head of a living Emperor before Nero.

Christ's College, Cambridge, 1969   Michael Crawford
Department of History, University College, London, 1994

A NOTE ON RELIGION

The Romans made no attempt to force their religion on other peoples, or to interfere with native religions, unless the latter involved inhuman or obscene practices. Thus they suppressed the human sacrifice associated with the cult of Baal in north Africa, and with Druidism in Gaul and Britain. Hence the opposition of the Druids to Rome. They did not rally popular opposition, and their political importance has been exaggerated.

The effect of the Roman presence varied. In remote rural areas Celtic religious practices undoubtedly survived little changed. (Inscriptions tell us nothing of this: their evidence is therefore partial and distorting.) Celtic religion does not seem to have advanced far beyond the merely propitiatory stage – appeasing vaguely-defined supernatural powers in advance, to avert disasters – and had only just begun to create individual deities. Roman influence, where it impinged, helped to "crystallise" Celtic deities as individual powers.

Roman religion had advanced further. Relations with gods involved a sort of contract. The dedicant vowed (in advance) to do something afterwards – usually to dedicate an altar – if the god would act for him (e.g. save his life in battle). After the desired end was achieved, the dedicant "paid his vow". The commonest formula is V.S.L.M. (*passim*).

Romans and Britons alike saw no real difference between Roman and Celtic deities, or deities originating elsewhere. Thus the Roman Mars and the Celtic Lenus (162) appeared to be the same war-god. (The Celts might have different names for the same god in different areas, cf. 231–3, 237). So we find Romans worshipping British gods (69, 173, 230, 240–2, 255, 259) and Britons worshipping Roman gods (137, 213, 221, 225, cf. 158); and Roman and native gods are often fused together (82, 148, 162, 206, 211, 228, 231–3, 237, 244, 250, 258).

The Romans made political use of religion in only two ways:

(a) by instituting the "Provincial Cult" honouring deified (former) emperors, the cult maintained by a council of delegates from the cities (which contributed according to wealth), which met probably at or near London (156, 224). This provided an outlet for the loyalty, and ambition, of leading provincials (the Council chose annually a "High Priest of the Province"), but its most important function was not religious: it formed a means of direct communication with the emperor, for petitions, complaints, etc., by-passing the governor.

(b) by instituting a very full military religious calendar of festivals, to promote the loyalty of troops to their unit, to the empire and especially to the emperor. The "official" deities cultivated – on fixed days – by units included both traditional Roman gods like Jupiter, Juno, Minerva and Mars, and even Hercules, and also new military aspects like Victoria (87, 211), Disciplina (e.g. *RIB* 1127) and the standards of the unit (111, cf. 222). The calendar included annual vows to Jupiter on 3 January (44, 45, 198, 218–20), and ceremonies on the birthday and accession-day of the emperor, or previous emperors (222), and the birthday of the unit.

In private life, while soldiers (and provincials) might thus be influenced to cultivate "official", or other, Roman deities (59, 221, 223, 226, 266), they often preferred non-Roman gods, both British, like Belatucadrus (230) or Veteris (255), and others from elsewhere, like Jupiter Dolichenus from Syria (263) or Serapis from Egypt (169). The official military religious policy probably had little effect.

A widespread and quite spontaneous development was the cult of the *numen* of the emperor. As defined by Varro and Festus, *numen* implies power – the god-like power of the emperor. The emperor was all-powerful – he could even banish gods – but refused to allow provincials to accord him divine status while yet living. Provincials got round this by creating a deity out of his enormous power. Dedications, whether to "official" gods (82, 131, 159, 218, 222–3) or others (162, 164, 234–6, 243), whether public dedications, e.g. by units (159, 218, 234–6, 243, cf. 156) or by private individuals (131, 146, 162, 223) are often accompanied, and reinforced, by a dedication to the *numen Augusti*. This development is a natural growth: it has nothing to do with the Provincial Cult.

But as imperial bureaucracy expanded, and government became more and more impersonal and crushing, so the ordinary provincial felt less and less direct personal involvement in the empire's fate. The old, mechanical paganism, in spite of some vague belief in a shadowy after-life (cf. the formula *Dis Manibus* and note 227), ceased to seem meaningful, and more and more people turned to systems of belief which did offer a place, and a commitment, to the individual: the "mystery religions", particularly Mithraism (264), and Christianity (265, note; 267, note; 269).

These have much in common, involving man in the struggle of good with evil, in which man is championed by a saviour who appears as divine. Mithraism taught bravery and honesty, and thus was popular with military officers and merchants, but it was expensive for its adherents, and excluded women.

Christianity had more to offer, to all ranks, and to both men and women. It spread slowly, in the cities at first, only beginning to win over the countryside after the middle of the fourth century. But when Roman rule came to an end the Britons were essentially a Christian people.

Durham 1971; Milton Keynes 1994   J. C. Mann

NOTES AND ABBREVIATIONS

Each entry in the collection consists of:

Title line: entry number; in brackets the equivalent number for the entry in editions 1 and 2 (where different) or (-) indicating a new entry; description of entry; date (usually the date of dedication or issue).

Publication details: publication reference; find-spot, with Latin name where known; nature of the inscription, when and where found; present location.

The text: the original Latin of the inscription (see Notes on Epigraphy for conventions used); translation into English. (A few terms, which do not translate easily, are left in the Latin and defined in the Glossary.)

Notes: brief comments on the significance of the inscription, drawing attention to recent work and, where appropriate, to alternative readings and interpretations. Full details of the publications to which reference is made appear in the Bibliography.

Line drawings have been provided of a representative sample of the texts, designed to show a building inscription, a tombstone, an altar, an example of ligatured letters etc. *RIB* contains line-drawings of all the entries published therein.

The Roman and Hellenic Societies maintain a large slide collection which contains material relevant to Roman Britain. Individual *slides* and *slide sets* may be hired by members only; but an increasing number of *filmstrips* (i.e. strips of unmounted slides) is now available for purchase by both members and non-members. For details write to: The Keeper of Slides, Joint Library of the Hellenic and Roman Societies, 31–34 Gordon Square, London WC1H 0PP.

Abbreviations used in the text

AE   *Annee Épigraphique.*

BMC   *Coins of the Roman Empire in the British Museum,* ed. H. Mattingley (1923–62). London.

CIL   *Corpus Inscriptionum Latinarum,* edd. T. Mommsen *et al.* (1866 cont.). Berlin.

CSIR   *Corpus Signorum Imperii Romani: Great Britain, Volume I.* Oxford.

DG   *Transactions of the Dumfries and Galloway Natural History and Antiquarian Society.*

G.   P. Grierson and M. Mays, *Catalogue of late Roman coins in the Dumbarton Oaks Collection* (1992). Washington (DC).

ILS   *Inscriptiones Latinae Selectae,* ed. H. Dessau (1892–1916). Berlin.

JRS   *The Journal of Roman Studies.*

L11   *Literary Sources for Roman Britain,* edd. J. Mann and R. G. Penman (1978–85) (LACTOR 11)

L15   *Dio: the Julio-Claudians*, ed. J. Edmondson (1992) (LACTOR 15)

OLD   *Oxford Latin Dictionary*

RIB   *The Roman Inscriptions of Britain.*
Vol. I: Inscriptions on Stone, edd. R. G. Collingwood and R. P. Wright (1967). Oxford.
Vol. II: Instrumentum Domesticum, fascs. 1–6, edd. S. S. Frere and R. S. O. Tomlin (1990–1994).

RIC   *Roman Imperial Coinage*, edd. H. Mattingley, E. A. Sydenham *et al.* (1923 cont.). London.

RMD   M. M. Roxan, *Roman Military Diplomas 1954–1977*. Institute of Archaeology Occasional Publication No. 2 (1978). London (Nos. 1–78).

RMD II   M. M. Roxan, *Roman Military Diplomas 1978–1984*. Institute of Archaeology Occasional Publication No. 9 (1985). London. (Nos. 79–135).

RMD III   M. M. Roxan, *Roman Military Diplomas 1985–1993*. Institute of Archaeology Occasional Publication No. 14 (1994). London. (Nos. 136–).

RPC   A. Burnett *et al., Roman Provincial Coinage. Vol. I.* (1992). London.

SHA   *Historia Augusta.*

Tab. Vindol. 1   A. K. Bowman and J. D. Thomas, *Vindolanda: the Latin Writing Tablets*. Britannia Monograph No. 4 (1983). London. (Nos. 1–117).

Tab. Vindol. 2   A. K. Bowman and J. D. Thomas, *The Vindolanda Writing Tablets (Tabulae Vindolandenses II)* (1994). London. (Nos. 118–573).

PART I: FROM CAESAR TO CLAUDIUS (55 BC–AD 43)

1   Gold stater of Tincommius   *c.* 20–10 BC

Van Arsdell 375

> *Obverse:* TINC(OMMIVS)
>
> *Reverse:* Horseman. Below, C(OMMI) F(ILIVS)
>
> The titulature runs continuously from obverse to reverse: "Tincommius son of Commius".

The fine lettering and well-cut horseman suggest a classically-trained die cutter who copied the horseman design from a Roman denarius. Cruder copies of this coin also exist (e.g. Van Arsdell 385). Tincommius must have succeeded Commius *c.* 30–20 BC and the adoption of Roman models in the later stages of his coinage implies that he was one of the British rulers who concluded treaties of friendship with the Roman authorities across the channel during Augustus's reign. He is later recorded by Roman sources as having sought the protection of the emperor, and we must assume that around the end of the 1st. century BC he was ejected from his kingdom south of the Thames by a rival.

2   Gold stater of Tasciovanus   *c.* 20–1 BC

Van Arsdell 1780

> *Obverse:* TASCIOV(ANVS) RICON (Some die varieties have RICONI)
>
> *Reverse:* Horseman.

Tasciovanus was a contemporary of Tincommius. He ruled a kingdom centred to the north of the Thames, and some of his coin types show similar traces of Roman influence. It is sometimes suggested that the word RICON on this stater is a British title, equivalent to the Roman REX, but this is uncertain. Many coins attributed to Tasciovanus bear the mint-mark VER or VERLAMIO, confirming that a British centre of importance preceded the Roman city at St. Albans. The horseman on this particular coin is apparently depicted wearing a coat of mail similar to the example found among the contents of a rich British tomb which was recently excavated there.

3   Silver coin of Eppillus   *c.* 10 BC–AD 10

Van Arsdell 415.

> *Obverse:* Crescent between two stars. REX and CALLE(VAE) above and below crescent.
>
> *Reverse:* Eagle. Behind, EPP(ILLVS).
>
> The titulature runs continuously from reverse to obverse: "Eppillus, king of Calleva".

Eppillus was another ruler who described himself on his coinage as a son of Commius. His reign probably overlapped that of Tincommius, and the mint-mark CALLEVA bears out the evidence of recent archaeological excavations which show that there was an important British settlement on the site of Roman Silchester well before the end of the 1st. century BC. Eppillus appears to be the first British ruler to use the Roman title REX on his coinage.

4   Gold stater of Verica   *c.* AD 20–40

Van Arsdell 520.

> *Obverse:* VIRI(CA), split by vine-leaf.

> *Reverse:* Horseman. Around, CO(MMI) F(ILIVS).

> The titulature runs continuously from obverse to reverse, "Virica, son of Commius".

This coin may be the work of a Roman-trained engraver, and the vine-leaf on the obverse has been suggested as symbolising the pro-Roman outlook of Verica's kingdom. Verica, the third southern ruler to style himself "son of Commius", probably succeeded Eppillus as the ruler of Calleva sometime in the early 1st. century AD. One of his earlier gold stater issues (Van Arsdell 500) bears the legend COM.F/VIR REX. Verica is undoubtedly synonymous with the British ruler called Berikos by the Roman historian Cassius Dio (see LACTOR 11 p. 32): his subsequent ousting in civil war was used by Claudius as a pretext for the Roman invasion in AD 43.

5   Gold stater of Cunobelinus   *c.* AD 20–40

Van Arsdell 2025.

> *Obverse:* Ear of corn. CA and MV(LODVNVM) on either side.

> *Reverse:* Horse. Below, CVNO(BELINVS).

Between *c.* AD 10 and 40 much of south-east England north and south of the Thames was ruled over by Cunobelinus, whose capital was at Camulodunum, pre-Roman and Roman Colchester, where this coin was apparently minted. The ear of barley on the obverse of Cunobelinus's gold is evidently a counterpart to the vine-leaf on Verica's issues, although the precise significance of this emblem is unclear.

6   Bronze coin of Cunobelinus   *c.* AD 25–40

Van Arsdell 2095.

> *Obverse:* Head (perhaps intended for that of Cunobelinus). Around, CVNOBELINVS REX.

> *Reverse:* Bull butting. Below, TASC(IOVANI FILIVS).

> The titulature runs continuously from obverse to reverse: "King Cunobelinus, son of Tasciovanus".

This is the only issue of Cunobelinus to bear the title REX and belongs to the later stages of his coinage. Unlike his coin types which carry the mint-mark CAMV, those with the legend TASCIOVANI F(ILIVS) are thought to have been issued from a second mint, possibly at Verlamion (St. Albans). There is no independent evidence to indicate whether Cunobelinus was actually a son of Tasciovanus, or whether he simply laid claim to the relationship to legitimate his succession to the domains previously ruled over by Tasciovanus.

PART II: THE FIRST CENTURY (AD 43–98)

(a) THE CLAUDIAN INVASION (AD 43–47)

7   Claudia Prima tombstone   Claudian or Neronian

CIL 13. 3542. *Boulogne* (Bononia). *A stone plaque found in the 18th. century near the Porte Gayole. In the Haigneré-Vaillant Museum.*

> Ti(berius) Claudius | Aug(usti) l(ibertus) Seleucus | tr(ierarchus) monument(um) | fecit Claudiae | Primae l(ibertae) suae.

> "Tiberius Claudius Seleucus, freedman of the emperor, ship's captain, erected this monument to Claudia Prima his freedwoman."

This is perhaps the oldest inscription from Boulogne, the port from which the Claudian invasion force set sail. Gaius had built a lighthouse here and it is the site of a first-century fort, probably the headquarters of the *classis Britannica*. Boulogne has a number of tombstones of naval personnel, suggesting that it was early (and continued to be) an important base for the fleet. Seleucus was freed by Claudius (whose names he took), which sets a limit on the date of the epitaph.

8   Longinus Sdapeze (ala I Thracum)   AD 43–49

RIB 201. *Colchester* (Camulodunum). *Tombstone found in 1928 near no. 18. Now in Colchester Museum.*

> Longinus Sdapeze | Matygi f(ilius) duplicarius | ala prima T(h)racum pago | Sardi(ca) anno(rum) XL aeror(um) XV | heredes exs testam(ento) [f(aciendum)] c(uraverunt) | h(ic) s(itus) e(st).

> "Longinus Sdapeze, son of Matygus, *duplicarius* in the first cavalry regiment of Thracians, from the district of Sardica, aged 40, of 15 years' service, lies buried here; his heirs had this set up under his will."

The relief shows a cavalryman in scale armour on a richly caparisoned horse, riding over a crouching naked barbarian. Above this relief is a winged sphinx flanked by lions; round each lion is twined a snake. Thracians are known to have served in the Roman army prior to the creation of the province of Thrace (the area now southern Bulgaria and northern Turkey) in AD 46 (Tac. *Ann.* 4.46), so the *ala I Thracum* could have come over with the initial invasion force in AD 43 and been stationed at Colchester some time between then and the creation of the colony in the winter of AD 49–50. Two military bases are known at Colchester: a fortress below the later city and, to the south, at Gosbecks, a fort. This unit perhaps occupied the fort, whether before, after or at the same time as Legion XX occupied the fortress is not known. The stone is in good condition but is defaced, suggesting overthrow, soon after erection, in the Boudican rebellion. An alternative reading of the name is "Longinus son of Sdapezematygus". The *duplicarius* was second-in-command of a cavalry *turma* (troop); his rank reflects his pay grade – he received double pay.

Vulgar Latin, such as *exs* for *ex*, is not uncommon (note also no. 11), and may reflect the spoken language; cf. Mann 1971.

9   Dannicus (ala Indiana)   Claudian–early Flavian

RIB 108. *Cirencester (Corinium). A tombstone found in 1835 at Watermoor near the south gate of Corinium, beside Ermin Street. Now in the Corinium Museum.*

> Dannicus eq(ues) alae | Indian(ae) tur(ma) Albani | stip(endiorum) XVI cives Raur(icus) | cur(averunt) Fulvius Natalis et | Fl[avi]us Bitucus ex testame(nto) | h(ic) s(itus) e(st).

> "Dannicus, cavalryman of the *ala Indiana*, from the troop of Albanus, served for 16 years, a citizen of the Raurici, lies buried here; Fulvius Natalis and Fl[avi]us Bitucus *(set this up)* according to his will."

The relief shows a cavalryman poising his lance over his prostrate enemy. The Raurici lived in the area around Augst (Augusta Raurica) on the upper Rhine. The *ala Indiana* was originally raised in Gaul; it was named after Julius Indus, a tribesman of the Treveri (from the Trier region), who led a band of native cavalry loyal to Rome, in the suppression of a native uprising in AD 21 (Tac. *Ann.* 3.42). Subsequently the band was incorporated as a regular unit of the Roman army and was stationed in upper Germany, where Dannicus was recruited. Dannicus died in service, so if the unit came to Britain in AD 43, he cannot have lived beyond the year AD 58. However, the stone may be later in date than this – AD 69 at earliest – if the name of one of Dannicus's heirs is correctly restored as Fl[avi]us; in this case the unit cannot have come over to Britain as early as AD 43. The fort at Cirencester was occupied from *c.* AD 45 to *c.* AD 75.

On Julius Indus see also no. 24.

10   Sex. Valerius Genialis (ala Thracum)   Claudian to early Flavian

RIB 109. *Cirencester (Corinium). A tombstone found in 1836 near no. 9. Now in Corinium Museum.*

> Sextus Vale|rius Genialis | eq(u)es alae Trhaec(um) | civis Frisiaus tur(ma) | Genialis an(norum) XXXX st(ipendiorum) XX | h(ic) s(itus) e(st) (h)e(res) f(aciendum) c(uravit).

> "Sextus Valerius Genialis, cavalryman of the *ala Thracum*, a citizen of the Frisiavones, in the troop of Genialis, aged 40 years, of 20 years' service, lies buried here; his heir had this set up."

A gabled tombstone with a relief which shows a cavalryman brandishing his lance above a fallen enemy. He carries a shield and also an enigmatic item which is probably a standard. The Frisiavones lived in the area of the lower Rhine, close to its mouth, so it is probable that Genialis was recruited to the *ala Thracum* when it was serving in Lower Germany, its base before it came to Britain. If that is so, Genialis, with 20 years' service, can have died no later than AD 62. Hence the Thracians may have been based at Cirencester before the *ala Indiana*. This is probably the same cavalry unit (the *ala I Thracum*) as is attested at Colchester (no. 8). Note that Genialis has the *tria nomina* of a Roman citizen.

11   Rufus Sita (cohors VI Thracum)   Mid-1st. century AD

RIB 121. *Gloucester* (Glevum). *A tombstone found in 1824 at Wootton, about a kilometre to the east of the site of the early military base at Kingsholm. Now in Gloucester City Museum.*

> Rufus Sita eques c(o)ho(rtis) VI | T(h)racum ann(orum) XL stip(endiorum) XXII | heredes exs test(amento) f(aciendum) curave(runt) | h(ic) s(itus) e(st).

> "Rufus Sita, cavalryman in the Sixth Cohort of Thracians, aged 40, of 22 years' service, lies buried here; his heirs had this stone erected according to his will."

A relief above this inscription shows a cavalryman with a shield in his left hand, a long sword (a *spatha*) at his right side, brandishing a spear over his fallen enemy. Above this scene is a sphinx, guardian of the tomb, flanked by lions, symbols of the consuming power of death. There is the same combination of motifs on the tombstone of a Thracian cavalryman from Colchester (above, no. 8). The unit in which Sita served is a mixed unit, a *cohors equitata*. *Cohors VI Thracum* is thought to have formed part of the garrison of Kingsholm, a military base founded in the 40s and evacuated in the late 60s, predating the Gloucester fortress. It possibly shared accommodation here with part of Legion XX, commemorated in the same cemetery by a fragmentary (and now lost) tombstone (*RIB* 122). Rufus (like Longinus in no.8) is a Latin "given" name. *Exs* in place of *ex* also appears on no.8, to which this stone bears several similarities.

12   Ti. Claudius Tirintius (cohors Thracum)   Before AD 72

RIB 291. *Wroxeter* (Viroconium). *Part of a tombstone, found in 1783 just north of the basilica. Now in Rowley's House Museum, Shrewsbury.*

> Tib(erius) Claud(ius) Tiri|ntius eq(ues) coh(ortis) [...] Thracum an[n]|orum LVII sti[p]|endior(um) XX[...] h(ic) s(itus) e(st).

> "Tiberius Claudius Tirintius, cavalryman of the ... Cohort of Thracians, aged 57 years, of [20+] years' service, lies buried here."

The relief above the tombstone shows a cavalryman riding over his fallen enemy. The number of the cohort is missing. It may be *cohors VI* (attested at Gloucester, no. 11) or *cohors I* which is known to have been in Britain by AD 122 (*CIL* 16.69). Tirintius had probably served at least 25 years since he has already received Roman citizenship. His names, Ti. Claudius, indicate a grant from either Claudius or Nero, so this inscription must date no later than early Flavian. A military base was established at Wroxeter in the mid-first century, presumably in connection with Ostorius Scapula's campaign against the Silures. A legionary fortress, an auxiliary fort and camps are known in the area.

13   L. Vitellius Tancinus (ala Vettonum)   c. AD 50–60

RIB 159. *Bath* (Aquae Sulis). *A tombstone found in 1736 in the old market place. Now in the Roman Baths Museum.*

L(ucius) Vitellius Malntai f(ilius) Tancinus I cives Hisp(anus) Caurie(n)sis
I eq(ues) alae Vettonum c(ivium) R(omanorum) I ann(orum) XXXXVI
stip(endiorum) XXVI I h(ic) s(itus) e(st).

"Lucius Vitellius Tancinus, son of Mantaius, a citizen of Caurium in Spain,
cavalryman of the *ala Vettonum*, Roman citizen, aged 46, of 26 years'
service, lies buried here."

The relief above the inscription shows a cavalryman riding over a prostrate
enemy. Tancinus probably took the names Lucius Vitellius on receiving Roman
citizenship in the year 47–48 when L. Vitellius was *censor* with Claudius. It
would be typical of Claudius to insist that his colleague should share fully in
the censorship, giving his names to some of the new citizens. The award could
have been made to Tancinus when he had completed 25 years' service; alternatively he may have earned it at any stage during his career, on the occasion
when the unit in which he was serving, the *ala Vettonum*, received its block grant
of citizenship, commemorated in the title *c(ivium) R(omanorum)* which it bears.
The dating of the inscription depends on which of these alternatives is correct,
lying somewhere between AD 48 and the late 60s. As a Spaniard serving in a
Spanish unit, he was probably recruited to the unit before it came to Britain.
This tombstone is one of the pieces of evidence suggesting that there may have
been a Roman fort at Bath.

14   C. Gavius Silvanus (cohors Praetoria)   Mid-1st.century AD

CIL 5.7003 = *ILS* 2701. *Turin* (Augusta Taurinorum), *Italy*.

C(aio) Gavio L(uci) f(ilio) I Stel(latina) Silvano I [p]rimipilari leg(ionis) VIII
Aug(ustae) I [t]ribuno coh(ortis) II vigilum I [t]ribuno coh(ortis) XIII
urban(ae) I [tr]ibuno coh(ortis) XII praetor(iae) I [d]onis donato a divo
Claud(io) I bello Britannico I [to]rquibus armillis phaleris I corona aurea I
[p]atrono colon(iae) I d(ecreto) d(ecurionum).

"To Gaius Gavius Silvanus, son of Lucius, of the voting tribe Stellatina,
formerly senior centurion of the Eighth Legion Augusta, tribune of the
Second Cohort of the City Fire Brigade, tribune of the Thirteenth Urban
Cohort, tribune of the Twelfth Praetorian Cohort, decorated by the deified
Claudius in the British war with necklets, armlets, medals and a gold crown.
(Set up) to the patron of the colony by decree of the decurions."

Gavius Silvanus was executed as a praetorian tribune in AD 65 (Tac. *Ann.*
15.71). Thus at the time of the British war he will have been at a relatively early
stage in his career, probably serving as an *evocatus* in the praetorian guard
(retained in service while awaiting promotion to a centurionate). The level of his
decorations is appropriate to that rank. Details of the early service of senior
centurions is often omitted from inscriptions. He will certainly not by AD 43 have
risen as high as *primus pilus* (senior centurion), a post which he held in Legion
VIII; this inscription does not therefore provide evidence for the participation of
Legion VIII in the British invasion, as has previously been argued. The decurions who decreed the inscription are local magistrates, members of the city council,
of what was Silvanus's home town, as the voting tribe shows. See nos. 150–152.

15 (–) M. Vettius Valens (cohors Praetoria)   AD 66

CIL 11.395 = *ILS* 2648. *Rimini* (Ariminum), *Italy.*

> M(arco) Vettio M(arci) f(ilio) Ani(ensi) I Valenti I mil(iti) coh(ortis) VIII
> pr(aetoriae) I benef(iciario) praef(ecti) pr(aetorio) I donis donato bello
> Britan(nico) I torquibus armillis phaleris I evoc(ato) Aug(usti) corona aurea
> donat(o) I (centurioni) coh(ortis) VI vig(ilum) (centurioni) stat(orum)
> (centurioni) coh(ortis) XVI urb(anae) (centurioni) coh(ortis) I II pr(aeto-
> riae) ...

> "Marcus Vettius Valens, son of Marcus, of the voting tribe Aniensis,
> soldier in the Eighth Praetorian Cohort, *beneficiarius* on the staff of the
> praetorian prefect, decorated in the British war with necklets, armlets and
> medals, *(appointed) evocatus* and awarded a gold crown, centurion of the
> Sixth Cohort of the City Fire Brigade, the *statores*, the Sixteenth Urban
> Cohort, the Second Praetorian Cohort ..."

Vettius Valens served in Claudius's British campaign as a member of the
emperor's bodyguard (the praetorian cohorts) and was decorated twice, once as
an orderly on the staff of the commanding officer of the guard (the prefect) and
once after he had been kept on (*evocatus*) beyond the normal 16-year term of
service – the same rank and the same scale of award as that at which Gavius
Silvanus (no. 14) was decorated in Britain. He was subsequently promoted centurion, rose high in the military service and went on to serve as a procurator in
Lusitania (posts recorded in the latter part of this inscription, not quoted). The
statores were based at the Praetorian camp in Rome: they functioned as military police.

16   P. Anicius Maximus (legio II Augusta)   Claudian

CIL 3. 6809 = *ILS* 2696. *Antioch in Pisidia* (Antiochia) *in the Roman province
of Galatia (modern Turkey).*

> P(ublio) Anicio I P(ublii) f(ilio) Ser(gia) Maxilmo praefecto I Cn(aei) Domiti
> Ahenobarlbi p(rimo) p(ilo) leg(ionis) XII Fulm(inatae) praef(ecto) I
> castror(um) leg(ionis) II Aug(ustae) in I Britannia praef(ecto) exercitu qui
> est in Aegypto I donato ab imp(eratore) donis I militaribus ob expediltionem
> honorato I corona murali et I hasta pura ob bellum I Britannic(um) civitas
> I Alexandr(iae) quae est I in Aegypto h(oc) c(onstituit).

> "To Publius Anicius Maximus, son of Publius, of the voting tribe Sergia,
> prefect of Gnaeus Domitius Ahenobarbus, senior centurion of Legion XII
> Fulminata, camp prefect of Legion II Augusta in Britain, prefect of the
> army in Egypt, awarded military decorations by the emperor on account
> of the expedition, honoured on the occasion of the British war with a mural
> crown and a ceremonial spear. The city of Alexandria which is in Egypt
> set this up."

The career of Anicius Maximus is dated by the references to Domitius
Ahenobarbus, who died in AD 40, and to the British War, which must be that of
Claudius in AD 43. Gnaeus Domitius Ahenobarbus, Nero's father, was probably

an honorary local magistrate at Antioch in Pisidia at an unknown date; if so, he would have served *in absentia* with a "prefect" acting as his deputy. The camp prefect was a member of the equestrian order, and was third in line of command of the legion, ranking only after the legate and the *tribunus laticlavius*, the senatorial tribune. (Poenius Postumus was camp prefect when left in command of Legion II, or part of it, presumably because his two superiors were absent with Paulinus in Wales: Tac. *Ann.* 14.37 = L11, 25.) The prefect of the army in Egypt seems to have been the senior military officer in Egypt, an imperial province where no senators (hence no legate nor laticlave tribune) were permitted to set foot. He served under the prefect of Egypt, one of the highest-ranking of equestrian officials. Anicius Maximus was awarded military decorations on two occasions: the cryptic reference to an emperor (unnamed) suggests an award by Gaius. The second occasion was the British war. The award of a crown and a spear is the one appropriate to his rank.

17   Gaius Saufeius (legio IX)   Claudio-Neronian

RIB 255. *Lincoln* (Lindum). *Tombstone found in 1865 on the west side of High Street. Now in the British Museum.*

> C(aio) Saufeio | C(ai) f(ilio) Fab(ia) Her(aclea) | militi legio(nis) | VIIII | annor(um) XXXX | stip(endiorum) XXII | h(ic) s(itus) e(st).

> "To Gaius Saufeius, son of Gaius, of the Fabian voting tribe, from Heraclea, soldier of the Ninth Legion, aged 40, of 22 years' service; he lies here."

Gaius Saufeius, like his comrade in Legion IX, Quintus Cornelius (no. 176), lacks a *cognomen*. Elsewhere in the empire soldiers without *cognomina* are almost all pre-Claudian, and the few examples in Britain should therefore date to the early years of the conquest, thus giving a *terminus ante quem* for the arrival of the legion at Lincoln (Keppie 1995). The Lincoln fortress (situated in the upper part of the city) is known to date no earlier than *c.* AD 60, so it is probable that there was an earlier military base nearby, probably on the lower ground to the south by the river, nearer to the cemetery area where this inscription was found. Heraclea was in Thrace.

18   M. Favonius Facilis (legio XX)   AD 43–49

RIB 200. *Colchester* (Camulodunum). *A tombstone found in 1868 in a Roman burial area on the west side of Colchester. Now in the Castle Museum, Colchester.* (Fig. 1).

> M(arcus) Favon(ius) M(arci) f(ilius) Pol(lia) Facilis c(enturio) leg(ionis) XX Verecundus et Novicius lib(erti) posuerunt h(ic) s(itus) e(st).

> "Marcus Favonius Facilis, son of Marcus, of the voting tribe Pollia, centurion of the Twentieth Legion; Verecundus and Novicius his freedmen set this up; here he lies."

Above the text is a relief of the soldier. It shows Facilis in military uniform, wearing a cuirass and *pteruges* and carrying a *vitis* (a vinestick), the staff of office of the centurion. The stone was originally painted. Near it was found a

Fig. 1

lead container with cremated bones inside, and a pottery cup of mid-first-century date. If Facilis was still a serving soldier at the time of his death (and this is by no means certain, as ex-centurions do not always call themselves veterans), it must have occurred while his legion was still based at Colchester, that is before the winter of 49–50, when, it may be inferred from Tacitus (*Ann.* 12.32 = L11, 16), it moved west. Note that the legion lacks its honorary titles, *Valeria Victrix*, Brave and Victorious, which it was probably awarded in AD 61 as a result of its conduct in the suppression of the Boudican rebellion (but cf. no. 129 note). This stone, together with no. 8, is thought to have been overthrown in the Boudican rebellion when Colchester was sacked (Tacitus *Ann.* 14.32 = L11, 22).

19   M. Petronius (legio XIV Gemina)   Mid-1st.century AD

RIB 294. *Wroxeter* (Viroconium). *A tombstone found in 1752 with RIB 293 (no. 129). Now in Rowley's House Museum, Shrewsbury.*

M(arcus) Petronius | L(uci) f(ilius) Men(enia) | Vic(etia) ann(orum) | XXXVIII | mil(es) leg(ionis) | XIIII Gem(inae) | militavit | ann(os) XVIII | sign(ifer) fuit | h(ic) s(itus) e(st).

"Marcus Petronius, son of Lucius, of the Menenian voting tribe, from Vicetia, aged 38 years, a soldier of the fourteenth Legion Gemina, served 18 years, was a standard-bearer and lies buried here".

Legion XIV Gemina received the honorary titles *Martia Victrix* in AD 61 in recognition of the part it played in the suppression of the Boudican rebellion. Although the titles are sometimes omitted from inscriptions even after this date, it is more likely that both this inscription and no.181 (also from Wroxeter) date to before AD 61. The absence of a *cognomen* for Petronius is consistent with a date in the early years of the conquest (Keppie 1995, and cf. no. 17). Archaeological evidence for the foundation of the known Wroxeter fortress now dates it to the late 50s. Vicetia is now Vicenza in north-east Italy. Italy continued to provide the majority of recruits to the legions until the early second century when provincials started to dominate.

20   Aureus of Claudius   AD 46–47

RIC Claudius 9 = BMC Claudius 32

Obverse: TI(BERIVS)   CLAVD(IVS)   CAESAR   AVG(VSTVS) P(ONTIFEX)   M(AXIMVS)   TR(IBVNICIA)   P(OTESTATE)   VI IMP(ERATOR) XI. Head of Claudius wearing laurel wreath.

"Tiberius Claudius Caesar Augustus, chief priest, in his sixth year of tribunician power, hailed *imperator* eleven times."

Reverse: No legend. Triumphal arch surmounted by equestrian statue flanked by two trophies: inscribed DE BRITANN(IS).
"*(Erected in commemoration of victory)* over the Britons."

Gold coin (*aureus*) minted in Lyons. For the commemorative arches set up in celebration of Claudius's British victory see no.22.

Silver coins were issued by Caesarea in Cappadocia with the legend DE BRITANNIS, which show Claudius in his triumphal chariot celebrating the conquest of Britain. (PJC).

21   Claudius to the athletes   AD 46

P. Lond. (Greek Papyri in the British Museum) 3.215

"Tiberius Claudius Caesar Augustus Germanicus Sarmaticus, *pontifex maximus*, in his sixth year of tribunician power, designated consul for the fourth time, acclaimed *imperator* twelve times, father of his country – Greetings to the association of touring athletes. I received with pleasure the gold crown which you sent me on account of the victory over the Britons, as a perpetual symbol of your loyalty to me. The delegates were Tiberius Claudius Hermas; Tiberius Claudius Cyrus; Dio son of Mykkalos, from Antioch."

For the full text in translation see Lewis and Reinhold 1966, 232.

22   Arch of Claudius   AD 51

ILS 216. Rome (Roma). Inscription above the arch of Claudius, over the Via Flaminia; still standing in the fifteenth century. Fragments now in the courtyard of the Palazzo dei Conservatori, Capitoline Museum.

Ti(berio) Clau[dio Drusi f(ilio) Cai]sari | Augu[sto Germani]co | pontific[i maximo trib(unicia) potes]tat(e) XI | co(n)s(uli) V im[p(eratori) XX patri pa]triai | senatus po[pulusque] Ro[manus q]uod | reges Brit[anniai] XI [devictos sine] | ulla iactur[a in deditionem acceperit] | gentesque b[arbaras trans Oceanum sitas] | primus in dici[onem populi Romani redegerit].

"Tiberius Claudius Caesar Augustus Germanicus, son of Drusus, *pontifex maximus*, in his eleventh year of tribunician power, consul five times, hailed as *imperator* (22 or 23) times, father of his country; erected by the Senate and people of Rome because he received the submission of eleven British kings, conquered without any loss, and because he first brought barbarian tribes beyond Ocean into the dominion of the Roman people."

Cf. Cassius Dio 60.22.1 (= L 11, 34; L 15, 98 and 219): "The Senate on hearing of his achievement voted him the title *Britannicus* and permission to celebrate a triumph. It was further enacted that ... two triumphal arches should be erected, one in Rome and the other in Gaul." Note also the coin (no.20) illustrating a triumphal arch. It was in fact Claudius's son who received the title *Britannicus*. The eleven British kings presumably include those who were won over by diplomacy as well as those who submitted to force. The arch in Gaul was perhaps erected at Boulogne whence the invasion army had set sail for Britain (see no.7). The achievements of Caesar in Britain seem to have been forgotten or brushed aside. Note the archaic spelling, typical of Claudius's antiquarianism. The arch carried statues of members of the imperial house.

(b) THE SETTLEMENT OF THE SOUTH (AD 47–69)

23 Mendip lead pig (?) AD 49

RIB 2.1.2404.1. Found near Wookey Hole, 8 kilometres south of Charterhouse on Mendip; described by Leland. Now lost.

> Ti(berius) Claud(ius) Caesar Aug(ustus) p(ontifex) m(aximus) tr(ibunicia) p(otestate) VIIII imp(erator) XVI de Britan(nicis).

> "Tiberius Claudius Caesar Augustus, *pontifex maximus*, in his ninth year of tribunician power, sixteen times acclaimed *imperator*, from the British *(mines)*."

Evidence that the lead/silver mines in the Mendips were being exploited under Roman control within six years of the Claudian invasion. Doubts have, however, recently been raised as to whether the object on which this text appeared was an ingot, as is generally assumed, suggesting rather that, given the word-length and complexity, it was a commemorative plaque (Whittick 1982, discussed in *RIB* 2.1.2404.1). Leland described it as "an oblong tablet of lead" (*oblonga plumbi tabula*).

24 Tombstone of Julius Classicianus, procurator *c.* AD 61–64

RIB 12. London (Londinium). Fragments of tomb found partly in 1852, partly in 1935 in a bastion of the Roman city wall. Now in the British Museum. (Fig. 2).

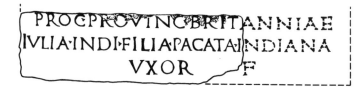

Fig. 2

Dis | [M]anibus | [C. Iul(ii) C(ai) f(ilii) F]ab(ia) Alpini Classiciani | ... | ... | proc(uratoris) provinc(iae) Brita[nniae] | Iulia Indi filia Pacata I[ndiana (?)] | uxor [f(ecit)].

"To the spirits of the departed and of Gaius Iulius Alpinus Classicianus, son of Gaius, of the Fabian voting tribe, ... procurator of the province of Britain. Julia Pacata I[ndiana], daughter of Indus, his wife, had this built."

A carved bolster (also found in 1852) probably belongs to this monument. In AD 61 Classicianus succeeded Catus Decianus as procurator (chief finance officer), sent by Nero after the Boudican rebellion. Having the power to report directly to the emperor, he criticised Suetonius Paulinus for his handling of the rebellion, and as a result, after a special commissioner had been sent to investigate, Suetonius was recalled (Tacitus, *Ann.* 14.38–39 = L11, 25). Classicianus was himself a provincial; he almost certainly came from northern Gaul (Birley 1981, 420) and had married the daughter of a Treveran noble (Julius Indus) who had helped to suppress the rebel Julius Florus in AD 21 (Tacitus, *Ann.* 3.42: cf. no. 9). For the date of the Boudican revolt see Syme 1958, Appendix 69, 762ff. The precise date of Classicianus's death is not known, but assuming a three- to four-year period of office as procurator, it probably occurred by the mid-60s. The fact that London was the place of Classicianus's burial suggests that he lived here and hence that London was already the seat of the procurator by the 60s.

(c)   THE FLAVIANS AND NERVA (AD 69–98)

25   Chester lead water-pipe   AD 79

RIB 2.3.2434.1. *Chester (Deva). Pieces of lead water-piping found in 1899 running east-west in the central range of the fortress, c. 23 metres north of Eastgate Street. Now in Grosvenor Museum, Chester.*

Imp(eratore) Vesp(asiano) VIIII, T(ito) imp(eratore) VII co(n)s(ulibus), Cn(aeo) Iulio Agricola leg(ato) Aug(usti) pro pr(aetore).

"*(Made)* in the ninth consulship of the emperor Vespasian and in the seventh of Titus, acclaimed *imperator*, in the governorship of Gnaeus Iulius Agricola."

The date is the first half of the year 79, providing a firm *terminus ante quem* for the foundation of the fortress. The inscription occurs twice on the 5.026-m long section of pipe which was exposed. The pipe was part of the water-supply put into the legionary fortress at Chester early in the governorship of Agricola. The construction of the fortress may well have begun during the term of office of his predecessor, Julius Frontinus, since a piped water supply is not a primary necessity. A further length of pipe with a similar inscription was found in 1969 below the courtyard of the elliptical building in the central range of the fortress (*RIB* 2.3.2434.3).

26 (25a) T. Valerius Pudens (legio II Adiutrix)   *c.* AD 71–78

RIB 258. *Lincoln (Lindum). Tombstone found in 1849. Now in the British Museum.*

T(itus) Valerius T(iti) f(ilius) I Cla(udia) Pudens Sav(aria) I mil(es) leg(ionis)
II A(diutricis) P(iae) F(idelis) I c(enturia) Dossenni I Proculi a(nnorum)
XXX I aera [V]I h(eres) d(e) s(uo) p(osuit) I h(ic) s(itus) e(st).

"Titus Valerius Pudens, son of Titus, of the Claudian voting tribe, from
Savaria, a soldier of the Second Legion Adiutrix Pia Fidelis, in the century
of Dossennius Proculus, aged 30 years, of 6 years' service; his heir set this
up at his own expense; here he lies."

In a gable above the text are two opposed dolphins and a trident; below it
an axe. Legion II Adiutrix was raised at the time of the Civil Wars of AD 69,
from sailors of the Ravenna fleet. The dolphins and trident are presumably an
allusion to this origin. It came to Britain in AD 71 with the new governor,
Cerealis, presumably replacing Legion IX at Lincoln, and was transferred to
Chester, forming its original garrison, in about 78. Dossennius was still in service
when he died and was buried at Lincoln, so his years of service are more likely
to have been six (VI) than eleven (XI) which would take us to AD 80. Savaria
is Szombathely, a Claudian colony in Pannonia Superior, modern Hungary.

27 (25b) C. Calventius Celer (legio II Adiutrix)   *c.* AD 78–87

RIB 475. Chester (Deva). *Tombstone found in 1891 built into the west wall of the
fortress. Now in the Grosvenor Museum, Chester.*

C(aius) Calventius I C(ai) f(ilius) Claud(ia) Celler Apro mil(es) leg(ionis)
II Ad(iutricis) P(iae) F(idelis) c(enturia) I Vibi Cleme[ntis I ...

"Gaius Calventius Celer, son of Gaius, of the Claudian voting tribe, from
Apri, soldier of the Second Legion Adiutrix Pia Fidelis, in the century of
Vibius Clemens [...]"

Legion II Adiutrix was based at Chester from about 78 until its move from
Britain to the Danube in about AD 87 to take part in Domitian's Dacian War.
Aprus is a Claudian colony in Thrace (in northern Turkey).

28 (26) Verulamium forum   AD 79 or 81

JRS 46 (1956), 146–7. St. Albans (Verulamium). *Fragments of an inscription
found during excavation in 1955. Now in the Verulamium Museum.*

[Imp(eratori) Tito Caesari divi] Vespa[siani] f(ilio) Ves[pasiano Aug(usto)
I p(ontifici) m(aximo) tr(ibunicia) p(otestate) VIIII imp(eratori) XV
co(n)s(uli) VII] desi[g(nato) VIII censori patri patriae I et Caesari divi
Vesp]asian[i f(ilio) Do]mi[tiano co(n)s(uli) VI desig(nato) VII principi I
iuventutis et] omn[ium collegiorum sacerdoti I Cn(aeo) Iulio A]gric[ola
legato Aug(usti) pr]o pr(aetore)I[municipium] Ve[rulamium basilica
or]nata.

"The Emperor Titus Caesar Vespasian Augustus, son of the deified
Vespasian, *pontifex maximus*, in his ninth year of tribunician power, hailed
imperator 15 times, consul 7 times, designated consul for the 8th. time,
censor, father of his country, and Caesar Domitian, son of the deified
Vespasian, consul 6 times, designated consul for the 7th. time, *princeps*

iuventutis and of all the colleges of priests, through Gnaeus Iulius Agricola, governor, the city of Verulamium to mark the building of the basilica."

Only five small fragments of this large (4.06m x 0.71m) inscription survive and so the detail of the wording is not absolutely certain. As restored above, lines 2–3 give a date of AD 79; an alternative restoration *[...tr.p.XI imp.XVII cos VIII] desi[gn. VIIII...]* and *[cos VII design. VIII]*, giving a date in AD 81, is also possible (Birley 1981, 73). The third and fourth lines which mention Domitian were erased after his death in AD 96, when his memory was officially damned. The inscription was found during excavations in the forum/basilica complex, and it is on this basis that the word *basilica* has been restored in line 5, assuming that the inscription commemorates the dedication of the building. The restoration *[... basilica or]nata* is far from certain. The surviving VE in the last line can be restored equally well as *[municipium] Ve[rulamium]* (as above) or *[civitas Catu]ve[llaunorum]*, so the inscription cannot be used as independent evidence to confirm Tacitus's statement, in his account of the Boudican rebellion, that Verulamium was a *municipium* (Tac. *Ann.* 14.33 = L11, 23). This is the only inscription attesting the sort of building activity alluded to by Tacitus (*Agr.* 21; cf. comment in L11, 75 note 47). For a fragment from Bath, attesting building activity in AD 76 during the governorship of Agricola's predecessor, see *RIB* 172.

PART III: THE SECOND CENTURY (AD 98–193)

(a)   TRAJAN (AD 98–117)

29 (28) Caerleon stone of Trajan   AD 100

RIB 330. *Caerleon* (Isca Silurum). *A marble commemorative slab found in 1928. It had been reused on the site of a stone-built exercise hall in the rear part of the fortress. Now in the Caerleon Legionary Museum.*

> Imp(eratori) Caes(ari) divi [Nervae f(ilio)] | Nervae Traia[no Aug(usto)] | Ger(manico) pontif(ici) maxim[o trib(unicia)] | potest(ate) p(atri) p(atriae) | co(n)s(uli) III | leg(io) II Aug(usta).

> "For the Emperor Caesar Nerva Trajan Augustus, son of the deified Nerva, conqueror of Germany, high priest, with tribunician power, father of his country, consul for the third time, the Second Legion Augusta."

Cos II was altered to cos III, suggesting that the stone was drafted in AD 99 and was brought up-to-date in AD 100. The inscription is made from imported Tuscan marble. Traces of the red paint which highlighted the letters still survive. It is not known which building it originally came from, though the internal bath-house was certainly undergoing important construction work at about this time.

30 (29) Rebuilding at York   AD 107–8

RIB 665. *York* (Eboracum). *Part of a commemorative tablet found in 1854 in King's Square near the Roman south-east gateway. Now in the Yorkshire Museum.* (Fig. 3).

> [I]mp(erator) Caesar | [divi N]ervae fil(ius) Ne[rva | Trai]anus Aug(ustus) Ger[m(anicus) Da]cicus po]ntifex maximu[s tribun|iciae po]testatis XII imp(erator) VI[I co(n)s(ul) V p(ater) p(atriae) | per leg(ionem) VIIII Hi[sp(anam)].

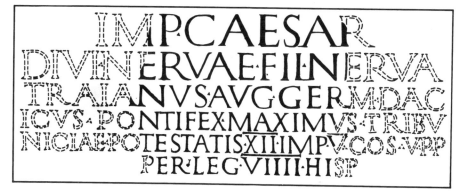

Fig. 3

"The Emperor Caesar Nerva Trajan Augustus, son of the deified Nerva, conqueror of Germany, conqueror of Dacia, *pontifex maximus*, in his twelfth year of tribunician power, acclaimed *imperator* seven times, consul five times, father of his country, by the Ninth Legion Hispana."

Trajan's twelfth year of tribunician power ran from 10 December 107 to 9 December 108. This is the last dated reference to Legion IX Hispana in Britain. Soon thereafter it was replaced at York by Legion VI Victrix, which probably came to Britain in AD 122. The last line of this inscription is sometimes restored to read: *portam per leg VIIII Hispanam fecit* on the assumption that the inscription referred to the rebuilding of a gate. In inscriptions of this date it is not common to specify what is being built; see for example the Caerleon inscription no.29.

If the fragmentary inscription *RIB* 464 is correctly restored to record building at Chester in AD 102–117, there is evidence from inscriptions for construction work going on under Trajan at all three legionary bases in Britain.

31 (30) Gelligaer dedication   AD 103–111

RIB 397. *Gelligaer, 21 kilometres north of Cardiff (Roman name unknown). A commemorative tablet found in 1909, near the south-east gate of Gelligaer fort. Now in the National Museum of Wales, Cardiff.*

[Imp(eratori) Ca]es(ari) divi | [Ner(vae) f(ilio) N]er(vae) Traiano | [Aug(usto) Ge]rm(anico) Dac(ico) pont(ifici) | [max(imo) t]rib(unicia) p(otestate) p(atri) p(atriae) co(n)s(uli) V | [imp(eratori) III]I | [leg(io) II Aug(usta)].

"For the emperor Caesar Nerva Trajan Augustus, son of the deified Nerva, conqueror of Germany, conqueror of Dacia, *pontifex maximus*, with tribunician power, father of his country, five times consul, acclaimed *imperator* four times, the Second Legion Augusta *(built this)*.

"Five times consul" = AD 103–111. The stone is broken off at the bottom, but the name of Legion II Augusta is restored on the assumption that it is normally the legions who were responsible for building work at this period, and Legion II, based at nearby Caerleon, is the likeliest candidate. The stone fort at Gelligaer, whose building is commemorated by this inscription, was laid out adjacent to its Flavian timber predecessor.

(b)   HADRIAN (AD 117–138)

32 (31) *As* of Hadrian   AD 119

RIC Hadrian 577a.

Obverse: IMP(ERATOR) TRAIANVS HADRIANVS AVG(VSTVS) Bust of Hadrian wearing laurel-wreath.

Reverse: PONT(IFEX) MAX(IMVS) TR(IBVNICIA) POT(ESTATE) CO(N)S(VL) III. S(ENATVS) C(ONSVLTO). BRITANNIA Britannia seated with right foot resting on a rock. Shield stands beside her.

The imperial titulature runs continuously from obverse to reverse: "Imperator Traianus Hadrianus Augustus, *pontifex maximus*, holding tribunician power, three times consul."

The Britannia motif is thought to be an allusion to the successful resolution of the problems Hadrian faced in Britain at the beginning of his reign (SHA *Hadrian* 5.1 = L11, 44 and cf. p. 70 note 19).

33 (32) A military diploma   AD 122

CIL 16.69. *O-Szöny, Hungary* (Brigetio). *Now in the British Museum.*

Imp(erator) Caesar divi Traiani Parthici f(ilius) divi Nervae nepos Traianus Hadrianus Augustus, pontifex maximus, tribu|nic(ia) potestat(e) VI, co(n)sul III, proco(n)s(ul)|

equitib(us) et peditib(us) qui militaverunt in alis decem et trib(us) et coh(or)|tib(us) triginta et septem quae appellantur I Pannonior(um) Sabinian(a)| et I Pannon(iorum) Tampian(a) et I Hispan(orum) Asturu(m) et I Tungror(um) et II Astur(um) | et Gallor(um) Picentiana et Gallor(um) et Thrac(um) Classiana c(ivium) R(omanorum) et Gallor(um) | Petriana (milliaria) c(ivium) R(omanorum) et Gallor(um) Sebosiana et Vetton(um) Hispan(orum) c(ivium) R(omanorum) et | Agrippiana Miniata et Aug(usta) Gallor(um) et Aug(usta) Vocontior(um) c(ivium) R(omanorum) et I | Nervia German(orum) (milliaria) et I Celtiberor(um) et I Thrac(um) et I Afror(um) c(ivium) R(omanorum) et I | Lingon(um) et I Fida Vardullor(um) (milliaria) c(ivium) R(omanorum) et I Frisiavon(um) et I Vangion(um) | (milliaria) et I Hamior(um) Sagitt(ariorum) et I Delmat(arum) et I Aquitan(orum) et I Ulpia Traia|na Cugern(orum) c(ivium) R(omanorum) et I Morin(orum) et I Menapior(um) et I Sunucor(um) et I B(a)etalsior(um) et I Batavor(um) et I Tungror(um) et I Hispan(orum) et II Gallor(um) et II | Vascon(um) c(ivium) R(omanorum) et II Thrac(um) et II Lingon(um) et II Astur(um) et II Delmatar(um) | et II Nervior(um) et III Nervior(um) et III Bracaror(um) et III Lingon(um) | et IIII Gallor(um) et IIII Breucor(um) et IIII Delmatar(um) et V Raetor(um) | et V Gallor(um) et VI Nervior(um) et VII Thrac(um) quae sunt in Britan|nia sub A(ulo) Platorio Nepote quinque et viginti stipendis | emeritis dimissis honesta missione per Pompeium | Falconem quorum nomina subscripta sunt ipsis libe|ris posterisq(ue) eorum civitatem dedit et conub(ium) cum uxo|rib(us) quas tunc habuissent cum est civitas iis data | aut siqui caelibes essent cum iis quas postea duxis|sent dumtaxat singuli singulas.

a.d. XVI k. Aug. | Ti(berio) Iulio Capitone Lucio Vitrasio Flaminino co(n)s(ulibus).|

alae I Pannonior(um) Tampianae cui pra(e)est | Fabius Sabinus, | ex sesquiplicario | Gemello Breuci f(ilio) Pannon(o) |

Descriptum et recognitum ex tabula aenea quae fixa est | Romae in muro post templum divi Aug(usti) ad Minervam. |

Ti. Claudi Menandri, | A.Fulvi Iusti, | Ti.Iuli Urbani, | L. Pulli Daphni, | L. Noni Victoris, | Q. Lolli Festi, | L. Pulli Anthi.

"The Emperor Caesar Trajan Hadrian Augustus, son of the deified Trajan Parthicus, grandson of the deified Nerva, high priest, in his sixth year of tribunician power, three times consul, proconsul

To the cavalrymen and infantrymen who served in the 13 alae and 37 cohorts named (*list follows*) which are in Britain under Aulus Platorius Nepos, who have served twenty-five years, given honourable discharge by Pompeius Falco, whose names are written below, has granted citizenship for themselves, their children and descendants, and the right of legal marriage with the wives they had when citizenship was granted to them, or, if any were unmarried, with those they later marry, but only a single one each.

17 July in the consulship of Tiberius Iulius Capito and Lucius Vitrasius Flamininus.

To Gemellus, son of Breucus, a Pannonian, formerly *sesquiplicarius* of the ala I Pannoniorum Tampiana, commanded by Fabius Sabinus.

Copied and checked from the bronze tablet set up at Rome on the wall behind the temple of the deified Augustus near *(the statue of)* Minerva.

[Witnessed by] Tiberius Claudius Menander, Aulus Fulvius Iustus, Tiberius Iulius Urbanus, Lucius Pullius Daphnus, Lucius Nonius Victor, Quintus Lollius Festus, Lucius Pullius Anthius."

This is the text of the outer faces of the two leaves of a military diploma (Cohors IV Lingonum omitted in error). The inner faces repeat the text (minus the names of the seven witnesses), but are less well inscribed and contain a number of errors. The two leaves of a diploma were wired together and sealed with the seals of the witnesses. This example was still wired together when found.

The inclusion of *proconsul* in the titles of Hadrian implies that he was away from Italy at the time of issue; he was probably in Britain. This diploma establishes, to within a few months, the date of arrival of Platorius Nepos as governor of Britain, for the soldiers whose grant is recorded had been discharged by Nepos's predecessor, Pompeius Falco. (For Platorius Nepos see no. 125.) The 50 units named on this diploma may represent a nearly complete tally of the auxiliary garrison of Britain in July 122.

A *sesquiplicarius* is a junior officer who received pay-and-a-half; he was third in command of a cavalry troop. Note that the recipient of this diploma was a Pannonian, who served in a Pannonian unit and who returned to the area of his birth after discharge – the document was found at the site of *Brigetio*, a frontier fort on the Danube in the province of Pannonia Superior (northern Hungary).

34 (33 and 34) Altars to Neptune and Oceanus   Early 120s AD

RIB 1319 and 1320. Newcastle upon Tyne (Pons Aelius). A pair of altars found in 1875 (a) and 1903 (b) in the river Tyne by the site of the Roman bridge (by the present Swing Bridge) at Newcastle. Now in the Museum of Antiquities.

(a)   Neptuno le(gio) | VI Vi(ctrix) | P(ia) F(idelis).

"To Neptune, the Sixth Legion Victrix Pia Fidelis *(set this up)*."

(b)   Ociano leg(io) I VI Vi(ctrix) I P(ia) F(idelis).

"To Ocianus, the Sixth Legion Victrix Pia Fidelis *(set this up)*."

The centrepiece of the inscription to Neptune is a dolphin entwined around a trident, of that to Ocianus (= Oceanus) an anchor. These two altars are thought to have been set up in a shrine on the bridge constructed across the Tyne by Hadrian at Newcastle *(Pons Aelius)*, the lowest bridging point of the river. Legion VI Victrix came to Britain from lower Germany in AD 122, along with the new governor, A. Platorius Nepos (see no.125); the "marine" dedications of these two altars may allude to the sea crossing which the legion had undertaken in travelling to Britain. Hadrian's Wall initially ran eastwards from Newcastle, and the construction of the bridge presumably formed an early part of the building programme.

35 (37) Milecastle 38 building inscription   *c.* AD 122–5

RIB 1638. Hadrian's Wall. A dedication slab found between 1751 and 1757 at Hotbank milecastle, No.38. Now in the Museum of Antiquities, Newcastle upon Tyne.

Imp(eratoris) Caes(aris) Traian(i) I Hadriani Aug(usti) I leg(io) II Aug(usta) I A(ulo) Platorio Nepote leg(ato) pr(o) pr(aetore).

"*(In honour of)* the emperor Caesar Trajan Hadrian Augustus, the Second Legion Augusta *(built this)* under Aulus Platorius Nepos, governor."

This is one of three surviving inscriptions recording the building of the milecastles of Hadrian's Wall, dating their completion (and probably their construction) to the governorship of Platorius Nepos (AD 122 to at least 124: see no. 125). The milecastles were part of the original scheme for Hadrian's Wall, and were built by the three legions, II Augusta (as this), VI Victrix and XX Valeria Victrix; each legion designed its milecastles slightly differently (Breeze and Dobson 1987, chap. 2).

36 (35) Halton Chesters dedication   *c.* AD 122–125

RIB 1427. Halton Chesters, Northumberland (Onnum). *A dedication slab, found in 1936 at the west gate of Halton Chesters fort. Now in the Museum of Antiquities, Newcastle upon Tyne.*

Imp(eratori) Caes(ari) T[ra(iano) Hadriano] I Aug(usto) leg(io) VI V(ictrix) [P(ia) F(idelis)] I A(ulo) Platorio N[epote] I leg(ato) Aug(usti) pr(o) [pr(aetore)].

"For the emperor Caesar Trajan Hadrian Augustus, the Sixth Legion Victrix Pia Fidelis *(built this)* under Aulus Platorius Nepos, governor."

Platorius Nepos was governor from AD 122 to at least 124. This inscription shows that the forts, though structurally secondary to Hadrian's Wall, were nevertheless added soon after the building began, and still within the governorship of Nepos.

37 (36) Benwell *classis Britannica* building inscription   *c.* AD 122–125

RIB 1340. *Benwell* (Condercum). *A building inscription found in 1937, in the portico of the granaries of Benwell fort. Now in the Museum of Antiquities, Newcastle upon Tyne.*

> Imp(eratori) Caes(ari) Traiano | Hadr[ia]n(o) Aug(usto) | A(ulo) Platorio N[epote l]eg(ato) Aug(usti) pr(o) p[r(aetore)] | vexillatio c[lassis] Britan(nicae).

> "For the emperor Caesar Trajan Hadrian Augustus, a detachment of the British fleet *(built this)* under the governor Aulus Platorius Nepos."

This is the earliest building inscription recording a unit other than a legion being involved in building work in Roman Britain (though note that *c[lassis]* is a restoration).

38   Great Chesters dedication   AD 128–138

RIB 1736. *Great Chesters, Northumberland* (Aesica). *A dedication slab found shortly before 1851, near the east gate of Great Chesters fort. Now in Chesters Museum.*

> Imp(eratori) Caes(ari) Trai(a)n(o) Had[ri]a|no Aug(usto) p(atri) p(atriae).

> "For the emperor Caesar Trajan Hadrian Augustus, father of his country."

Hadrian took the title *pater patriae* in AD 128; assuming that this title is correctly used (and this is not invariably the case, cf. no.141) this inscription dates the construction of Great Chesters fort to the latter part of the reign. The fort was built entirely to the south of the Wall instead of projecting across it as was the case with the early forts such as Halton Chesters and Benwell. Cf. also Carrawburgh (no.39), built in *c.* AD 130–132.

39 (-) Carrawburgh dedication   *c.* AD 130–132

RIB 1550. *Carrawburgh, Northumberland* (Brocolitia). *Part of a dedication-slab found in 1838 in the north-east corner of Carrawburgh fort. Now in Chesters Museum.*

> [...? Iulio Se]vero leg(ato) | [Aug(usti) pr(o) p]r(aetore) coh(ors) I Aquit|[anorum] fecit | [sub ...]io Nepote | [pra]ef(ecto).

> "... under Iulius Se]verus as governor, the First Cohort of Aquitanians built *(this)* under [...]ius Nepos, prefect."

This fragmentary text dates building work at Carrawburgh fort to a governorship, almost certainly that of Iulius Severus, later than that of Platorius Nepos. (Julius Verus is virtually ruled out as *coh. I Aquitanorum* was at Brough-on-Noe during his governorship (no.62)). This is consistent with the fact that Carrawburgh fort, like Great Chesters, is not built straddling the line of Hadrian's Wall (as is the case with all of the clearly early forts, where topography permitted), but is attached to its south side. This (together with no.41 and possibly no.42) is one of the earliest building inscriptions set up by an auxiliary unit in Britain, though it is known from one of the Vindolanda tablets (*Tab. Vindol.* 1.1) that auxiliary soldiers were engaged in construction work in the early Trajanic period (*c.* AD 95–105).

40 (39) Netherby dedication   AD 122–128

RIB 974. *Netherby, Cumbria* (Castra Exploratorum). *An inscription seen in 1601, built into the house at Netherby. Now lost.*

Imp(eratori) Caes(ari) Tra(iano) | Hadriano | Aug(usto) | leg(io) II Aug(usta) fec(it).

"For the emperor Caesar Trajan Hadrian Augustus, the Second Legion Augusta built *(this)*."

This inscription from the outpost fort of Netherby is not sufficiently closely datable to indicate whether the outposts formed part of the initial scheme for Hadrian's Wall, or whether they were part of the secondary plan when forts were built on the line of the Wall. The terminal date of AD 128 is based on the absence of *p(ater) p(atriae)* in the emperor's titles (but see comment on no.38). Inscriptions from the other two Hadrianic outpost forts provide dates of before 128 for Birrens (*DG* 38, 142ff) and ? AD 124/30 for Bewcastle (*RIB* 995).

41 (40) Bowes dedication   *c.* AD 130–132

RIB 739. *Bowes, Yorkshire* (Lavatrae). *A dedication-slab seen before 1600 in the church at Bowes, where it had been used as an altar slab. Recorded by Camden (1600). Now lost.*

Im[p(eratori)] Caesari divi Traiani [Parthici f(ilio)] | divi Nervae nepoti Traia[no Hadria]lno Aug(usto) pontifici maxi[mo tr(ibunicia) pot(estate) ...] lco(n)s(uli) I[II] p(atri) p(atriae) coh(ors) IIII B[reucorum | sub Sex(to) Iul]io Sev[ero leg(ato) Aug(usti) pr(o) pr(aetore)]

"For the emperor Caesar Trajan Hadrian Augustus, son of the deified Trajan Parthicus, grandson of the deified Nerva, *pontifex maximus*, in his ... year of tribunician power, three times consul, father of his country, the Fourth Cohort of B[reuci] under the governor Sextus Iulius Severus *(built this)*."

Camden gave the name of the unit as IIII F[...]. There is no likely candidate in Britain so Birley (cited in *RIB*) suggested it should read IIII B[reucorum]. IIII Delmatarum, another possibility, was stationed at this time at Hardknott (below, no.42).

42 (41) Hardknott fragments   *c.* AD 119–38

JRS 55 (1965), 222. *Hardknott, Cumbria* (Mediobogdum). *Fourteen scattered fragments of a dedication slab, found in 1964 at the south-east gate (porta praetoria).*

[Imp(eratori) Ca]es(ari) d[ivi Traiani] Part[hici | fil(io) div]i Ne[rvae nep(oti) Tr]aian[o | Hadrian]o [Augusto pont(ifici)] m[ax(imo) | ... co(n)s(uli) III

... | ... le]g(ato) Aug(usti) p[r(o)] pr(aetore) | coh(ors) II[II De]lmatar(um) | [fecit]

"For the emperor Caesar Trajan Hadrian Augustus, son of the deified Trajan Parthicus, grandson of the deified Nerva, *pontifex maximus* ... three times consul, ... governor, the Fourth Cohort of Delmatians built *(this)*."

This inscription probably dates the original construction of the fort at Hardknott (though some have argued for a Trajanic foundation). Hadrian took his third consulship in AD 119; he did not take a fourth. The name of the governor is not recoverable. *Cohors IIII Delmatarum* is first attested in Britain on a diploma of AD 103 (*RIB* 2.1.2401.1 = *CIL* 16.48).

43 (42) Moresby dedication   AD 128–38

RIB 801. *Moresby, Cumbria. A sandstone tablet in three parts found in 1822 near the east gate of Moresby fort. Now at Lowther Castle.*

Imp(eratoris) Caes(aris) | Traian(i) Hadri|ani Aug(usti) p(atris) p(atriae) | leg(io) XX V(aleria) V(ictrix).

"*(In honour)* of the emperor Caesar Trajan Hadrian Augustus, father of his country, the Twentieth Legion Valeria Victrix *(built this)*."

The date is given by the title *pater patriae* taken by Hadrian in AD 128. The construction of Moresby was presumably linked with the extension of the Hadrianic frontier down the Cumberland coast.

44 (45) Maenius Agrippa altar   Hadrianic

RIB 823. *Maryport, Cumbria* (Alauna). *Altar found before 1725 outside the Roman fort at Maryport. Now at the Senhouse Museum, Maryport.*

I(ovi) O(ptimo) M(aximo) | coh(ors) I His(panorum) | cui prae(est) | M(arcus) Maeni|us Agrip(pa) | tribu(nus) | pos(uit).

"To Jupiter, Best and Greatest, the First Cohort of Spaniards commanded by Marcus Maenius Agrippa, tribune, set this up."

For the career of Maenius Agrippa see no.46. This altar is one of a remarkable collection of dedications to Jupiter Optimus Maximus (sixteen in total), set up by the *cohors I Hispanorum equitata*. These altars were found, buried in several pits around the parade ground at the Maryport fort. It seems probable, as Wenham suggested (1939, 28), that these altars were a record of the annual oath of allegiance of the soldiers, and as they all show so little weathering the previous year's altar was buried as the new one was set up. Alternatively, perhaps they were buried in batches having stood under shelter. *Cohors I Hispanorum* was resident at Maryport in the Hadrianic period, the first of five different units to occupy the site (which remained in use from *c.* 122 to *c.* 400). Some of the conmmanding officers named on these altars are tribunes (as here), others prefects (as no. 45); the former commanded units 1000-strong, the latter 500-strong. This indicates that *I Hispanorum* changed in establishment strength during its sojourn at Maryport, and the fact that the fort appears originally to have been built for a large unit (Jarrett 1976, 21) suggests that the unit was reduced in size.

45 (44) Maryport altar   Hadrianic

RIB 816. *Maryport, Cumbria* (Alauna). *Altar found with nos. 44 and 218. Now at the Senhouse Museum, Maryport.*

> I(ovi) O(ptimo) M(aximo) | coh(ors) I Hisp(anorum) | eq(uitata) cui praeest | L(ucius) Antistius L(uci) f(ilius) | Quirina Lupus | Verianus praef(ectus) | domu Sic|ca ex Africa.

> "To Jupiter Best and Greatest, the First Cohort of Spaniards *equitata* commanded by Lucius Antistius Lupus Verianus, son of Lucius, of the tribe Quirina, prefect, from Sicca in Africa *(set this up)*."

Antistius Lupus Verianus held the rank of prefect when he commanded *I Hispanorum*. Sicca Veneria lay in the province of Africa Proconsularis (in modern Tunisia), about 120 kilometres inland from Carthage. For another Maryport altar, in this case set up by the *cohors I Baetasiorum*, see no.219.

46   Maenius Agrippa statue base   Mid-2nd.century AD

ILS 2735 = *CIL* 11.5632. *Camerini* (Camerinum), *Italy. A statue base found in the 17th.century.*

> M(arco) Maenio C(ai) f(ilio) Cor(nelia) Agrip|pae L(ucio) Tusidio Campestri | hospiti divi Hadriani patri | senatoris praef(ecto) coh(ortis) II Fl(aviae) | Britton(um) equitat(ae) electo | a divo Hadriano et misso | in expeditionem Brittan|nicam trib(uno) coh(ortis) I Hispanor(um) | equitat(ae) praef(ecto) alae Gallor(um) | et Pannonior(um) catafracta|tae proc(uratori) Aug(usti) praef(ecto) classis | Brittannicae proc(uratori) provin|ciae Brittanniae equo pu|blico patrono municipi | vicani Censorglacenses | consecuti ab indulgentia | optimi maximique imp(eratoris) Anto|nini Aug(usti) Pii beneficio inter|pretationis eius privi- legia | quibus in p[e]rpetuum aucti | confirmatique sunt. | L(ocus) d(atus) d(ecreto) d(ecurionum).

> "Marcus Maenius Agrippa Lucius Tusidius Campester, son of Gaius, tribe Cornelia, host of the deified Hadrian, father of a senator, prefect of the *cohors II Flavia Brittonum equitata*, chosen by the emperor Hadrian and sent on an expedition to Britain, tribune of *cohors I Hispanorum equitata*, prefect of the *ala Gallorum et Pannoniorum catafractata*, imperial procu- rator, prefect of the British fleet, procurator of the province of Britain, *equo publico*, patron of his city; the people of the village of Censorglacum erected this in recognition of the privileges they obtained by favour of the excellent and all-powerful emperor Antoninus Augustus Pius as a result of his intervention, privileges which are a perpetual source of strength and comfort. The site was given by decree of the decurions."

The *expeditio Britannica* in which Maenius Agrippa took part is either the war which Hadrian waged against the Britons at the start of his reign or another campaign later within the reign. The very existence of this supposed later campaign depends wholly on the disputed dating of this inscription and that of no.47 (for the various views cf. Birley 1961, 26–29; Jarrett 1976, 145–51; Dobson 1978, 236; Maxfield 1981, 196–97). *Equo publico* means that Agrippa had been granted the honour of taking part in the ceremonial ride-past in Rome, a relic of the days when the equestrian nobility were Rome's cavalry force.

47   Titus Pontius Sabinus   Hadrianic

ILS 2726. *Ferentini* (Ferentinum), *Italy. A tombstone inscribed front and back. Found in 1851. Now in the museum at Ferentini.*

Front: T(ito) Pontio T(iti) f(ilio) Pal(atina) I Sabino I p(rimo) p(ilo) II proc(uratori) provinc(iae) I Narb(onensis) IIIIvir(o) i(ure) d(icundo) quinq(uennali) I flamin(i) et patron(o) I municipi I Valeria L(uci) f(ilia) Procula I uxor I l(ocus) d(atus) d(ecreto) d(ecurionum).

Back: T(itus) Pontius T(iti) f(ilius) Pal(atina) Sabinus I praef(ectus) coh(ortis) I Pann(oniorum) et Dalmat(arum) I eq(uitatae) c(ivium) R(omanorum) trib(unus) mil(itum) leg(ionis) VI Ferrat(ae) I donis donatus expeditione Parlthica a divo Traiano hasta pura I vexillo corona murali (centurio) leg(ionis) XXII I Primig(eniae) (centurio) leg(ionis) XIII Gemin(ae) primus pillus leg(ionis) III Aug(ustae) praepositus vexillaltionibus milliaris tribus expediltione Brittannica leg(ionis) VII Gemin(ae) I VIII Aug(ustae) XXII Primig(eniae) trib(unus) coh(ortis) III I vig(ilum) coh(ortis) XIIII urb(anae) coh(ortis) II praet(oriae) I p(rimus) p(ilus) II proc(urator) provinc(iae) Narbonens(is) I IIIIvir i(ure) d(icundo) quinq(uennalis) flamen patron(us) I municipi.

Front: "Titus Pontius Sabinus, son of Titus, of the tribe Palatina, *primus pilus II*, procurator of the province of Narbonensis, magistrate, priest and patron of the city. *(Erected by)* Valeria Procula, daughter of Lucius, (his) wife. The site was given by decree of the decurions.

Back: Titus Pontius Sabinus, son of Titus, of the tribe Palatina, prefect of *cohors I Pannoniorum et Dalmatarum equitata*, Roman citizens, tribune of the Sixth Legion Ferrata, decorated on the Parthian expedition by the deified Trajan with a ceremonial spear, a standard and a mural crown, centurion of Legion XXII Primigenia, centurion of Legion XIII Gemina, senior centurion of Legion III Augusta, in command of detachments of a thousand men from each of Legions VII Gemina, VIII Augusta and XXII Primigenia on the British expedition, tribune of the Third Cohort of Vigiles, tribune of the Fourteenth Urban Cohort, tribune of the Second Praetorian Cohort, *primus pilus II*, procurator of the province of Narbonensis, magistrate, priest, patron of the city."

The front of the inscription gives the high spots of Sabinus's career; the reverse gives the full details. After starting service as an equestrian military commander, Sabinus obtained a direct commission into the legionary centurionate and rose from there into the ranks of the procurators. (On career changes of this sort see Dobson 1972). The three legions which sent detachments to the British war were based in Spain (VII Gemina) and Upper Germany (VIII Augusta and XXII Primigenia). Sabinus's career can be approximately dated by the reference to the Parthian War which began in 114 and in which Trajan was engaged at the time of his death in 117. The date of the British expedition depends on the length of time Sabinus is estimated to have taken to advance from tribune of Legion VI (the post he held in 117) to the senior centurionate and his appointment in charge of the detachments sent to Britain. Estimates vary considerably, allowing for participation in the troubles at the start of Hadrian's reign or in a campaign anywhere up to the mid-120s. The nature of the post *primus pilus II* is obscure.

48   Sestertius of Hadrian   AD 134–138

RIC Hadrian 845. *Sestertius.*

> *Obverse:* Bust of Hadrian wearing a laurel wreath.
> HADRIANVS AVG(VSTVS) CO(N)S(VL) III P(ATER) P(ATRIAE)
> "Hadrian Augustus, three times consul, father of his country."

> *Reverse:* Britannia seated with right foot resting on a rock, holding a spear in crook of left arm. Shield stands beside her. Around, BRITANNIA. Below, S(ENATVS) C(ONSVLTO)

A large series of coins issued at the end of Hadrian's reign recapitulated his provincial tours and commemorated the armies of the provinces visited. (PJC)

49   Carvoran altar   AD 136–137

RIB 1778. *Carvoran, Northumberland* (Magnis). *An altar, found in 1831 in the bathhouse at Carvoran fort. Now in the Museum of Antiquities, Newcastle upon Tyne.*

> Fortunae Aug(ustae) | pro salute L(uci) Aeli | Caesaris ex visu | T(itus) Fla(vius) Secundus | praef(ectus) coh(ortis) I Hamiorum sagittar(iorum) | v(otum) s(olvit) l(ibens) m(erito).

> "To the Fortune of the Emperor for the welfare of Lucius Aelius Caesar, Titus Flavius Secundus, prefect of the First Cohort of Hamian Archers, because of a vision, fulfilled his vow willingly and deservedly."

Lucius Aelius was adopted Caesar in 136 and died on 1 January 138. This, together with the following inscription, date a rebuilding of the fort rampart at Carvoran to *c.* 136–137, indicating that construction work on the Hadrianic frontier was continuing right down to the end of the reign. Dedications to the goddess Fortuna are not uncommon finds in bathhouses where their presence is often associated with the practice of using the bathhouse for gambling; it is as likely to be due to the need to avert the evil eye from the naked soldiers.

50   Carvoran building-stone   *c.* AD 136–138

RIB 1820. *Carvoran, Northumberland* (Magnis). *A building-stone found in 1940 near Carvoran fort. Now in the Museum of Antiquities, Newcastle upon Tyne.*

C(enturia) Silvani | vallavit | p(edes) CXII sub | Fla(vio) Secundo | [pr]aef(ecto).

"The century of Silvanus built 112 feet of rampart under the command of Flavius Secundus, prefect."

This stone is dated by the reference to Flavius Secundus, known from no.49 (above) to have been in command when Lucius Aelius was Caesar. The verb *vallare* to build a *vallum*, a rampart, occurs in Britain only on this and two other stones from Carvoran, *RIB* 1816 and 1817, which are therefore almost certainly contemporary.

(c)   ANTONINUS PIUS (AD 138–161)

51   Corbridge, probably from the west granary   AD 139

RIB 1147. *Corbridge, Northumberland* (Coria?). *A dedication-slab found in 1935 reused as a paving-stone in the west granary at Roman Corbridge. Now in Corbridge Museum.*

[Imp(eratori)] T(ito) Aelio Anionino | [Au]g(usto) Pio II co(n)s(uli)| [sub] cura Q(uinti) Lolii Urbici | [leg(ati) A]ug(usti) pr(o) pr(aetore) leg(io) II Aug(usta) f(ecit).

"For the Emperor Titus Aelius Antoninus Augustus Pius, consul for the second time, under the charge of the governor, Quintus Lollius Urbicus, the Second Legion Augusta built this."

Note that the mason has incorrectly inscribed ANIONINO, LOLII and VRBIC.I. The stone is dated by the consulship. Together with no.52 it points to the rebuilding of the fort at Corbridge, at the very beginning of Pius's reign, in connection with the move forward into Scotland and the construction of a new frontier across the Forth-Clyde isthmus. For Lollius Urbicus as governor of Britain cf. SHA, *Antoninus Pius* 5.4 (L11, 44). His name appears also on an inscription recording the building of a fort on the Antonine Wall (no.55) and on one from the area between Hadrian's Wall and the Antonine Wall (no.54). The governor is not named on the distance slabs from the Wall itself (cf. nos.56–58).

The Roman name for Corbridge, formerly taken to be *Corstopitum* (Rivet and Smith 1979), now appears, from evidence in the Vindolanda tablets, to be *Coria* (no. 273; Bowman and Thomas 1991, 71; 1994, 96–97).

52   Corbridge, probably from the east granary   AD 140

RIB 1148. *Corbridge, Northumberland* (Coria?). *Part of a dedication-slab found in 1907 reused as a paving-stone in the east granary at Roman Corbridge. Now in Corbridge Museum.*

Imp(eratori) Caes(ari) [T(ito)] Ael[io] | Antonino A[ug(usto)] Pi[o] | III co(n)[s(uli) p(atri)] p(atriae) | sub cura Q(uinti) [Lolli Urbici] | leg(ati) Au[g(usti) pr(o) pr(aetore)] leg(io) II A[ug(usta) fecit].

"For the Emperor Caesar Titus Aelius Antoninus Augustus Pius, in the year of his third consulship, father of his country, under the charge of the governor, Quintus Lollius Urbicus, the Second Legion Augusta built this."

Note that *III cos* has been altered from *II cos* (cf. no.29 from Caerleon).

53   Sestertius of Antoninus Pius   AD 143–144

RIC Antoninus Pius 719. *Sestertius.*

Obverse: Head of Antoninus Pius wearing laurel-wreath.
ANTONINVS AVG(VSTVS) PIVS P(ATER) P(ATRIAE) TR(IBVNI-CIA) P(OTESTATE) CO(N)S(VL) III.

Reverse: Victory standing on globe, holding wreath and palm-branch.
IMPERATOR II. BRITAN(NICA).
Below: S(ENATVS) C(ONSVLTO)

The imperial titulature runs continuously from obverse to reverse: "Antoninus Augustus Pius, father of his country, having tribunician power, three times consul, twice hailed *imperator*."

Pius's second imperial salutation was no doubt on account of his British victory, alluded to here by the figure of Victory. The earliest dated reference to Pius's salutation as *imperator II* is in AD 142 (*CIL* 10.515 = *ILS* 340).

54   High Rochester building-slab   AD 139–*c*.143

RIB 1276. *High Rochester, Northumberland* (Bremenium). *A dedication-slab found in 1852 reused in the floor of a water-tank in front of the headquarters building; original position unknown. Now at Alnwick Castle.*

Imp(eratori) Caes(ari) T(ito) Aelio I H[a]d(riano) Antonino Aug(usto) Pio p(atri) p(atriae) I sub Q(uinto) Lol(lio) Urbico I leg(ato) Aug(usti) pro prae(tore) I coh(ors) I Ling(onum) eq(uitata) f(ecit).

"For the Emperor Caesar Titus Aelius Hadrianus Antoninus Augustus Pius, father of his country, under Quintus Lollius Urbicus, governor, *cohors I Lingonum equitata* built this."

High Rochester lies on Dere Street, a day's march north of Corbridge. Between Corbridge and High Rochester lies Risingham, where a new fort was constructed in the Antonine period (no building inscription).

55 (56)   Balmuildy slab   AD 139–*c*.143

RIB 2191. *Balmuildy, Lanarkshire. Part of a commemorative tablet found built into a byre at Balmuildy. Now in the Hunterian Museum, Glasgow.*

[Imp(eratori) C(aesari) T(ito) Ael(io) Hadr(iano) I Antonino Aug(usto) Pio I p(atri)] p(atriae) leg(io) II Au[g(usta) sub] I Q(uinto) Lollio Ur[bico] I leg(ato) Aug(usti) pr(o) pr(aetore) [fec(it)].

"For the Emperor Caesar Titus Aelius Hadrianus Antoninus Augustus Pius, father of his country, the Second Legion Augusta built *(this)* under Quintus Lollius Urbicus, governor."

The fort of Balmuildy lies on the Antonine Wall but was constructed before it. Urbicus does not appear on any of the distance-slabs (cf. nos.56–58) and may not have been involved in the construction. Auxiliaries, as well as legionaries, are attested building forts on the Antonine Wall: cf. *RIB* 2145 (Rough Castle), 2155 (Castlecary) and 2170 (Bar Hill).

56 (55) The Bridgeness slab   Early 140s AD

RIB 2139. *Bridgeness, West Lothian. A dedication slab found in 1868 on Windmill Hill immediately overlooking the Firth of Forth and the site of the end of the Antonine Wall. Now in the National Museums of Scotland, Edinburgh. (There is also a cast in the Hunterian Museum, Glasgow.)*

> Imp(eratori) Caes(ari) Tito Aelio | Hadri(ano) Antonino | Aug(usto) Pio p(atri) p(atriae) leg(io) II | Aug(usta) per m(ilia) p(assuum) IIIIDCLII | fec(it).

> "For the Emperor Caesar Titus Aelius Hadrianus Antoninus Augustus Pius, father of his country, the Second Legion Augusta built 4652 paces."

There is a relief on either side of the inscribed central panel, each in a pillared niche. On the left, representing the campaigning which preceded the building of the Wall, is a helmeted cavalryman with spear and shield, thrusting at four naked enemies. One is headless, one falling dead, one crawling and one sitting defence-less. On the right is a representation of the *suovetaurilia* – a ceremonial sacrifice of a pig (*sus*), sheep (*ovis*) and bull (*taurus*) – which inaugurated the construc-tion of the Wall. The animals move towards a seated figure. In the background are five figures: one plays a double flute, one is holding a *patera* over the altar, and one holds a *vexillum* inscribed LEG II AVG.

This is one of a series of inscriptions (20 are now known) recording lengths of the Antonine Wall built by the three legions involved in its construction. On these inscriptions Legion II is recorded as complete (as here), the other two only as detachments. Note that this text records the building length in paces (*passus*); compare nos. 57 and 58 where the unit used is feet (*pedes*). For a text and commentary on this and all the other distance-slabs from the Antonine Wall cf. *CSIR* I.4, 27–28, no. 68 and Keppie 1979, 9–10.

57   Duntocher distance-slab   Early 140s AD

RIB 2200. *Duntocher, Lanarkshire. A commemorative tablet, found in 1812 on the line of the Antonine Wall at Braidfield Farm. Original position must have been about 1100 metres south-east of Duntocher fort. Now in Hunterian Museum, Glasgow.*

> Imp(eratori) C(aesari) T(ito) Aelio Hadrliano Antonino Aug(usto) | p(atri) p(atriae) vex(illatio) leg(ionis) VI | Victric[i]s p(iae) f(idelis) | opus valli p(edum) | MMMCCXL f(ecit).

> "For the Emperor Caesar Titus Aelius Hadrianus Antoninus Augustus, father of his country, a detachment of the Sixth Legion Victrix Pia Fidelis built 3240 feet of rampart."

The inscribed panel is supported by two winged Victories in relief, each standing on a globe. They are flanked left by Mars Victor (the victorious god of war) and right by Virtus Augusta (the valour of the emperor), who holds in her left hand a sheathed ceremonial sword inverted, and in her right a *vexillum* inscribed *Virtus Aug(usti)*. Note the use of the expression *opus valli* for the work of building the turf wall (or rampart). The distance recorded here (and on no.58 and on all other slabs from the westernmost four miles of the Wall) is recorded in feet, contrasting with the paces used further east. This is perhaps a reflection of the dislocation caused by the change in plan when it was decided to add extra forts to the Wall line.

58 Duntocher distance-slab   Early 140s AD

RIB 2204. *Duntocher, Lanarkshire. A commemorative tablet found before 1699 on the line of the Antonine Wall near the farm of Carleith, about 1600 metres west of Duntocher fort. Now in the Hunterian Museum, Glasgow.*

Imp(eratori) Anton(ino) | Aug(usto) Pio | p(atri) p(atriae) | leg(io) | II | Aug(usta) | f(ecit) p(edum) III (milia) CCLXXI.

"For the emperor Antoninus Augustus Pius, father of his country, the Second Legion Augusta built 3271 feet."

The tablet is adorned with a capricorn, a winged pegasus and rosettes. Note that there is no mention here of a detachment of the legion; contrast no. 57 of the Sixth Legion.

59 Altar from Newstead   Antonine

RIB 2122. *Newstead* (Trimontium). *Altar found in 1909 in the fort. Now in the National Museums of Scotland, Edinburgh.*

Dianae Reg|nae, o[b] pros|pero[s] eventus | C(aius) Arrius | Domitianus | c(enturio) leg(ionis) XX V(aleriae) V(ictricis) | v(otum) s(olvit) l(aetus) l(ibens) m(erito).

"To Diana the queen, on account of successful ventures, Gaius Arrius Domitianus, centurion of the Twentieth Legion Valeria Victrix, fulfilled his vow joyfully, willingly and deservedly."

Arrius Domitianus dedicated three altars at Newstead (this and *RIB* 2123–4). His presence, together with that of another legionary centurion (L. Maximus Gaetulicus, *RIB* 2120) suggests that a detachment of Legion XX was in residence at Newstead in the early Antonine period, together with a cavalry unit, the *ala Vocontiorum*. Newstead lies on Dere Street (near Melrose) and is a key fort in the occupations of Scotland.

60 Dupondius of Antoninus Pius   AD 154–155

RIC Antoninus Pius 930. *Dupondius.*

Obverse: Head of Antoninus Pius, wearing a radiate crown.
ANTONINVS AVG(VSTVS) PIVS P(ATER) P(ATRIAE) TR(IBVNI-CIA) P(OTESTATE) XVIII

"Antoninus Augustus Pius, father of his country, in his eighteenth year of tribunician power."

Reverse: Britannia seated on a rock. Shield and spear stand beside her. Around, BRITANNIA; below, S(ENATVS) C(ONSVLTO)

Dupondii and Asses of this type are found only in Britain, and are common on military sites. They appear to be a special donative given only to the army of Britain. (PJC)

61   Newcastle, Julius Verus slab   *c.* AD 158

RIB 1322. Newcastle upon Tyne (Pons Aeli). A dedication slab found in 1903 in dredging the north channel of the Tyne below the Swing Bridge. Now in the Museum of Antiquities, Newcastle upon Tyne. (Fig. 4).

Imp(eratori) Antonilno Aug(usto) Pio p(atri) | pat(riae) vexil(l)atio | leg(ionis) II Aug(ustae) et leg(ionis) | VI Vic(tricis) et leg(ionis) | XX V(aleriae) V(ictricis) con(t)rl(i)buti ex(ercitibus) Ger(manicianis) dulobus sub Iulio Velro leg(ato) Aug(usti) pr(o) p(raetore).

"For the Emperor Antoninus Augustus Pius, father of his country, the detachment(s) of Legion II Augusta, Legion VI Victrix and Legion XX Valeria Victrix for the armies of the two Germanies, under Julius Verus, governor, *(set this up)*."

Fig. 4

VEXILLATIO(NES) is also possible. The interpretation EX(ERCITIBVS) GER(MANICIANIS) DVOBVS proposed is recent, replacing the less satisfactory EX GER(MANIIS) DVOBVS, "from the two Germanies", which involves a grammatical error, as GERMANIIS are feminine, and DVOBVS masculine. It has also been suggested that EX, "from", has dropped out before EX(ERCITIBVS), preserving the old theory that the troops are coming from the Germanies to Britain; the text as expanded above implies that the troops are being sent to the German armies.

There is no clear way of deciding between these two possibilities. This inscription, on the old interpretation, has been used as evidence for a "Brigantian revolt" in the 150s AD. The case for the "revolt" is far from proven; for a discussion contrast Breeze and Dobson 1987, 112–115 with Frere 1987, 135–137. If the troops are actually leaving Britain this would argue against the notion of a revolt.

62   Brough-on-Noe dedication   *c.* AD 158

RIB 283. Brough-on-Noe, Derbyshire (Navio). *A commemorative slab found in 1903 in the strongroom of the fort's headquarters. Now in Buxton Museum.*

Imp(eratori) Caesari T(ito) [Ael(io) Hadr(iano) | An]tonino Au[g(usto) Pio p(atri) p(atriae)] | coh(ors) I Aquitan[orum] | sub Iulio V[ero leg(ato)] Aug(usti) | pr(o) pr(aetore) inst[ante] | [C]apitoni[o…]sco prae(fecto).

"For the Emperor Caesar Titus Aelius Hadrianus Antoninus Augustus Pius, father of his country, the First Cohort of Aquitanians under Julius Verus, governor, under the charge of Capitonius […]scus, prefect, *(built this)*."

The fort was rebuilt on a deserted Flavian site. This reoccupation has been linked to the "Brigantian revolt", on which see above, under no. 61.

63   Birrens rebuilding   AD 157–158

RIB 2110. Birrens, Dumfriesshire (Blatobulgium). *A dedication slab found in 1895 in the fort's headquarters building. Now in the National Museums of Scotland, Edinburgh.*

Imp(eratori) Caes(ari) T(ito) A[el(io)] Hadr(iano) | An[to]nino Aug(usto) [Pio po]nt(ifici) | max(imo) [tr]ib(unicia) pot(estate) XXI co(n)s(uli) IIII | coh(ors) II [Tung]r(orum) m[i]l(liaria) eq(uitata) C L | sub Iu[lio Vero] leg(ato) Aug(usti) pr(o) pr(aetore).

"For the Emperor Caesar Titus Aelius Hadrianus Antoninus Augustus Pius, *pontifex maximus*, in his twenty-first year of tribunician power, four times consul, the Second Cohort of Tungrians, *milliaria, equitata*, C. L., *(set this up)* under Julius Verus, governor."

The Tungrians lived around Tongres, in Belgium. Pius's TRIB POT XXI lasted from 10 December 157 to 9 December 158. The letters C L cannot be expanded with confidence. The frequently suggested C(IVIVM) L(ATINORVM), "Latin citizens", would be unique and has no evidence to justify it. C(ORAM) L(AVDATA), "publicly praised" i.e. in the presence of the emperor, has been suggested, but this is also unparalleled for a unit, though known for an individual, *AE* 1956, 124. This inscription has been linked to the "Brigantian revolt"; see above under no. 61.

64   Heddon-on-the-Wall stone (Legio VI Victrix)   AD 158

RIB 1389. ? Near Heddon-on-the-Wall, on the line of Hadrian's Wall. A building-stone found in 1751. Now lost.

Leg(io) VI V(ictrix) P(ia) | F(idelis) ref(ecit) Te|r(tullo) et Sac(erdote) co(n)s(ulibus) | S(...) F(...).

"The Sixth Legion Victrix Pia Fidelis rebuilt *(this)* in the consulship of Tertullus and Sacerdos; S(...) F(...)."

S. F. are presumably the initials of the centurion in charge of the work. The consuls give the date. This attests repair or reconstruction to the curtain of Hadrian's Wall in AD 158, implying possibly an intention to return to it; cf. no. 189, from the same area, which also refers to rebuilding.

(d)   MARCUS AURELIUS (AD 161–180)

65   Corbridge rebuilding   *c.* AD 161–166

RIB 1149. *Corbridge, Northumberland* (Coria?). *A dedication-slab, part of which was found before 1702 and parts in 1912, 1937 and 1938 at Corbridge. Now in Corbridge Museum.*

Imperato[ribus Caesaribus] | M(arco) Aurelio A[ntonino Aug(usto) tribuni-ciae] | potestati[s XVII] co(n)s(uli) [III et L(ucio) Aur|elio Vero Aug(usto)] A[rmeniaco trib|uniciae potestati]s I[[II] co(n)s(uli) II| [vexillatio leg(ionis) XX] V(aleriae) V(ictricis) fecit su[b c]ura | [Sexti Calpurni] Agrico[l]ae | [legati Augustoru]m pr(o) pr(aetore).

"For the Emperors Caesars Marcus Aurelius Antoninus Augustus, in his seventeenth year of tribunician power, three times consul, and Lucius Aurelius Verus Augustus, conqueror of Armenia, in his third year of tribunician power, twice consul, a detachment of the Twentieth Legion Valeria Victrix built *(this)* under the charge of Sextus Calpurnius Agricola, governor."

The inscription is restored as in *RIB* for autumn – 9 December 163, but is only certainly dated between Verus's second consulship in 161 and his third in 167. Calpurnius Agricola's governorship of Britain is attested by SHA *Marcus* 8.7–8 (L11, 44), where he is said to have been sent specifically to deal with a threat of war in Britain. For the possibility that the Roman name of Corbridge was Coria see under no. 51.

For other inscriptions of Calpurnius Agricola see no. 66 (also Corbridge), no. 67 (Carvoran), *RIB* 1703 (Vindolanda), *RIB* 589 (Ribchester) and note also *RIB* 793 (Hardknott) as a possible example.

66   Invincible Sun-god (Legio VI Victrix)   *c.* AD 161–166

RIB 1137. *Corbridge, Northumberland* (Coria?). *A dedication-slab found in 1911 incorporated in the roadway south of Site XI. Now in Corbridge Museum.*

Soli Invicto | vexillatio | leg(ionis) VI Vic(tricis) P(iae) F(idelis) f(ecit) | sub cura Sex(ti) | Calpurni Agrico|lae leg(ati) Aug(usti) pr(o) pr(aetore).

"To the Invincible Sun-god, a detachment of the Sixth Legion Victrix Pia Fidelis set *(this)* up, under the charge of Sextus Calpurnius Agricola, governor."

Flanking panels which once carried the figures of Victory are now lost. Line 1 was later erased, possibly after the death of Elagabalus in AD 222. Sun-worship came from the East, but is rare in Britain, except when later associated with the cult of Mithras.

67   Carvoran Dea Syria altar
c. AD 161–166

RIB 1792. Carvoran, Northumberland (Magnis). Altar seen in 1599 at Melkridge, about 8 kilometres east of Carvoran. Now at Cambridge.

> Deae Surila[e s]u[b] Calp[urnio] Ag[r]licol[a le]g(ato) Au[g(usti)] | pr(o) pr(aetore) Lic[in]ius | [C]lem[ens praef(ectus) | c]oh(ortis) I Ha[miorum].

> "To the Syrian Goddess, under Calpurnius Agricola, governor, Licinius Clemens, prefect of the First Cohort of Hamians, *(set this up)*."

The altar has a decorated capital. The Hamians were a unit of Eastern archers. They came from Syria, and have brought with them the worship of their homeland goddess. This special type of unit appears to have continued to recruit from the original homeland (*contra* Haynes 1993, 145 but the evidence referred to is unpublished, so difficult to assess). Note that the same unit was at Carvoran in *c.* AD 136–137 (nos. 49, 50) and at Bar Hill on the Antonine Wall under Pius (*RIB* 2172).

68   Ilkley Lucanus dedication
AD 161–169

RIB 636. Ilkley, Yorkshire. A dedication found in, or before, 1603 built into the parish church. Later destroyed, perhaps during repair work.

> [Pro salute | Imperato]|rum Caes(arum) | Aug(ustorum) | Antonini | et Veri | Iovi dilect(orum) | Caecilius | Lucanus | praef(ectus) coh(ortis).

> "For the welfare of the Emperors Caesars, the Augusti, Antoninus and Verus, beloved by Jupiter, Caecilius Lucanus, prefect of the cohort, *(set this up)*."

The common identification of Ilkley with Olicana is rejected by Rivet and Smith 1979, 430f. They suggest Verbeia (493) but there is no evidence that this river-name was also used for the fort. Further inscriptions recording activity under Marcus and Verus are known from Stanwix (AD 167, *RIB* 2026) and Great Chesters (AD 166–169, *RIB* 1737).

69   Anociticus altar
c. AD 177–180

RIB 1329. Benwell (Condercum). An altar found in 1862 in a Roman temple outside the fort. Now in the Museum of Antiquities, Newcastle upon Tyne.

> Deo Anocitico | iudiciis Optimo|rum Maximorum|que Imper(atorum) N(ostrorum) sub Ulp(io) | Marcello co(n)s(ulari) Tinelius Longus in p[re]-|lfectura equitu[m] | lato clavo exorna|tus et q(uaestor) d(esignatus).

> "To the god Anociticus Tineius Longus *(set this up)* having, while prefect of cavalry, been adorned with the *(senatorial)* broad stripe and designated quaestor by the decrees of our best and greatest Emperors, under Ulpius Marcellus, consular governor."

The fortunate discovery of a diploma (*RMD* 3, 184), showing Ulpius Marcellus as governor in AD 178, has cleared up an old problem. Ulpius Marcellus was sent against the Britons by Commodus (Dio 72.8.2 = L11, 38). This seemed to imply that Commodus as sole emperor had appointed him as governor. The inscription however refers to Marcellus as governor under the joint reign of Marcus and Commodus, AD 176–180. The designation as quaestor would have been on 23 January, so 177–180 are the possible years. Now that it is clear that Ulpius Marcellus was already governor under Marcus and Commodus, a fact obscured by Dio, there is no need to argue for a second governor called Ulpius Marcellus in order to explain the inscription. Jarrett 1978 discusses the problem as it existed before the discovery of the diploma.

RIB 1327 and 1328 give the god's name as Antenociticus. His life-sized stone statue stood in the temple, and fragments including the notable head survive. The portrayal is Celtic rather than classical. He is an interesting example of a local god worshipped by a commanding officer, a legionary centurion (1327) and an auxiliary unit (1328).

(e)   COMMODUS (AD 180–192)

70   Chesters aqueduct   *c.* AD 178–184

RIB 1463. *Chesters, Northumberland* (Cilurnum). *A dedication-slab found in 1897 in the south-east part of the fort. Now in the Chesters Museum.*

> Aqua adducta | alae II Astur(um)| sub Ulp(io) Marcello | leg(ato) Aug(usti) pr(o) pr(aetore).

> "Water brought for the Second Cavalry Regiment of Asturians under Ulpius Marcellus, governor."

The presence of the *ala II Asturum* (originally raised in north-west Spain) under Ulpius Marcellus is significant, as the regiment continues to be stationed at Chesters throughout the third century and is still there *c.* AD 400, if that date for the Wall section in the Notitia Dignitatum is accepted. At this Wall fort at least there appears to be continuity of unit from the 180s. At Old Carlisle the *ala Augusta ob virtutem appellata* is found in AD 188, AD 191, AD 197 and AD 242 (*RIB* 893–5, 897).

71 (71 and 72) Sestertii of Commodus   AD 184

(a) RIC Commodus 437.

> *Obverse:* Head of Commodus wearing laurel-wreath. Around, M(ARCVS) COMMODVS ANTON(INVS) AVG(VSTVS) PIVS BRIT(ANNICVS).

> *Reverse:* Britannia standing, holding sword. Around, P(ONTIFEX) M(AXIMVS) TR(IBVNICIA) P(OTESTATE) VIIII IMP(ERATOR) VII CO(N)S(VL) IIII P(ATER) P(ATRIAE). S(ENATVS) and C(ONSVLTO) on either side of Britannia, BRITT(ANNIA) below her.

> The imperial titulature runs continuously from obverse to reverse: "Marcus Commodus Antoninus Augustus Pius Britannicus, *pontifex*

maximus, in his ninth year of tribunician power, hailed *imperator* for the seventh time, consul for the fourth time, father of his country."

(b) *RIC Commodus* 440.

Obverse: Same as on *(a)*.

Reverse: Victory seated on a pile of weapons, holding a shield in left hand and a palm-branch in right hand. S(ENATVS) and C(ONSVLTO) on either side of Victory, VICT(ORIA) BRIT(ANNICA) below her.

These two coins commemorate Commodus's victory in Britain, won by Ulpius Marcellus: cf. comment under no. 69.

For a medallion of AD 185 still celebrating this victory see Frere 1987, Pl. 31, 5.

72 (74) Kirksteads altar   Later 2nd.century AD

RIB 2034. Kirksteads, Cumbria. An altar found in 1803 near Kirksteads Farm. Now at Lowther Castle.

[...] I L(ucius) Iunius Vicltorinus Fl[av(ius)]l Caelianus leg(atus) I Aug(usti) leg(ionis) VI Vic(tricis) I P(iae) F(idelis) ob res trans I vallum prolspere gestas.

"To ..., Lucius Junius Victorinus Flavius Caelianus, commander of the Sixth Legion Victrix Pia Fidelis, *(set this up)* because of successful achievements beyond the Wall."

The inscription clearly belongs to a period when Hadrian's Wall was the frontier, and is probably later than Hadrian. It names the Wall as the VALLVM, strictly "rampart". For a discussion of the possible dates and identifications of Caelianus, see Birley 1981, 254.

The suggestion of military activity north of Hadrian's Wall may be compared with *RIB* 946, from Carlisle, which has been restored to refer to "the slaughter of a band of barbarians".

73 (–) Legio VI at Castlecary   *c.* AD 175–190?

RIB 2148. Castlecary. Altar found in or before 1845 between the west rampart of Castelcary fort and the Red Burn. Now in the National Museums of Scotland, Edinburgh.

Deo I Mercurio I milites leg(ionis) VI I Victricis Pi(a)e F(idelis) I (a)ed(em) et sigillum I cives Italici I et Norici I v(otum) s(olverunt) l(aeti) l(ibentes) m(erito).

"To the god Mercury, soldiers of the Sixth Legion Victrix Pia Fidelis, being citizens of Italy and Noricum, set up this shrine and statuette, gladly, willingly and deservedly fulfilling their vow."

The significance of this inscription depends upon its dating. The argument may be summarised thus: a mixture of Italians and Noricans would be only likely to occur in a legion newly-raised in Italy and stationed in Noricum. The only possibility is *legio II Italica*, and it must be assumed that a detachment of that legion has been transferred into *legio VI Victrix*. The dating given here is that in Mann 1969, 92, cf. Jarrett and Mann 1970, 194, being the period when *legio II Italica* would have contained such a mixture of original Italian recruits and local Norican recruits.

The inscription would then show activity on the Antonine Wall at a time when it is generally thought to have been abandoned.

PART IV: SEVERUS AND THE THIRD CENTURY
(AD 193–284)

(a)   SEVERUS (AD 193–211)

74 (–) Denarius of Clodius Albinus   AD 196–7

RIC Albinus 19. Mint of Lugdunum.

> *Obverse:*   IMP(ERATOR)   CAE(SAR)   D(IDIVS)   CLO(DIVS)
> SEP(TIMIVS) ALB(INVS) AVG(VSTVS).
> "The Emperor Caesar Didius Clodius Septimius Albinus Augustus."

> *Reverse:* Legionary eagle between two standards. Around FIDES
> LEGION(VM) CO(N)S(VL) II
> "The fidelity of the legions, twice consul."

Clodius Albinus as self-proclaimed emperor. (PJC)

75   Brough-under-Stainmore rebuilding   AD 197

RIB 757. Brough-under-Stainmore, Cumbria (Verterae). *A dedication-slab found
in 1879 in restoring the church. Now built into the porch.*

> Imp(eratori) Caesa[r]i L(ucio) Sep(timio) Severo P(io) P[[ertin]aci
> Aug(usto) et | [M(arco) Aur(elio) Anto]nino Caes(ari)|[...|... Later]a[n(o)]
> et R[uf]in(o) co(n)s(ulibus).

> "For the Emperor Caesar Lucius Septimius Severus Pius Pertinax
> Augustus and for Marcus Aurelius Antoninus Caesar ... in the consulship
> of Lateranus and Rufinus."

The consuls are for AD 197. Marcus Aurelius Antoninus Caesar was
Septimius's son, the future emperor Caracalla.

It has been suggested that there was a disaster in AD 197, when the governor
Clodius Albinus was defeated at Lyons by Severus. The assumption was that
when Albinus withdrew troops from Britain the northern barbarians broke into
the province. Building activity under the early governors of Severus, e.g. nos.
75–81 and 83–86, and even 88–89 (from Wales), has then been explained as
repairs to damage caused by this. There was trouble in the north at this time,
cf. Dio 75.5.4=L11, 39, but this is not necessarily the reason for all, or indeed
any, of the rebuilding. Some at least may be simply part of a normal repair
programme which carries on at least into the 240s AD (nos. 100–107, 109–110).
Repairs of ageing buildings are referred to specifically in nos. 83, 89, 90, 103,
107 and 110.

76   Ilkley rebuilding   AD 197–198

*RIB 637. Ilkley, Yorkshire. A dedication-slab found before 1600 near the church.
Now lost.*

[Imp(erator) Caes(ar) L(ucius) Sept]lim[ius] Severus [P(ius) P(ertinax)] I Aug(ustus) et Antoninus I Caes(ar) (imp(erator)) destinatus resltituerunt curante Virlio Lupo leg(ato) eorum pr(o) pr(aetore).

"The Emperor Caesar Lucius Septimius Severus Pius Pertinax Augustus and Antoninus Caesar destined (to be emperor) restored *(this)* under the charge of Virius Lupus, governor."

See 68 *note* for doubts on the Roman name of Ilkley. IMP after ANTON-INVS CAESAR was apparently omitted by a mason's error. This is dated between the defeat of Clodius Albinus on 19 February AD 197, and Caracalla becoming Augustus on 28 January AD 198.

77   Bowes bath-house   AD 197–198

RIB 730. Bowes, Yorkshire (Lavatrae). An altar found before 1600 at Bowes. Now at the Museum of Archaeology, Cambridge.

D(e)ae Fortunae I Virius Lupus I leg(atus) Aug(usti) pr(o) pr(aetore) I balineum vi I ignis exustlum coh(orti) I Thrlacum restiltuit curanlte Val(erio) Fronltone praef(ecto) I eq(uitum) alae Vetto(num).

"To the goddess Fortuna Virius Lupus, governor, restored this bath-house, burnt by the violence of fire, for the First Cohort of Thracians; Valerius Fronto, prefect of the Vettonian cavalry regiment, had charge of the work."

The dating is based on the fact that Lupus refers to himself as legate for one emperor, Severus, cf. no. 76 above. Dedications to Fortuna commonly appear in fort bath-houses. The *ala Vettonum*, originally recruited in west-central Spain, appears to be at Binchester during the third century. It is not clear why its commander is in charge here. For Virius Lupus see also no.76 and *RIB* 1163 (Corbridge).

78   Bainbridge barracks   AD 205

JRS 51 (1961), 192. Bainbridge, Yorkshire (Virosidum?). Dedication-slab found in 1960 in the east gateway of the fort. Now at the School of Classics, University of Leeds; to be deposited in the Yorkshire Museum, York.

Imp(eratori) Caesari Lucio Septimio I Severo Pio Pertinaci Aug(usto) et I Imp(eratori) Caesari M(arco) Aurelio I Antonino Pio Felici Aug(usto) et I P(ublio) Septimio Getae nolbilissimo Caesar(i), D(ominis) I N(ostris) Imp(eratoribus) Antonino II et I Geta Caesare co(n)s(ulibus), centurias I sub cura C(ai) Valeri Pudentis I amplissimi co(n)sularis coh(ors) I VI Nervior(um) fecit, cui praeest I L(ucius) Vinicius Pius praef(ectus) coh(ortis) eiusd(em).

"For the Emperor Caesar Lucius Septimius Severus Pius Pertinax Augustus and for the Emperor Caesar Marcus Aurelius Antoninus Pius Felix Augustus and for Publius Septimius Geta most noble Caesar, in the consulship of Our Lords the Emperor Antoninus (for the second time) and Geta Caesar, the Sixth Cohort of Nervians built these barrack-blocks, under the charge of Gaius Valerius Pudens, most illustrious consular governor, overseen by Lucius Vinicius Pius, prefect of the said cohort."

The text is flanked by reliefs, reading downwards: on the left panel a Capricorn, Victory on a globe holding palm-branch in left, and wreath in right hand, an eagle on a thunderbolt with wreath in its beak; on the right panel a "lunula", a draped Genius holding over his left arm a cornucopia and in his right hand a wreath above a small altar, a bull facing left. CAESARI and DDNN have been erased (Geta's name and/or titles were erased after his murder by Caracalla in 212, though not consistently). CENTVRIAM (barrack-block) has been altered to CENTVRIAS. Alternative readings are CAES AVGG for CAESAR DD, "Our Augusti" not "Our Lords" and CENTVRIAM (unaltered), "barrack-block" (Alföldy in *JRS* 1969, 246). The Nervii, from whom the cohort was originally raised, came from modern Belgium, around Bavay.

79 Bainbridge defences *c.* AD 205–208 (206?)

RIB 722. *Bainbridge, Yorkshire* (Virosidum?). *A dedication-slab found shortly before 1600 at the Roman fort. Now lost.*

Imp(eratori) Caesari L(ucio) Septimio [Severo] | Pio Pert[i]naci Augu[sto et] | Imp(eratori) Caesari M(arco) Aurelio A[ntonino] | Pio Feli[ci] Augusto et P(ublio) S[eptimio Getae nobilissimo Caesari vallum cum] | bracchio caementicium [fecit coh(ors)] | VI Nervio[ru]m sub cura L(uci) A[lfeni] | Senecion[is] amplissimi [co(n)s(ularis) instituit] | operi L(ucius) Vinic[ius] Pius praef(ectus) [coh(ortis) eiusd(em)].

"For the Emperor Caesar Lucius Septimius Severus Pius Pertinax Augustus and for the Emperor Caesar Marcus Aurelius Antoninus Pius Felix Augustus and for Publius Septimius Geta, most noble Caesar, the Sixth Cohort of Nervians built this [rampart] with annexe-wall of uncoursed masonry under the charge of Lucius Alfenus Senecio, most illustrious consular governor; Lucius Vinicius Pius, prefect of the said cohort, had direction of the work."

The slab was flanked on both sides by a panel carrying a winged Victory. The name Geta and his title were erased. The name of the prefect is restored on the analogy of no. 78, as read by Alföldy in *JRS* 1969, 246. It may be possible to restore the consuls for AD 206, cf. Birley 1988, 170 and 254 fn. 2. For the Nervii see under no. 78. *RIB* 723 (Brough-by-Bainbridge) may also be restored to show the names of Senecio and of Lucius Vinicius Pius; Alföldy 1969.

80 Bowes rebuilding *c.* AD 205–208

RIB 740. *Bowes, Yorkshire* (Lavatrae). *A dedication-slab found in 1929 outside vicarage. Now in north transept of church.*

Imp(eratoribus) Caes(aribus) L(ucio) Septim(io) | Severo Pio Pertinaci | Arab(ico) Adiab(enico) Part(hico) Max(imo) | et M(arco) Aur(elio) Anton(ino) Pio Aug(ustis) [et P(ublio) Sept(imio) Getae nob(ilissimo) Caes(ari)] ius|su L(uci) Alfeni Senecionis leg(ati) | Aug(ustorum) pr(o) pr(aetore) coh(ors) I Thrac(um) eq(uitata).

"For the Emperors Caesars Lucius Septimius Severus Pius Pertinax, Conqueror of Arabia, Conqueror of Adiabene, Most Great Conqueror of

Parthia, and Marcus Aurelius Antoninus Pius, both Augusti, and for the most noble Caesar Publius Septimius Geta, on the order of Lucius Alfenus Senecio, governor, the First Cohort of Thracians, *equitata, (set this up)*."

Compare no.77. The three new titles of Severus were gained from his victorious campaigns in the East (AD 197–201). Adiabene was a small vassal-kingdom of Parthia, east of the Upper Tigris. For the origins of Thracian units see under no. 8.

81   Greta Bridge rebuilding   *c.* AD 205–208

RIB 746. *Greta Bridge, Yorkshire. A dedication-slab found in 1793 near north gate of fort. Now in the Bowes Museum, Barnard Castle.*

Imp(eratoribus) Caes(aribus) L(ucio) Sep(timio) Severo | Pio Pert(inaci) et M(arco) Aur(elio) Antoni|no Pio Aug(ustis) et P(ublio) Sept(imio) Getae | nob(ilissimo) Caes(ari) sub cura L(uci) | Alfeni Senecionis | leg(ati) eorum pr(o) pr(aetore).

"For the Emperors Caesars Lucius Septimius Severus Pius Pertinax and Marcus Aurelius Antoninus Pius, both Augusti, and for Publius Septimius Geta, most noble Caesar, under the charge of Lucius Alfenus Senecio, governor."

The sides of the slab are decorated. Geta's names have been erased, but his title remains.

82   The Greetland Victoria Brigantia   AD 208

RIB 627. *From Greetland, 3 kilometres south of Halifax. An altar found in 1597. Now at Museum of Archaeology, Cambridge.*

D(eae) Vict(oriae) Brig(antiae) | et Num(inibus) Aug(ustorum) | T(itus) Aur(elius) Aurelian|us d(edit) d(edicavit) pro se| et suis, s(e) mag(istro) s(acrorum). (*Right side:*) – Antonin[o] | III et Geta [II] | co(n)s(ulibus).

"To the goddess Victoria Brigantia and to the Divine Powers of the two Emperors, Titus Aurelius Aurelianus gave and dedicated *(this altar)* for himself and his family, while he himself was master of the sacred rites, in the third consulship of Antoninus and the [second] of Geta."

For Brigantia see also nos. 173, 238, 263 and notes. This victory if it refers to Britain may be one won by a Severan governor, cf. Dio 76.10.6=L11, 39f., 72. For *Numina Augustorum* see Note on Religion (p. 19).

83   Risingham rebuilding   *c.* AD 205–7

RIB 1234. *Risingham, Northumberland* (Habitancum). *Dedication-slab found in 1844 at south gateway. Now in Museum of Antiquities, Newcastle upon Tyne.*

[Imp(eratoribus) Caes(aribus) L(ucio) | Sept(imio) Severo Pio Pertin|aci Arab(ico) Adi]ab(enico) Part(h)[i]co Maxi(mo) | co(n)s(uli) III et M(arco) Aurel(io) Antonino Pio | co(n)s(uli) II Aug(ustis) [et P(ublio) Sept(imio) Getae nob(ilissimo) Caes(ari)] | portam cum muris vetustate di|lapsis iussu

Alfeni Senecionis v(iri) c(larissimi) I co(n)s(ularis) curante Oclatinio Advento proc(uratore) I Aug(ustorum) n(ostrorum) coh(ors) I Vangion(um) m(illiaria) eq(uitata) I cum Aem[i]l(io) Salviano trib(uno) I suo a solo rest(ituit).

"For the Emperors Caesars Lucius Septimius Severus Pius Pertinax, Conqueror of Arabia, Conqueror of Adiabene, Most Great Conqueror of Parthia, three times consul, Augustus, and Marcus Aurelius Antoninus Pius, twice consul, Augustus, and for Publius Septimius Geta, most noble Caesar, the First Cohort of Vangiones, *milliaria*, *equitata*, restored from ground-level this gate with its walls, which had fallen in through age, on the order of Alfenus Senecio, of senatorial rank and consular governor, under the charge of Oclatinius Adventus, procurator of our Emperors, together with its own tribune Aemilius Salvianus."

The inscription is inside a circle with patterned rim; on left side Mars (?), on right Victory (?) with globe at feet. The top of the relief has been lost, including heads of both figures. Caracalla was consul for the second time in 205, and for the third time in 208. No. 84 may be the same tribune. The unit of Vangiones was originally raised in Germania Superior, around Worms. The description "collapsed through old age" is not uncommon, and there is no reason not to take it literally, cf. above under no. 75.

84 (83n.) A *numerus* at Risingham   *c.* AD 205–207 ??

RIB 1216. *Altar found about 1751 at Risingham, Northumberland* (Habitancum). *Now lost.*

I(ovi) O(ptimo) M(aximo) I v[e]xi[l](latio) g(aesatorum) R(aetorum) I q(uorum) c(uram) a(git) I Aemil(ius) Aemilianus I trib(unus) coh(ortis) I Vang(ionum).

"To Jupiter Best and Greatest, the detachment of *gaesati Raeti* under the command of Aemilius Aemilianus, tribune of the First Cohort of Vangiones, *(set this up)*."

There is a knife and axe on the right-hand side of the altar. AEMILIANVS could have been miscopied from an original SALVIANVS, and the inscription refer to the same officer as no. 83. The *gaesati Raeti* came from Switzerland, and were definitely at Risingham in AD 213: *RIB* 1235.

85 (84) Birdoswald granary   *c.* AD 205–208

RIB 1909. *Birdoswald, Cumbria* (Banna). *A dedication-slab found in 1929 reused in the floor of a barrack-block in the fort. Now in Tullie House Museum, Carlisle.*

Imp(eratoribus) Caes(aribus) L(ucio) I Sept(imio) Severo Pio I Pert(inaci) et M(arco) Aur(elio) A[nt]o[n]ino Aug(ustis) [et P(ublio) Sep(timio) I Geta nob(ilissimo) Caes(ari)] hor[reum fecer(unt) coh(ortes) I Ael(ia) I Dac(orum) et I T(h)racum c(ivium) R(omanorum) sub I Alfeno Senecione co(n)s(ulari) I per Aurel(ium) Iulianum tr(ibunum).

"For the Emperors Caesars Lucius Septimius Severus Pius Pertinax and Marcus Aurelius Antoninus, both Augusti, and for Publius Septimius Geta, most noble Caesar, the First Aelian Cohort of Dacians and the First Cohort of Thracians, Roman citizens, built this granary under Alfenus Senecio, consular governor, through the agency of Aurelius Iulianus, the tribune."

The Roman name of Birdoswald is now thought to be Banna, not Camboglanna (Rivet and Smith 1979, 261f.). Geta's name is erased. The title "Roman citizens" marks an occasion on which the unit's men at the time were granted citizenship *en masse* for valour; it was retained as a battle-honour. There appears to have been more than one *cohors I Thracum*, and this unit is not necessarily the same as nos. 77 and 80, both at Bowes.

86 (85) Corbridge granary   *c*. AD 205–208

RIB 1151. *Corbridge, Northumberland (Coria?). A dedication-slab, part of which was found in 1725 reused as a roofing slab in crypt of Hexham Abbey, where it still is, and part in 1907 among the foundations of the south-west tower, now built into north wall of the nave.*

Imp(erator) Caes(ar) L(ucius) Sep(timius) [S]everus Pi(us) | Pertinax et Imp(erator) C[a]esar M(arcus) | Aur(elius) Antoninu[s] Pius Aug|usti et P(ublius) Septi[mi]us Geta | Caesar horre[u]m [per] | vexillatione[m leg(ionis) ...] | fecerunt su[b L(ucio) Alfeno | Senecione leg(ato) Aug(ustorum) pr(o) pr(aetore)].

"The Emperor Caesar Lucius Septimius Severus Pius Pertinax Augustus and the Emperor Caesar Marcus Aurelius Antoninus Pius Augustus and Publius Septimius Geta Caesar built this granary through the agency of a detachment of the ... Legion under Lucius Alfenus Senecio, governor."

Geta's name is damaged but readable. The name of C. Valerius Pudens (no. 78) is an alternative restoration as governor to L. Alfenus Senecio. For the Roman name of Corbridge see no. 51.

87 (86) Benwell dedication   *c*. AD 205–208

RIB 1337. *Benwell, Northumberland (Condercum). A dedication-slab found c. 1669 among ruined walls of the fort. Now lost.*

Victoriae | [Au]g(ustorum) Alfe|no Senecio|n[e] co(n)s(ulari) felix | ala I Asto(rum) | [...] M pra(efecto).

"To the Victory of the Emperors while Alfenus Senecio was consular governor, the Fortunate First Cavalry Regiment of Asturians *(set this up)*, when ... M(...) was prefect."

Birley 1981, 157 suggests the reading ASTO|[RV]M, and interprets PRA as *pra(etoria?)*, a possible extra title of the unit. A winged Victory flanked both sides of the slab. The emperors were Septimius Severus and his son Caracalla. The victory may be one of those won in Britain before the arrival of Severus, referred to by Dio 76.10.6=L11, 39f., but it need not be one in Britain. Alfenus Senecio also appears on nos. 79–81, 83, 86?, *RIB* 723 (Bainbridge), *RIB* 1462

(Chesters) and *Britannia* 8 (1977), 432 (Vindolanda). *RIB* 1277 (High Rochester) and *RIB* 1612 (Housesteads), both of AD 198–209, may also belong to this governor. The *ala I Asturum* was originally raised in north-west Spain.

88 (87) Quarrying inscriptions AD 207

(a) *RIB* 1008. *Cumbria quarries. An inscription seen c. 1604 cut on the rock-face about 9 metres above the river on the north side of the river Gelt, 1 kilometre south-east of Low Gelt Bridge.*

> vex(illatio) l<i>eg(ionis) II Aug(ustae) of(ficina) Apr(...) l sub Agricola optione.

> "A detachment of the Second Legion Augusta; the working-face of Apr(...), under Agricola, the optio."

Above the inscription is a naively drawn face. Roman quarries were usually state-owned; here under military control. An *optio* was the second-in-command of a century.

(b) *RIB* 1009. *Cumbria quarries. An inscription seen before 1607 c. 30 cm beyond the end of RIB 1008.*

> Apro et Maximo l consulibus l of(f)icina Mercati.

> "In the consulship of Aper and Maximus, the working-face of Mercatius".

The consuls are those of AD 207.

89 (88) Caerleon rebuilding AD 198–209

RIB 333. *Caerleon, Gwent (Isca). Fragments of a block forming a medial part of a frieze found between 1845 and 1850 in the churchyard, perhaps from the headquarters building of the fortress. Now in Caerleon Museum.*

> [Imperatores] Caesares L(ucius) Septi(mius) [Severus Pius Pertinax Aug(ustus) et M(arcus) Aurelius l Antoninus A]ug(ustus) et [P(ublius)] Septimius [Geta nobilissimus Caesar ... l vetustate c]orruptum [restituerunt].

> "The Emperors Caesars Lucius Septimius Severus Pius Pertinax Augustus and Marcus Aurelius Antoninus Augustus and Publius Septimius Geta, most noble Caesar, [restored the building] ruined by age."

90 (89) Caernarfon aqueduct AD 198–209

RIB 430. *Caernarfon (Segontium). Fragments of a commemorative slab, reused in the Roman fort as cover-slabs in a hypocaust, found partly in 1845, partly in 1852, in Llanbeblig Vicarage garden. Now in Segontium Museum.*

> [Imp(eratores) Caes(ares) L(ucius)] Sept(imius) Severus Pius Perl[tinax et M(arcus) A]urel(ius) Antoninus l [Pius Aug(usti)] et [P(ublius) Sep]t(imius) [Geta no]b(ilissimus) C[aes(ar) l rivos aq]uaeductium vetusl[tate conla]bs(os) coh(orti) I Sunic(orum) restit(uerunt) l ... RE ... l ... NL ...

"The Emperors Caesars Lucius Septimius Severus Pius Pertinax Augustus and Marcus Aurelius Antoninus Pius Augustus and Publius Septimius Geta most noble Caesar, restored the channels of the aqueducts fallen in through age for the First Cohort of Sunicians ..."

The Sunici, better Sunuci, originated in Lower Germany. Casey, Davies and Evans 1993, 72f., discusses a large drain near the find-spot of the inscription, which they think might be overflow from the *castellum aquae*, the collecting-point from which the water of an aqueduct is distributed.

91 (90) An unknown soldier   *c.* AD 208–209?

ILS 9123. *Amiens* (Samarobriva). *Limestone slab found in 1848 reused on the road to Nazon. Now in the Mowat Museum.*

[D(is)] M(anibus) | [...]ius Se[[...] miles | [leg(ionis) ...] p(iae) f(idelis), vex[ill(arii)] l]eg(ionis) eiusdem | [m]onime[n]tum euntes | [ad] expedi[t(ionem)] Britan(n)icam | [d(e)] s(uo) f(aciendum) c(uraverunt).

"To the departed: -ius Se-, soldier of the Legion *(perhaps Twenty-Second Primigenia)* ... Pia Fidelis, soldiers of the detachment of the same legion going on the British campaign had this memorial erected out of their own funds."

The style of the lettering makes it probable that the *expeditio Britannica* referred to is that beginning in AD 208 by Severus and his sons Caracalla and Geta. The soldier commemorated was a member of a legionary detachment, perhaps from Legion XXII Primigenia, based at Mainz. Herodian 3.14.3 = L11, 42 says that troops came from everywhere for the campaign; cf. no. 96. It has been suggested that the centurion of *legio I Italica* who set up an altar at Old Kilpatrick on the Antonine Wall while temporarily in command of an auxiliary cohort (*Britannia* 1 (1970), 310f., n.20) had come to Britain on the Severan *expeditio*. (The legion was stationed in Lower Moesia, modern Bulgaria) (Birley 1983, 73–77). An earlier date was suggested in Breeze and Dobson 1969–70, 120 fn. 48.

92 (91) A Corbridge granary officer   AD 209–211

RIB 1143. *Corbridge, Northumberland* (Coria?). *An altar, found in 1908, in the west granary. Now in the Corbridge Museum.*

[... | ...]sit[... | ...]norus | [... pr]aep(ositus) cu[[ram] agens | horr(eorum) tempo[[r]e expeditio]nis felicissi(mae) | Britannic(ae) | v(otum) s(olvit) l(ibens) m(erito).

"... norus ... officer in charge of the granaries at the time of the most successful expedition to Britain, gladly and deservedly fulfilled his vow."

"Granaries" seems more likely than "granary". This is most probably the campaign under Severus. For the Roman name of Corbridge see no. 51.

93 (92) "Setting-out" denarius of Caracalla AD 208

RIC Caracalla 107. *Denarius.*

> *Obverse:* Head of Caracalla wearing laurel-wreath. Around, ANTON-
> INVS PIVS AVG(VSTVS).

> *Reverse:* Caracalla on horseback. Around, PONT(IFEX) TR(IBVNICIA)
> P(OTESTATE) XI CO(N)S(VL) III. Below, PROF(ECTIO) = "setting-
> out".

The Imperial titulature runs continuously from obverse to reverse:
"Antoninus Pius Augustus, *pontifex*, in the eleventh year of his possession of
tribunician power, consul for the third time".

94 (93) "Setting-out" denarius of Caracalla with captive AD 208

RIC Caracalla 108.

> *Obverse:* Same as on no.93.

> *Reverse:* Same as on no.93, with the addition of a captive on the ground
> in front of the horse.

95 (94) *As* or medallion of Caracalla AD 209

RIC Caracalla 441.

> *Obverse:* Bust of Caracalla wearing laurel-wreath. Around, ANTONINVS
> PIVS AVG(VSTVS).

> *Reverse:* Bridge of boats, with soldiers crossing. Around, PONTIF(EX)
> TR(IBVNICIA) P(OTESTATE) XI (or XII) CO(N)S(VL) III. Below,
> TRAIECTVS = "Crossing".

> The Imperial titulature runs continuously from obverse to reverse:
> "Antoninus Pius Augustus, *pontifex*, in the eleventh (or twelfth) year of
> tribunician power, consul for the third time."

Illustrated in Frere 1987, pl. 31.9.
This coin is sometimes interpreted as a literal reference to bridge building during
the campaigns in Scotland (e.g. Robertson 1980; Hanson and Maxwell 1983, 206);
a more elaborate structure, with triumphal arches at each end, is depicted on an
as of Severus (*RIC* 786; Frere 1987, pl. 31.8). Elsewhere TRAIECTVS is used on
the coinage as an alternative form of PROFECTIO, the setting forth from Rome
of an imperial expedition. In the present case the bridge is an alternative symbol
for a journey in place of the more usual ship. (PJC)

96 (95) Tombstone of Cesennius Senecio *c.* AD 209–211

ILS 2089. *Rome* (Roma). *A marble urn, found near St. Peter in Vincola. Now at
Palermo.*

> D(is) m(anibus) | C. Cesennio Selnecioni c(enturioni) c(o)hor(tis) II |
> pr(aetoriae) p(iae) v(indicis), exercitatori | equitum pr(aetoriae), fecit C.
> Celsernius Zonysius livelrtus et heres, atferlente Zotico a Brittlania.

"To the departed: Gaius Cesennius Senecio, centurion of the Second Praetorian Cohort *pia vindex*, trainer of the praetorian cavalry: erected by Gaius Cesernius Zonysius his freedman and heir: Zoticus brought his body from Britain."

Cesennius could have come to Britain with Severus in AD 208. The date is suggested by the fact that a Caes. Senecio was a centurion of the *vigiles* in AD 205 (*CIL* 6.1057). Promotion of centurions of the *vigiles* to centurions of the urban cohorts and then to centurions of the praetorian cohorts is well attested. The titles *pia vindex* were given to the praetorian cohorts by Severus. The inscription is inconsistent in spelling, and reflects the spoken language.

(b)   SEVERUS'S SUCCESSORS (AD 211–284)

97 (–) Building at Carpow   AD 212–?

JRS 55 (1965), 223f., no. 10; *cf. Wright 1974. Carpow. Two portions of a monumental dedication found in 1964 on the south roadway of the east gate of the base. Now in Dundee Museum.*

Imp(erator) e[t D(ominus) N(oster) M(arcus) Aur(elius) Antoninus I Piu]s F[elix ...]

"The Emperor and Our Lord Marcus Aurelius Antoninus Pius Felix ..."

The left-hand sculptured panel, which includes the I of IMP, carries the emblems of the Legion II Augusta, a Capricorn and two Pegasi. The restoration is controversial, cf. Wright 1974. If correct it would indicate work still in progress at Carpow after the death of Severus and before the presumed withdrawal from the lands which Severus had conquered (Dio 77.1.1 = L11, 41; Herodian 3.15.6 = L11, 44). Over 200 tiles from Carpow of the Legion VI Victrix give it the title *B(ritannica)*, only otherwise attested at York by a single example (*RIB* 2.4.2460.71–74, Carpow; *RIB* 2.4.2460, 75, York). The title was presumably taken in AD 210 when the three emperors took the title BRITANNICVS, and dropped not long afterwards.

98 (96) High Rochester declaration of loyalty   AD 213

RIB 1278. *High Rochester* (Bremenium). *Fragment, found in 1852, at the fort. Now in the Museum of Antiquities, Newcastle upon Tyne.*

[Imp(eratori) Caes(ari) L(uci) Sept(imi) Severi Pii I Pertinacis Aug(usti) Arabici I Adiabenici Parth(ici) Max(imi) I fil(io) divi Antonini Sarm(atici) I nep(oti) divi Antonini Pii I pron(epoti)] di[vi Hadr(iani) abnep(oti) I divi] Tr[aiani Parth(ici) I et di]vi N[ervae adnep(oti) I M(arco)] Aure[lio Antonino I Pi]o Fel(ici) [Aug(usto) Parthico I M]axim[o Brit(annico) Maximo I p]ontif(ici) [maximo tr(ibunicia) pot(estate) I X]VI imp(eratori) [II p(atri) p(atriae) proco(n)s(uli) I pr]o pie[tate et devotione I communi ...]

"For the Emperor Caesar, son of Lucius Septimius Severus Pius Pertinax Augustus, conqueror of Arabia, conqueror of Adiabene, Most Great

Conqueror of Parthia, grandson of the deified Antoninus, conqueror of Sarmatia, great-grandson of the deified Antoninus Pius, great-great-grand-son of the deified Hadrian, great-great-great-grandson of the deified Trajan, conqueror of Parthia, and of the deified Nerva, Marcus Aurelius Antoninus Pius Felix Augustus, Most Great Conqueror of Parthia, Most Great Conqueror of Britain, *pontifex maximus*, in his sixteenth year of tribunician power, twice acclaimed *imperator*, father of his country, proconsul, out of their joint duty and devotion ...''

It would appear that the loyalty of the army in Britain was suspect after the murder of Geta by Caracalla at the end of AD 211. Geta had acted as civil governor in Britain during the campaigns of Severus and Caracalla in AD 208–211. Protestations of loyalty to Caracalla and his mother Julia Domna are found at Risingham (*RIB* 1235), Vindolanda (*RIB* 1705), Old Penrith (*RIB* 928), Whitley Castle (*RIB* 1202), Newcastle (*Britannia* 11 (1980), 405 no. 6) and South Shields (*Britannia* 16 (1985) 325f. no. 11). The *damnatio memoriae* of C. Iulius Marcus, governor in AD 213, see under no. 99, may be linked to unrest in the army of Britain.

99 (97) Netherby declaration of loyalty   AD 213

RIB 976. *Netherby* (Castra Exploratorum). *The jamb of a doorway, of perhaps the shrine of the headquarters building, found in 1609 in building Arthuret Church. Since lost.*

...] Iuliae Au[g(ustae)]l <M> matri Au[g(usti) l nostri M(arci) Aur]leli<i> Anton[ini] l et castr(orum) [et] l senatus et l patriae pro l [pietate ac] devo-tione l [communi] l num(ini) eius l [curante C(aio) Iul(io)] l Marc[o] l[eg(ato) Aug(ustorum)] l pr(o) pr(aetore) coh(ors) [I] Ael(ia) l [Hisp(anorum) m(illiaria) e(quitata)] l posuit.

"... for Julia Augusta, mother of our emperor Marcus Aurelius Antoninus and of the army and senate and country, our of their common duty and devotion to his Divine Power, under the charge of Gaius Julius Marcus, governor, the First Aelian Cohort of Spaniards, *milliaria*, *equitata*, set this up."

The first half of the text, recording Caracalla and his full style, may have been on the corresponding jamb. The name of C. Iulius Marcus seems to have been erased on a number of these inscriptions, cf. *RIB* 1202, 1235, *Britannia* 11 (1980), 405 no. 6; 16 (1985), 325f., no. 11. *RIB* 2298 (Welton milestone) gives his name as governor in AD 213. It is not clear how much of Britain he was governing. Herodian asserts that Severus divided Britain into two provinces in or shortly after AD 197 (3.8.2 = L11, 42). The governors mentioned under Severus operating in the north are still consular (nos. 76–81, 83, 85–87), so if the province is divided the senior governor is in the northern province. Shortly after the situation was reversed, with the senior governor in the southern province. See for full discussion Birley 1981, 168–172.

100 (98) High Rochester rebuilding   AD 216

RIB 1279. *High Rochester* (Bremenium). *Dedication-slab, found in 1744, at High Rochester. Now in the Museum of Antiquities, Newcastle upon Tyne.*

Imp(eratori) Caes(ari) M(arco) Aurelio | Severo Antonino | Pio Felici
Aug(usto) Parthic(o) | Max(imo) Brit(annico) Max(imo) Germ(anico) |
Max(imo) pontifici maxim(o) | trib(unicia) potest(ate) XVIIII imp(eratori)
II | co(n)s(uli) IIII proco(n)s(uli) p(atri) p(atriae) coh(ors) I | Fida
Vardul(lorum) c(ivium) R(omanorum) eq(uitata) m(illiaria) Anto|niniana
fecit sub cura [... | ...] leg(ati) Aug(usti) pr(o) p[r(aetore)].

"For the Emperor Caesar Marcus Aurelius Severus Antoninus Pius Felix
Augustus, Most Great Conqueror of Parthia, Most Great Conqueror of
Britain, Most Great Conqueror of Germany, *pontifex maximus*, in his nineteenth year of tribunician power, twice acclaimed *imperator*, four times
consul, proconsul, father of his country, the First Loyal Cohort of Vardulli,
Roman Citizens, *equitata, milliaria, Antoniniana*, built this under the charge
of ..., governor."

The governor's name has been erased. This is probably Gordianus, later the
emperor Gordian I; see *RIB* 1049 (Chester-le-Street), AD 216: (line 6) ... DIANI
LEG.
   Note the difference between honorary titles given to units (e.g. AELIA),
formed usually from the emperor's *nomen*, and given when the unit was raised
or decorated, and the third-century and later practice of adding to the unit's
name a title derived from the emperor's *cognomen* (e.g. ANTONINIANA) which
was replaced at the end of that emperor's reign by one derived from the new
emperor's *cognomen*. The Vardulli originate in northern Spain.

101 (–) Troops from the two Germanies   *c.* AD 217

JRS 57 (1967), 205 no. 16. *Piercebridge. Statue base, found in 1966 in the field
east of Piercebridge fort. Now in Bowes Museum, Barnard Castle.*

I(ovi) O(ptimo) M(aximo) | Dolicheno pro | salute vexil(lationum)
leg(ionis)| VI V(ictricis) et exer(citus) G(ermaniae) utri|usq(ue) c(uram)
a(gente) M(arco) Loll(io) Ve|natore (centurione) leg(ionis) II Aug(ustae) |
(vexillarii) v(otum) s(olverunt) l(ibentes) m(erito).

"To Jupiter Dolichenus Best and Greatest, for the welfare of the detachments of the Sixth Legion Victrix and the armies of both the Germanies,
under the charge of Marcus Lollius Venator, centurion of the Second
Legion Augusta, the members of the detachments willingly and deservedly
fulfilled their vow."

A centurion from Germania Superior dedicated to Dolichenus at Piercebridge
in AD 217 (*RIB* 1022). *RIB* 1026 is the undated tombstone of a further centurion from Germania Superior, and *Britannia* 17 (1986), 438 no. 20 seems to refer
to a soldier from the same province.

102 (99) High Rochester artillery   AD 220

RIB 1280. *High Rochester* (Bremenium). *Two parts of a dedication-slab found by
1810 and in 1855 respectively, outside the fort. Now at Museum of Antiquities,
Newcastle upon Tyne.*

Imp(eratori) Caes(ari) M(arco) Au[r]elio | Antonino Pio Fel(ici) Aug(usto) | trib(unicia) pot(estate) III co(n)s(uli) III p[roco(n)s(uli)] | p(atri) p(atriae) ballist(arium) a sol[o] coh(ors) I F(ida) | Vardul(lorum) A[nt(oniniana) s]ub cura | Tib(eri) Cl(audi) Paul[ini le]g(ati) Aug(usti) | pr(o) pr(aetore) fe[cit insta]nte | P(ublio) Ael[io Erasino trib(uno)].

"For the Emperor Caesar Marcus Aurelius Antoninus Pius Felix Augustus, in his third year of tribunician power, in his third consulship, proconsul, father of his country, the First Loyal Cohort of Vardulli, *Antoniniana*, built this *ballistarium* from ground-level under the charge of Tiberius Claudius Paulinus, governor, under the direction of Publius Aelius Erasinus, tribune."

The conjunction of TRIB POT III and COS III does not fit Caracalla, and therefore the titles of Elagabalus are restored, which give the date AD 220. The traditional interpretation of *ballistarium* as artillery-platform has recently been challenged, and artillery-shed suggested (Donaldson 1990, 210–213).

103 (100) Chesters rebuilding   30 October AD 221

RIB 1465. Chesters (Cilurnum). *A dedication-slab, found in Chesters fort. Now in Chesters Museum.*

Imp(erator) Caes[a]r M(arcus) Aurel(ius) [Antoninus P(ius) F(elix)] | A[ug(ustus) sacerdos ampliss(imus) Dei Invicti Solis Elagabali] p(ontifex) [m(aximus) tr]ib(unicia) p(otestate) [IIII] co(n)s(ul) [III] p(ater) p(atriae) div[i Anton(ini) f(ilius)] | divi Sever(i) nep(os) et M(arcus) [Aur]el(ius) [Alexander nobiliss(imus)] | Caesar imper[i consors ...] | alae II Astur(um) [Anton(inianae)] v[et]ustate [dilapsum restitu]erunt per Marium Valer[ianum leg(atum) Aug(ustorum) pr(o) pr(aetore)] | instante Septimio Ni[l]o prae[f(ecto) equitum] | dedicatum (ante diem) III Kal(endas) Novem(bres) Gr[at]o et Sele[uco co(n)s(ulibus)].

"The Emperor Caesar Marcus Aurelius Antoninus Pius Felix Augustus, most honourable priest of the Invincible Sun-God Elagabalus, *pontifex maximus*, in his fourth year of tribunician power, three times consul, father of his country, son of the deified Antoninus, grandson of the deified Severus, and Marcus Aurelius Alexander, most noble Caesar, partner of empire, for the Second Cavalry Regiment of Asturians, *Antoniniana*, restored [this building], fallen in through age, through the agency of Marius Valerianus, governor, under the direction of Septimius Nilus, prefect of cavalry: dedicated on 30 October in the consulship of Gratus and Seleucus."

Parts of the names and titles of Elagabalus and Severus Alexander and the honorific ANTONINIANA have been erased. The gap of about 11 letters after CONSORS presumably indicated the building which was restored.

104 (101) Netherby drill-hall   AD 222

RIB 978. Netherby (Castra Exploratorum). *A dedication-slab, found in 1762 in use as a drain-cover at Netherby. Now in Carlisle Museum.*

Imp(eratori) Caes(ari) M(arco) Aurelio | Severo Alexandro Pio [F]el(ici) Aug(usto) | pont(ifici) maximo trib(unicia) pot(estate) co(n)s(uli) p(atri) p(atriae) coh(ors) I Ael(ia) | Hispanorum m(illiaria) eq(uitata) devota numini | maiestatique eius baselicam | equestrem exercitatoriam | iam pridem a solo coeptam | aedificavit consummavitque | sub cura Mari Valeriani leg(ati) | Aug(usti) pr(o) pr(aetore) instante M(arco) Aurelio | Salvio trib(uno) coh(ortis) Imp(eratore) D(omino) N(ostro) | Severo Alexandro Pio Fel(ice) | Aug(usto) co(n)s(ule).

"For the Emperor Caesar Marcus Aurelius Severus Alexander Pius Felix Augustus, *pontifex maximus*, with tribunician power, consul, father of his country, the First Aelian Cohort of Spaniards, *milliaria, equitata*, devoted to his Divine Power and majesty, built a cavalry drill-hall, whose foundations were already laid, and completed it, under the charge of Marius Valerianus, governor, under the direction of Marcus Aurelius Salvius, tribune of this cohort, in the consulship of our Lord the Emperor Severus Alexander Pius Felix Augustus."

For AELIA see no.100.

105 (102) South Shields aqueduct   AD 222–223

RIB 1060. *South Shields* (Arbeia). *A dedication-slab, found in 1893, in South Shields fort. Now in Arbeia Fort Museum, South Shields.* (Fig. 5).

Imp(erator) Caes(ar) divi Severi | nepos divi Magni Antonini fil(ius) | M(arcus) Aurel(ius) Severus [Alexander] | Pius Felix Aug(ustus) pontif(ex) max(imus) | trib(unicia) pot(estate) p(ater) p(atriae) co(n)s(ul) aquam | usibus mil(itum) coh(ortis) V Gallo(rum) in|duxit curante Mario Valeriano | leg(ato) eius pr(o) pr(aetore).

"The Emperor Caesar Marcus Aurelius Severus Alexander Pius Felix Augustus, grandson of the deified Severus, son of the deified Antoninus the Great, *pontifex maximus*, with tribunician power, father of his country, consul, brought in this supply of water for the use of the soldiers of the Fifth Cohort of Gauls, under the charge of Marius Valerianus, governor."

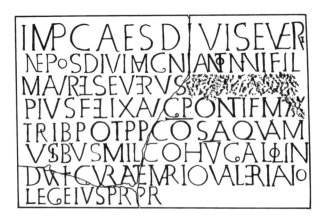

Fig. 5

ALEXANDER has been erased when the emperor's memory was damned. Cf. *RIB* 1049 (Chester-le-Street) for an aqueduct built in AD 216, and nos.70 and 90 above.

106 (103) Chesterholm gate with towers   AD 223–225

RIB 1706. *Chesterholm (Vindolanda). A dedication-slab, found before 1702, at Vindolanda fort. Since lost.*

> [... coh(ors) IIII] Gallor(um) | [Severianae Alexandrianae de]vota nul[mi]ni eius por[tam cum tu]rribus [a] | fundamen[tis restitu]erunt sub | Cl(audio) Xenepho[nte l]eg(ato) [Aug(usti)] n(ostri) pr(o) [pr(aetore) Br(itanniae) Inf(erioris)] | curante [...].

> "... the Fourth Cohort of Gauls, *Severiana Alexandriana*, devoted to his Deity, restored from the foundations this gate with its towers under Claudius Xenephon, governor of Lower Britain, under the charge of ..."

The titles SEVERIANAE ALEXANDRIANAE have been erased, cf. no. 105. The first part of the text, recording the names and titles of Severus Alexander, must have been on a corresponding stone.

107 (104) Great Chesters granary   AD 225

RIB 1738. *Great Chesters (Aesica). A dedication-slab, found in 1767 in Great Chesters fort. Now in the Museum of Antiquities, Newcastle upon Tyne.*

> Imp(erator) Caes(ar) M(arcus) Aur(elius) Sevelrus Alexander P(ius) Fel(ix) | Aug(ustus) horreum vetulstate conlabsum mil(itibus) | coh(ortis) II Asturum S(everianae) A(lexandrianae) | a solo restituerunt | provincia(m) regente [...] | Maximo leg(ato) [Aug(usti) pr(o) pr(aetore) cur(ante)] | Val(erio) Martia[le c(enturione) leg(ionis) ... | F]us[co II et Dextro co(n)s(ulibus)].

> "The Emperor Caesar Marcus Aurelius Severus Alexander Pius Felix Augustus for the soldiers of the Second Cohort of Asturians, *Severiana Alexandriana*, restored from ground level this granary fallen in through age, while the province was governed by ... Maximus, governor, under the charge of Valerius Martialis, centurion of the ... Legion, in the consulship of Fuscus for the second time and Dexter."

The inscription contains a grammatical error; either the emperor should be in the dative, with MIL(ITES) as the subject, or the verb should be RESTITVIT (*RIB*).

108 (105) The Reculver inscription   3rd.century AD

Antiquaries Journal 41 (1961), 224. *Reculver (Regulbium). A dedicatory tablet, found in 1960 in a cellared room below the shrine of the headquarters building of the fort.*

> [...] aedem pr[inci]piorum | cu[m b]asilica | su[b ...]r[...]io Rufino | c[o](n)s(ulari) | [... For]tunatus | [... dedicavi]t.

"... Fortunatus dedicated the shrine of the headquarters building, together with the basilica, under the consular governor, ...r...ius Rufinus".

A. Triarius Rufinus was restored in the original publication, but he was *consul ordinarius* in AD 210, a socially elevated person not likely to have governed one of the emperor's provinces; Q. Aradius Rufinus, consul a little later, has also been suggested. The date could in fact be considerably later in the third century, as few of the consuls are known, and Rufinus is not an uncommon name: see further Mann 1977. The first part of the text, on a separate slab, never recovered, must have indicated the emperor for whom the building was set up. The inscription nevertheless may confirm archaeological indications of an earlier date for Reculver (and Brancaster) than the other Saxon Shore forts (Maxfield 1989, 136–139).

This is the first inscription ever to mention the term AEDES PRINCIPI-ORVM where it can be identified with the official shrine of the headquarters building. For literary references to such shrines, see Herodian, *Histories* 4.4.5 (in Greek) and Statius *Thebaid* 10.176–7. This inscription is also the first certain application of the term BASILICA to a military cross-hall, though in form it resembles a civil basilica.

109 (106) Lanchester baths and basilica   AD 238–244

RIB 1091. *Lanchester* (Longovicium). *A dedication-slab, found before 1700 just outside Lanchester fort. Now in the Old Fulling Mill Museum, Durham.*

Imp(erator) Caes(ar) M(arcus) Ant(onius) Gordia|nus P(ius) F(elix) Aug(ustus) balneum cum | basilica a solo instruxit | per Egn(atium) Lucilianum leg(atum) Aug(usti) | pr(o) pr(aetore) curante M(arco) Aur(elio) | Quirino pr(a)ef(ecto) coh(ortis) I L(ingonum) Gor(dianae).

"The Emperor Caesar Marcus Antonius Gordianus Pius Felix Augustus erected from ground level this bath-building with basilica through the agency of Egnatius Lucilianus, governor, under the charge of Marcus Aurelius Quirinus, prefect of the First Cohort of Lingones, *Gordiana*."

The name of the unit is expanded from *RIB* 1075, LING(ONVM). The unit was originally raised from the *Lingones* of the Langres area of eastern France.

110 (107) Lanchester headquarters and armouries   AD 238–244

RIB 1092. *Lanchester* (Longovicium). *A dedication-slab, found in 1715 inside Lanchester fort. Now in the Old Fulling Mill Museum, Durham.*

Imp(erator) Caesar M(arcus) Antonius | Gordianus P(ius) F(elix) Aug(ustus) | principia et armamen|taria conlapsa restituit per Maecilium Fuscum leg(atum) | Aug(usti) pr(o) pr(aetore) curante M(arco) Aur(elio) | Quirino pr(aefecto) coh(ortis) I L(ingonum) Gor(dianae).

"The Emperor Caesar Marcus Antonius Gordianus Pius Felix Augustus restored the headquarters building and armouries, which had fallen in, through the agency of Maecilius Fuscus, governor, under the charge of Marcus Aurelius Quirinus, prefect of the First Cohort of Lingones, *Gordiana*."

111 (108) Egnatius Lucilianus altar   AD 238–244

RIB 1262. *High Rochester* (Bremenium). *An altar, found in 1852, in the strong-room of the headquarters building of the fort. Now in Museum of Antiquities, Newcastle upon Tyne.*

G(enio) D(omini) n(ostri) et | Signorum | coh(ortis) I Vardul[l(orum)] | et n(umeri) Explora|tor(um) Brem(eniensium) Gor(diani) | Egnat(ius) Lucili|anus leg(atus) Aug(usti) pr(o) pr(aetore) | curante Cassio | Sabiniano trib(uno).

"To the Genius of our Lord and of the Standards of the First Cohort of Vardulli and of the Unit of Scouts of Bremenium, *Gordianus*, Egnatius Lucilianus, governor, *(set this up)* under the charge of Cassius Sabinianus, tribune."

Place-names are not infrequently found as part of the title of irregular units, cf. nos. 148, 235, 243 and *venatores Bannienses, RIB* 1905, from Birdoswald (Banna).

112 (109) Nonius Philippus altar   AD 242

RIB 897. *Old Carlisle* (Maglona?). *An altar, found about 1550. Now at the Museum of Archaeology, Cambridge.*

I(ovi) O(ptimo) M(aximo) | pro salu[te] Imperatoris | M(arci) Antoni Gordiani P(ii) [F(elicis)] | Invicti Aug(usti) et Sab[in]iae Fur|iae Tranquil(lin)ae coniugi eius to|taque domu divin(a) eorum a|la Aug(usta) Gordia(na) ob virtutem| appellata posuit cui pra(e)est | Aemilius Crispinus pr(a)ef(ectus) | eq(uitum) natus in pro(vincia) Africa de | Tusdro sub cur(a) Nonii Ph|ilippi leg(ati) Aug(usti) pro pr(a)e[to(re)] | [At]tico et Praetextato | co(n)s(ulibus).

"To Jupiter Best and Greatest, for the welfare of the Emperor Marcus Antonius Gordianus Pius Felix Invictus Augustus and for his wife Sabinia Furia Tranquillina and for their whole Divine House, the Cavalry Regiment styled *Augusta* for valour, *Gordiana*, set this up, when commanded by Aemilius Crispinus, prefect of cavalry, born in the province of Africa, at Thysdrus, under the charge of Nonius Philippus, governor, in the consulship of Atticus and Praetextatus."

Thysdrus, spelt TVSDRVS in the inscription, was where Gordian III was proclaimed emperor. Maglona is suggested as the Roman name for Old Carlisle by Rivet and Smith 1979, 407; cf. no. 158.

113 (110) Caerleon barracks   AD 253–257

RIB 334. *Caerleon* (Isca). *A commemorative tablet, found in or before 1845, outside the east angle of the fortress. Now in Caerleon Museum.*

Imp(eratores) Valerianus et Gallienus | Aug(usti) et Valerianus nobilis-simus | Caes(ar) cohorti VII centurias a sollo restituerunt per Desticium Iubam | v(irum) c(larissimum) leg(atum) Aug(ustorum) pr(o) pr(aetore) et

I Vitulasium Laetinianum leg(atum) leg(ionis) I II Aug(ustae) curante Domit(io) Potentino I praef(ecto) leg(ionis) eiusdem.

"The Emperors Valerian and Gallienus, Augusti, and Valerian, most noble Caesar, restored from ground-level barrack-blocks for the Seventh Cohort through the agency of Desticius Juba, of senatorial rank, governor, and of Vitulasius Laetinianus, legate of the Second Legion Augusta, under the charge of Domitius Potentinus, prefect of the said legion."

This is the last example anywhere in the empire of a legionary legate. Henceforth all legions were commanded by prefects.

114 (111) Lancaster baths and basilica   Between AD 263 and 268

RIB 605. Lancaster. A dedication-slab, found in 1812 reused in a Roman bath-building inside the late fort. Now at St. John's College, Cambridge.

[... I ... ob] balineum refect(um) I [et] basilicam vetustate conlabsum I a solo restitutam eq(uitibus) alae Sebussian(ae) I [Po]s[t]u[mi]anae sub Octavio Sabino v(iro) c(larissimo) I praeside n(ostro) curante Fla(vio) Ammaulsio praef(ecto) eq(uitum) d(e)d(icata) (ante diem) XI Kal(endas) Septem(bres) I Censore II et Lepido II co(n)s(ulibus).

"[For the Emperor ... Postumus ...] on account of the bath-house rebuilt and the basilica restored from ground-level, when fallen in through age, for the troopers of the Sebosian Cavalry Regiment, *Postumiana*, under Octavius Sabinus, of senatorial rank, our governor, and under the charge of Flavius Ammausius, prefect of cavalry; dedicated on 22 August, in the consulship of Censor and Lepidus, both for the second time."

POSTVMIANAE is erased but some letters are legible. The consuls were of Postumus' Gallic Empire; the year in which they held office cannot be more closely dated. Note the spelling *conlabsum* rather than *conlabsam*.

PART V: CARAUSIUS AND THE FOURTH CENTURY

(a) CARAUSIUS TO CONSTANTIUS (AD 284–306)

115 (112) Antoninianus of Carausius   AD 290–292

Numismatic Chronicle 1959, 10.

> *Obverse:* Busts side by side of Maximian, Diocletian and Carausius, each wearing radiate crown and cuirass. Around, CARAVSIVS ET FRATRES SVI = "Carausius and his brothers".

> *Reverse:* Moneta standing with scales and cornucopiae. Around, MONETA AVGGG = MONETA (TRIVM) AVGVSTORVM = "Moneta, the patron goddess of the coinage of the Augusti".

Illustrated Frere 1987, Pl. 32. 3.

116 (113) Denarius of Carausius   AD 290–292

RIC Carausius 555.

> *Obverse:* Bust of Carausius wearing laurel-wreath and cuirass. IMP(ERATOR) CARAVSIVS P(IVS) F(ELIX) AV(GVSTVS)

> *Reverse:* Britannia shaking hands with Emperor. Around, EXPECTATE VENI = "come, awaited one". Below, RSR (name of mint).

Illustrated Frere 1987, Pl. 32. 2.

117 (113 n.) Milestone of Carausius   AD 286–293

RIB 2290–2. *Milestone found in 1894 in the bed of the River Petterill, Gallows Hill, about 1 ¹⁄₂ kilometres south of Carlisle. Inscribed three times. Now in Carlisle Museum.*

> *RIB* 2290 *Text in centre:* [I]m[p...]s[...]c

> *RIB* 2291 *Text at broader end:* Imp(eratori) C(aesari) M(arco) | Aur(elio) Maus(aeo) | Carausio P(io) F(elici) | Invicto Aug(usto).

> *RIB* 2292 *Text at narrower end:* Fl(avio) Val(erio) | Cons|tant[i]|no nob(ilis-simo) | Caes(ari)

Constantine I as Caesar, AD 306–307. For milestones only bearing the emperor's name and title in the third and fourth centuries see above, *Notes on Roman Epigraphy*, 3 (e) (page 12).

118 (114) The Arras medallion   AD 296

RIC 6, *Mint of Trier* 34 *(Constantius Chlorus). Gold medallion of ten aurei.*

> *Obverse:* Bust of Constantius Chlorus wearing laurel-wreath and cuirass. Around, FL(AVIVS) VAL(ERIVS) CONSTANTIVS NOBIL(ISSIMVS) CAES(AR) = "Flavius Valerius Constantius, most noble Caesar"

Reverse: Constantius Chlorus riding along the edge of a river (the Thames) towards the gate of a city (identified as LON(DINIVM) on the coin). Woman (personifying Britain) kneels before the gate. Around, REDDI-TOR LVCIS AETERNAE = "restorer of eternal light". Below, PTR (name of mint).

Illustrated, Frere 1987 Pl. 32. 5. This commemorates Constantius Chlorus's arrival in London after his army had defeated Allectus.

119 (115) Birdoswald restorations   *c.* AD 296–305

RIB 1912. *Birdoswald (Banna). Dedication-slab, found 1929, reused face down-wards as a paving-stone in the floor of a barrack-block in the fort. Now in Carlisle Museum.*

[D(ominis)] n(ostris) Dioc[letiano] et I M[axim]iano Invictis Aug(ustis) et I Constantio et Maximiano I n(obilissimis) C(aesaribus) sub v(iro) p(erfec-tissimo) Aur(elio) Arpagio pr(aeside) I praetor(ium) quod erat humo copert(um) I et in labe(m) conl(apsum) et princ(ipia) et bal(neum) rest(ituit) I curant(e) Fl(avio) Martino cent(urione) p(rae)p(osito) c(ohors) [...]

"For our Lords Diocletian and Maximian, Invincible Augusti, and for Constantius and Maximianus, most noble Caesars, under His Perfection Aurelius Arpagius, the governor, the ... Cohort restored the commanding officer's house, which had been covered with earth and had fallen into ruin, and the headquarters building and the bath-house, under the charge of Flavius Martinus, centurion in command."

Cf. *RIB* 1613 (Housesteads), which also may be a Diocletianic inscription. Excavations at Haltonchesters and Rudchester, also forts on Hadrian's Wall, have produced just such a picture of decay as is described here. There is there-fore no need to explain it as a covert reference to destruction caused by a barbarian invasion in AD 296.

This inscription was the first discovered to draw a clear distinction between PRINCIPIA and PRAETORIVM.

(b)   THE FOURTH CENTURY (AD 306–410)

120 (–) Visit of Constantine the Great to Britain   AD 311–312

RIC 6, *Mint of Londinium 133 etc. (London).*

Obverse: Bust of Constantine facing left, wearing helmet and armour, holding shield and spear. Around, CONSTANTINVS P(IVS) F(ELIX) AVG(VSTVS)

Reverse: Emperor, riding down captive, hand raised in greeting. Around, ADVENTVS AVG(VSTI) N(OSTRI) = "The coming of our emperor". Below, PLN = "Struck at London"

This visit to Britain is associated with the preparations for the civil war fought in Italy in 312. The garrisons of the outpost forts of Hadrian's Wall were withdrawn for this campaign. Other visits to Britain are attested by *Adventus* coins issued in 307 and 314. (PJC)

121 (120) Gold solidus of Magnus Maximus AD 384–385

RIC 9. *Mint of Londinium* 2b *(Magnus Maximus)*

> *Obverse:* Bust of Magnus Maximus wearing diadem and cuirass. Around, D(OMINVS) N(OSTER) MAG(NVS) MAXIMVS P(IVS) F(ELIX) AVG(VSTVS) = "our Lord Magnus Maximus Pius Felix Augustus."

> *Reverse:* Two Emperors (Magnus Maximus and Theodosius) on throne, holding a globe. Victory stands behind with outspread wings. Around, VICTORIA AVGG = VICTORIA AVGVSTORVM = "Victory, the patron goddess of the Augusti." Below, AVG(VSTA) = LONDINIVM (name of mint) and OB(RYZA) = "purified gold."

This is a specimen of Maximus's fourth issue of gold coins. The mint mark indicates that it was produced by the mint operating at the imperial court which must have been in London at the time. The coinage dates to 384/5 and shows that Maximus returned to Britain, presumably to fight the Pictish campaign noted in the Gallic Chronicle. (PJC)

Illustrated in Frere 1987, pl. 32.7.

122 (119) Ravenscar tower Late 4th.century AD

RIB 721. *Ravenscar. A dedication-slab, found in 1774, on site of Roman "signal-station" of Ravenscar (also called Peak). Now in Whitby Museum.*

> Iustinianus p(rae)p(ositus) | Vindicianus | magister (?) turr[e]|m (et) castrum fecit | a so(lo).

> "Justinianus, commander; Vindicianus, *magister*, built this tower and fort from ground level".

The "signal-stations" of the Yorkshire coast were built in the late fourth century: the Theodosian reorganisation and the time of Magnus Maximus have both been suggested as possible contexts (Casey 1979) and probably abandoned soon after AD 400. MAGISTER is a low rank in the army of the late fourth century. The identification of Justinianus as the man who later became one of Constantine III's generals remains controversial, but more likely if the towers were built during the reign of Maximus (383–88).

123 (116–118) Restorations on the Wall by *civitates* Date unknown

Durotriges

(a) *RIB* 1672. *Cawfields milecastle (MC 42). Building-stone found at foot of crags north of Wall. Now in Chesters Museum.*

> C(ivitas) Dur(o)|tr(i)g(um) L|endin(i)e(n)sis

> "The *civitas* of the Durotriges of Lindinis"

(b) *RIB* 1673. *Housesteads* (Vercovicium). *Uninscribed altar reused as a building stone found in Wall west of fort. Now in Chesters Museum.*

Ci(vitas) Duro|trag(um) Lendi|nie(n)sis

"The *civitas* of the Durotriges of Lindinis"

The Durotriges were located in Dorset and eastern Somerset. Dorchester (Durnovaria) was the original centre for the *civitas*, which may have been split in the third century AD, with Ilchester (Lindinis) becoming the centre of a separate *civitas* (Stevens 1941, 359).

Dumnonii

(c) *RIB* 1843. *Carvoran* (Magna). *Building stone found in or before 1760, near Carvoran. Now in private possession, at Castleton.*

Civitas | Dum(no)ni(orum)

"The *civitas* of the Dumnonii"

The Dumnonii had their centre at Exeter (Isca).

Brigantes

(d) *RIB* 2022. *Blea Tarn. Building stone, recorded before 1794. Now lost.*

Capud pe[d(aturae)] | civitat(i)s Brig<ig>

"The beginning of the length in feet built by the Brigantian *civitas*"

The Brigantes had their centre at Isurium (Aldborough).
For a similar stone referring to the Catuvellauni see *RIB* 1962. *RIB* 1629 and 2053 seem to refer to individuals. None can be dated.

124 (–) Gold solidus of Constantine III   AD 407–411

G.792 *Mint of Lugdunum, 407–8.*

Obverse: Bust of Constantine wearing imperial mantle and diadem. Around, D(OMINVS) N(OSTER) CONSTANTINVS P(IVS) F(ELIX) AVG(VSTVS)

Reverse: Emperor standing right, holding labarum and globe, spurning captive at his feet. Around, VICTORIA AVGGGG = Victoria Augustorum, "Victory of the four emperors".

The usurper who usurped the throne in Britain, claims his own legitimacy by associating the three legitimate emperors, Arcadius, Honorius and Theodosius II, with himself in the reverse legend. (PJC)

PART VI: GOVERNMENT AND ADMINISTRATION

(a) THE IMPERIAL STAFF

125 (-) A. Platorius Nepos, governor   *c.* AD 125

ILS 1052. *Aquileia* (Aquileia). *Statue base. Now in the Archaeological Museum, Aquileia.*

> A(ulo) Platorio A(uli) f(ilio) | Serg(ia tribu) Nepoti | Aponio Italico | Maniliano | C(aio) Licinio Pollioni | co(n)s(uli) auguri legat(o) Aug(usti) | pro praet(ore) provinc(iae) Br|tanniae leg(ato) pro pr(aetore) pro|vinc(iae) German(iae) Inferior(is) | leg(ato) pro pr(aetore) provinc(iae) Thrac(iae) | leg(ato) legion(is) I Adiutricis | quaest(ori) provinc(iae) Maced(oniae) | curat(ori) viarum Cassiae Clodiae Ciminiae novae | Traianae candidato divi | Traiani trib(uno) mil(itum) leg(ionis) XXII | Primigen(iae) P(iae) F(idelis) praet(ori) trib(uno) | pleb(is) IIIvir(o) capitali | patrono | d(ecreto) d(ecurionum).

> "To Aulus Platorius, son of Aulus, of the voting tribe Sergia, Nepos Aponius Italicus Manilianus Gaius Licinius Pollio, consul, augur, governor of the province of Britain, governor of the province of Lower Germany, governor of the province of Thrace, legate of the First Legion Adiutrix, quaestor of the province of Macedonia, curator of the Cassian, Clodian, Ciminian and New Trajanic Roads, a candidate nominated by the deified emperor Trajan, military tribune of the Twenty-Second Legion Primigenia *Pia Fidelis*, praetor, tribune of the plebs, one of the board of three men in charge of capital sentences, patron, by decree of the councillors."

Inscription on the base of a statue set up in honour of Platorius Nepos, the governor responsible for the building of Hadrian's Wall (see above, nos. 35–37), by the councillors of Aquileia, a city of which he was patron. It gives Nepos's career in reverse order, though the consulate (the supreme magistracy of Rome) and the post of *augur* (a religious official) are highlighted at the start, and there is some misordering of the early posts from *IIIvir capitalis* to *quaestor*. The date of Nepos's move to Britain is known very precisely from a military diploma (no. 33); he moved here from Lower Germany, bringing with him Legion VI Victrix, formerly based at Xanten (*Vetera*). The career is typical of that of a governor of an imperial province such as Britain, which, having three legions based within it, was regarded as a senior posting. The governor was appointed by, and was responsible directly to, the emperor.

126 (27) Governor's headquarters   3rd. century AD?

RIB 662–3. *York* (Eboracum). *Two bronze plates stuck back-to-back, found c. 1840 on the site of the Old Railway Station. Now in the Yorkshire Museum.*

(a)   θεοῖς | τοῖς τοῦ ἡγε|μονικοῦ πραι|τωρίου Σκριβ(ώνιος) | Δη[μ]ήτριος.

(b)   Ὠκεανῶι | καὶ Τηθύι | Δημήτρι[ος]

(a)   "To the deities of the governor's headquarters, Scribonius Demetrius (*set this up*)."

(b)   "To Ocean and Tethys, Demetrius (*set this up*)."

Demetrius is often identified with Demetrius of Tarsus, the *grammaticus* who took part in Plutarch's dialogue *De Defectu Oraculorum* in AD 83–4, having just returned from a visit to Britain and having, on Imperial orders, joined a voyage to the isles of Scotland. It is thought that he spent some years in York, probably on the staff of Caristanius Fronto, commander of Legion IX, subsequently joining Agricola's circumnavigation in AD 83. However at this time the "governor's headquarters" lay at London; there was none at York until the division of Britain into two provinces by Septimius Severus. Hence these dedications may well date to the third century: Demetrius is a common enough name.

127 (-) A judicial official   80s AD

ILS 1015. *Nadin* (Nedinum, Dalmatia).

> C(aio) Octavio ǀ Tidio Tossialno Ia[v]oleno ǀ Prisco l[e]g(ato) leg(ionis) IV Fla[v(iae)] leg(ato) leg(ionis) III Aug(ustae) ǀ iuridic(o) provinc(iae) Brittaniae leg(ato) ǀ consulari provin[c(iae)] Germ(aniae) Superioris ǀ legato consulari provinc(iae) Syriae ǀ proconsuli provinc(iae) Africae pontifici ǀ P(ublius) Mutilius P(ublii) f(ilius) Cla(udia tribu) [C]rispinus t(estamento) p(oni) i(ussit) ǀ amico carissimo.

> "For Gaius Octavius Tidius Tossianus Iavolenus Priscus, legate of the Fourth Legion Flavia, legate of the Third Legion Augusta, judicial official of the province of Britain, governor of the province of Upper Germany, governor of the province of Syria, governor of the province of Africa, priest: Publius Mutilius Crispinus, son of Publius, of the Claudian voting tribe, ordered this to be set up under his will, to his dearest friend."

This stone honours Iavolenus Priscus, the distinguished jurist, who served as *iuridicus* in Britain in the later first century. *Iuridici* were judicial officials of praetorian status, appointed to help the governor with judicial business. Only seven are at present known and none is recorded within Britain. The restoration of the very fragmentary *RIB* 8 from London (L4, 1st. ed., no. 121) to refer to a *iuridicus* is dubious (see Birley 1981, 206 no. 10).

128 (122) A speculator at London   1st. century AD

RIB 19. *London* (Londinium). *Tombstone found in 1843 in Playhouse Yard, Blackfriars. Now in the British Museum.*

> [Dis Mani]bus ǀ [...]r L(uci) f(ilius) C[l(audia tribu)] Celsu[s] ǀ [...s]pec(ulator) leg(ionis) [II A]ug(ustae) Anǀ[ton(ius)] Dardan[i]us Cu[r]sor R]ubrius Pudens ǀ [...]s Probus, sp[e]c(ulatores) l[eg(ionis)].

> "To the spirits of the departed, ...r Celsus, son of Lucius, of the Claudian voting tribe, from ..., *speculator* of the Second Augustan Legion, An[tonius?] Dardanius Cursor, Rubrius Pudens and ...s Probus, *speculatores* of the legion *(set this up)*."

The head of the deceased is carved in relief in a niche. *Speculatores* functioned as military police, served only on the staffs of governors, and thus are based at provincial capitals. The fact that Celsus's tombstone was set up by his fellow *speculatores* suggests that he died at base, and hence that London was already the provincial capital by the end of the first century AD, the probable date of this stone. *RIB* restores the legion's title as *leg(ionis) [II A]ugustae An[toninia]n(a)e.* This is not possible, as the title *Antoniniana* was used only in the early third century (AD 211–222) while all the other characteristics of the inscription put it firmly in the first (cf. Birley 1966, 228).

129 (123) A beneficiarius at Wroxeter   ? Before AD 61

RIB 293. *Wroxeter* (Viroconium). *Tombstone found in 1752 along with no. 19 in the Roman cemetery outside the east gate of the city. Now in Rowley's House Museum, Shrewsbury.*

C(aius) Mannius | C(ai) f(ilius) Pol(lia tribu) Secu|ndus Pollent(ia) | mil(es) leg(ionis) XX | an(n)oru(m) LII | stip(endiorum) XXXI | ben(eficiarius) leg(ati) pr(opraetore) | h(ic) s(itus) e(st).

"Gaius Mannius Secundus, son of Gaius, of the Pollian voting tribe, from Pollentia, a soldier of the twentieth legion, aged 52 years, served for 31 years, *beneficiarius* on the staff of the governor, lies here."

The text of this inscription is full of uncertainties. Mannius's rank at the time of his death has been variously restored as *beneficiarius legati pro praetore*, i.e. on the staff of the governor, or as *beneficiarius legati praetorii*, on the staff of the legionary legate. In the former case it can be argued that his presence at Wroxeter does not prove that legio XX was based there since he will have been seconded from the legion to the governor's staff, whence he could have been sent anywhere in the province. In the latter case he is much more likely to be at the legionary base, hence the tombstone can be used as evidence for the garrison of Wroxeter at the time of its erection. This problem is linked with another, the date of the stone. The absence of the honorific *Valeria Victrix* from the legion's name should point to a date before the title was awarded, most probably in AD 61 following the suppression of the Boudican rebellion. At this date, however, Legion XIV is thought to have been based at Wroxeter. For a discussion of this problem see Tomlin 1992, where doubt is cast on the idea that the honorific titles relate to the events of AD 61. Other *beneficiarii* appear in nos. 130–131, 165, 172, 226 and 245. Above the gable of the inscription is a relief of two lions, one on either side of a pine cone. Pollentia (modern Pollenza) is in Liguria in north-west Italy.

130 (124) A beneficiarius at Winchester   ?3rd. century AD

RIB 88. *Winchester* (Venta Belgarum). *Altar found in 1854 near south end of Jewry Street. Now in the British Museum (cast in Winchester Museum).*

Matrib(us) | Italis Ger|manis | Gal(lis) Brit(annis) | [A]ntonius | [Lu]cretianus | [b(ene)]f(iciarius) co(n)s(ularis) rest(ituit).

"To the Italian, German, Gallic and British Mother Goddesses, Antonius Lucretianus, *beneficiarius* of the governor, restored *(this)*."

The governor's *beneficiarii* were sent, not only to military sites (as no. 131), but also to civilian. For Mother Goddesses see nos. 175 and 246. The association here of the German, Gallic and British Mothers may be a reflection of Lucretianus's origin and of the places where he served, or, given the fact that this is the restoration of an earlier dedication, the associations of whoever originally set it up.

131 (125) A beneficiarius at Dorchester   2nd. or 3rd. century AD

RIB 235. Dorchester, Oxon. Altar found in 1731 at Dorchester in Court, or Bishop's, Close. Now lost.

> I(ovi) O(ptimo) M(aximo) I et N(u)minib(us) Aug(usti) I M(arcus) Vari(us) Severus I beneficiarius co(n)s(ularis) I aram cum I cancellis I d(e) s(uo) p(osuit).

> "To Jupiter Best and Greatest and to the Divine Powers of the Emperor, Marcus Varius Severus, *beneficiarius* of the governor, set up this altar with screens from his own funds."

As in no. 137, the worship of the Emperor's power is coupled with worship of the supreme deity of the Roman state. For *Numen Augusti* see the Note on Religion, p. 19.

132 (126) A strator consularis at Irchester   ?3rd. century AD

RIB 233. Irchester, Northants. Slab from a monumental tomb found about 1853, at Irchester, reused at the site of the Roman town. Now in the British Museum.

> D(is) M(anibus) s(acrum) I Anicius Saturn(inus) I strator co(n)s(ularis), m(onumentum) s(ibi) f(ecit).

> "Sacred to the spirits of the departed, Anicius Saturninus, *strator* of the governor, made this memorial to himself."

A *strator* is a junior officer in charge of horses. On the strength of this inscription it has been suggested that Irchester was a centre for horse rearing for the Roman army, a notion doubted in the most recent discussion of the site (Burnham and Wacher 1990, 147). The term *equisio cos* is used in one of the Vindolanda tablets (see below, no. 275) for a post equivalent to that of *strator cos*.

133 (127) An eques singularis   ?3rd. century AD

RIB 714. Malton (Derventio). Tombstone found in 1753, about 200 metres north of the Roman fort. Now lost.

> D(is) M(anibus) I Aur(elius) Malcrinus ex I eq(uite) sing(ulari) Au[g(usti)].

> "To the spirits of the departed, Aurelius Macrinus, formerly cavalryman in the emperor's bodyguard."

The *equites singulares Augusti*, the emperor's bodyguard, were recruited from soldiers in the auxiliary cavalry. Macrinus could have served in this capacity when an emperor (e.g. Severus) was present in Britain, or he could have served abroad and then retired to the fort whence he had originally come. A cavalry unit, the *ala Picentiana*, is attested at Malton in the mid-late 2nd. century (*Britannia* 2 (1971), 291 no. 9). For a *singularis consularis* (in the provincial governor's bodyguard) see no. 165.

134 (128) Naevius, procurators' assistant   AD 212–217

RIB 179. Combe Down, Monkton Combe. Dedication slab found in 1854 near the Roman villa. Now in Roman Baths Museum, Bath.

> Pro salute imp(eratoris) C(a)es(aris) M(arci) Aur(eli) | Antonini Pii Felicis Invic|ti Aug(usti) Naevius Aug(usti) | lib(ertus) adiut(or) proc(uratorum) princi|pia ruina op(p)ress(a) a solo res|tituit.

> "For the welfare of the Emperor Caesar Marcus Aurelius Antoninus Pius Felix Invictus Augustus, Naevius, imperial freedman, procurators' assistant, restored from ground level these ruined headquarters."

Principia here must denote the centre of local procuratorial administration, perhaps of an imperial estate, and not, as is more usual, the headquarters building of a fort. Note no. 149 for a *centurio regionarius* at Bath. The inscription had been reused as a cover-slab for a coffin.

135 (129) A governor in a divided Britain   3rd. or 4th. century AD

RIB 103. Cirencester (Corinium). *Base of a Jupiter Column found in 1891 in the garden of "The Firs", Victoria (or New) Road. Now in Corinium Museum.*

> *Face:* I(ovi) O(ptimo) [M(aximo)] | L(ucius) Sept(imius) [...] | v(ir) p(erfectissimus) pr(aeses) B[r(itanniae) pr(imae)] | resti[tuit] | civis R[...].

> *Back:* [Si]gnum et | [e]rectam | [p]risca rel[li]gione col[l]umnam.

> *Left side:* Septimius | renovat | primae | provinciae | rector.

> *Right side: missing*

> "To Jupiter Best and Greatest, his perfection Lucius Septimius [...], governor of Br[itannia ...] restored (this monument), being a citizen of R[...]"

> "This statue and column erected under the ancient religion, Septimius, governor of Britannia Prima, renewed."

Jupiter-worship was part and parcel of the official religion of Rome, though the creation of Jupiter columns is something which is particularly characteristic of the Rhineland and Danubian areas where it is most common in the later second to mid-third centuries. The reference to *Britannia Prima* is generally taken to date the inscription to after the Diocletianic reorganisation of Britain into four separate provinces, each governed by a *praeses*. (For a *praeses* of Britannia Secunda see no. 119). However Birley argues (1981, 179) that *primae provinciae* could be a non-technical allusion to Britannia Superior, while the fact that the governor has a *praenomen* favours a 3rd.- rather than a 4th.-century date. The most likely context would then lie between the recovery of Britain by Aurelian and the usurpation of Carausius, 274–86.

(b) LOCAL GOVERNMENT

136 (130) Chichester dedication to Nero   AD 59

RIB 92. Chichester (Noviomagus). Dedication slab found in 1740 on corner of St Martin's Lane and East Street. Now lost.

> Neroni I Claudio divi I [Claudi f(ilio) G]ermani[ci I Caesaris n]epoti Ti(beri) [Caes(aris) I Aug(usti) p]ronepoti div[i Aug(usti) I ab]n(epoti), Caesari Aug(usto) [Germ(anico) I t]r(ibuniciae) p(otestatis) IV imp(eratori) IV co(n)s(uli) IV I s(enatus) c(onsulto) v(otum) m(erito).

> "For Nero Claudius Caesar Augustus Germanicus, son of the deified Claudius, grandson of Germanicus Caesar, great-grandson of Tiberius Caesar Augustus, great-great-grandson of the deified Augustus, in his fourth year of tribunician power, four times acclaimed *imperator*, consul for the fourth time, by decree of the senate the vow was deservedly fulfilled."

Here is perhaps an example of the regular annual public vow for the emperor's safety. Compare Pliny's record of a similar vow for Trajan (*Epist.* 10.35). This is one of two major inscriptions erected in Chichester in the middle years of the first century AD, when it still presumably lay in the territory of the allied king Cogidubnus. (For the other see no. 137.)

137 (156) Cogidubnus   2nd. half of 1st. century AD

RIB 91 + Bogaers 1979. Chichester (Noviomagus). Dedication-slab found in 1723 in Lion Street at junction with North Street. Now built into the west face of the council chamber, Chichester. (Fig. 6).

> [N]eptuno et Minervae I templum I [pr]o salute do[mus] divinae I ex auctoritat[e Ti(beri)] Claud(i) I [Co]gidubni r(egis) mag(ni) in Brit(annia) I [colle]gium fabror(um) et qui in eo I [sun]t d(e) s(uo) d(ederunt) donante aream I [...]ente Pudentini fil(io).

> "To Neptune and Minerva for the welfare of the Divine House, by authority of Tiberius Claudius Cogidubnus, great king in Britain, the guild of smiths and those who belong to it gave this temple from their own resources, the site having been given by [...]ens, son of Pudentinus."

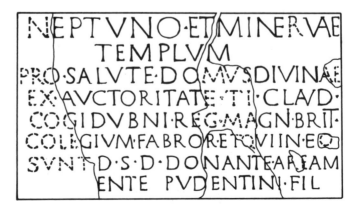

Fig. 6

Cogidubnus, the British ruler referred to by Tacitus (*Agricola* 14), is shown by this inscription to have acquired Roman citizenship from Claudius. His title *rex magnus* indicates his eminence (compare Herod the Great); see the discussion in Bogaers 1979. His philo-Roman stance is indicated by the development of the city of Chichester during his reign, when it stood within a friendly kingdom, independent of the authority of the governor of Britain. For a dedication to Nero set up at Chichester during the (assumed) lifetime of Cogidubnus see no. 136.

138 (131) Wroxeter forum dedication   AD 129–130

RIB 288. Wroxeter (Viroconium). Fragments of a commemorative slab found in 1924 to east of the main entrance to the forum. Now in Rowley's House Museum, Shrewsbury.

> Imp(eratori) Ca[es(ari)] divi Traiani Parthilci fil(io) di[vi N]ervae nepoti Traliano H[a]driano Aug(usto) ponti[fi]lci maximo trib(unicia) pot(estate) XIII[I co(n)s(uli) III p(atri) p(atriae)] I civitas Cornov[iorum].

> "For the Emperor Caesar Trajan Hadrian Augustus, son of the deified Trajan conqueror of Parthia, grandson of the deified Nerva, *pontifex maximus*, in his fourteenth year of tribunician power, three times consul, father of his country, the *civitas* of the Cornovii *(set this up)*."

This records the building of the forum by the corporate act of the whole community through its government. This is the one Hadrianic civilian public building in Britain whose construction is attested epigraphically, though building activity in the early- to mid-second century is well known from excavation; e.g. the fora at Caerwent, Caistor by Norwich and Leicester, and the replacement in stone of the original (timber) forum at Silchester. The town at Wroxeter developed later than many of the other Romano-British *civitates*, as the site remained that of a legionary fortress until *c.* AD 90. It is one of only two early fortresses (the other is Exeter) to be developed as a *civitas* rather than a *colonia*. The forum was built on the site of an unfinished baths. Other forum building inscriptions come from St. Albans (no. 28) and possibly Cirencester (*RIB* 114).

139 (133) Decree of the civitas of the Silures   Shortly before AD 220

RIB 311. Caerwent (Venta Silurum). Pedestal found in 1903 on the village green. Now in Caerwent church.

> [Ti(berio) Claudio] I Paulino I leg(ato) leg(ionis) II I Aug(ustae) proconsul(i) I provinc(iae) Narl<r>bonensis I leg(ato) Aug(usti) pr(o) pr(aetore) provin(ciae) I Lugudunen(sis) I ex decreto I ordinis reslpubl(ica) civit(atis) I Silurum.

> "To Tiberius Claudius Paulinus, legate of the Second Legion Augusta, proconsul of the province of Narbonensis, governor of the province of Lugudunensis, by decree of the council, the commonwealth of the *civitas* of the Silures *(set this up)*."

The pedestal probably held a statue of Tiberius Claudius Paulinus, who went on, after the posts named here, to become governor of Lower Britain under

Elagabalus. (He is attested in post in AD 220; cf. no. 102). The honour done Paulinus by the council of the Silures presumably stems from connections he had with the city when he was commanding officer of the locally based legion at Caerleon. This inscription, like that of Wroxeter (no. 138), records a corporate act of the community through its elected council. For the career of Paulinus cf. Birley 1981, 188–90.

140 (132) Kenchester milestone   AD 283–284

RIB 2250. *Kenchester* (Magnis). *Milestone found in 1796 on the site of the north wall of the Roman town. Now in Hereford City Museum.*

> Imp(eratori) C(aesari) | Mar(co) Aur(elio) | Numorianlo | r(es)p(ublica) c(ivitatis) D(obunnorum) | [...]

> "For the Emperor Caesar Marcus Aurelius Numerianus, the commonwealth of the *civitas* of the Dobunni [...]."

Milestones, in default of boundary stones, are valuable as evidence for the extent of city territories. The size and prosperity of the city of Cirencester is perhaps not unconnected with the large area of Dobunnian territory, as evidenced by this milestone (Kenchester lies *c.* 80 km. from Cirencester).

141 (159) Thurmaston milestone   AD 119–120

RIB 2244. *Thurmaston, Leicestershire. Cylindrical milestone found in 1771 on the west side of the Fosse Way, three kilometres from Leicester. Now in the Jewry Wall Museum, Leicester.*

> Imp(erator) Caes(ar) | div(i) Traian(i) Parth(ici) f(ilius) div[i Ner(vae)] nep(os) | Traian(us) Hadrian(us) Aug(ustus) p(ater) p(atriae) t(ri)b(uniciae) | pot(estatis) IV co(n)s(ul) III. A Ratis | m(ilia passuum) II.

> "The Emperor Caesar Trajan Hadrian Augustus, son of the deified Trajan, conqueror of Parthia, grandson of the deified Nerva, father of his country, in his fourth year of tribunician power, three times consul. From Ratae 2 miles."

Leicester (*Ratae*) is the urban centre of the *civitas* of the Corieltauvi (see no. 142) in which this milestone was found and from which its distance was measured. The emperor is here wrongly credited with the title *pater patriae* which he did not assume until AD 128.

142 (-) Tile naming the Corieltauvi   Date unknown

Britannia 14 (1983), 349–50. *Cave's Inn, Warwickshire* (Tripontium). *Tile found in 1965 during excavation.*

> [ci]vitatis Corieltavvorom[...]

> "... of the *civitas* of the Corieltauvi ..."

Line 1 of a graffito of at least four lines (too few letters survive to make any sense of lines 2–4). *Tripontium* lies about 24 kilometres from *Ratae* (Leicester). The graffito gives a more correct form of what has until now been known as the *civitas Coritanorum*. The form *Ratae Coritanorum* was based on Ptolemy's *Geography* (2.3.2: *Coritanoi*), and the Ravenna Cosmography which records *Ratecorioneltavori*, easily amended to *Rat(a)e Corielta(u)vorum* (Rivet and Smith 1979, 324; Tomlin 1983; Tomlin 1993, 137–8).

143 (136) Brougham milestone   AD 258–268

JRS 55 (1965), 224 no. 11. *Brougham, Cumbria* (Brocavum). *Milestone found in 1964 in Frenchfield, beside the Roman Road to Carlisle. Now at Brougham Castle.*

> Imp(eratori) Caes(ari) Ma|r(co) Casianio | Latinianio | Postimo | Aug(usto) Pio | Felici R(es) P(ublica) C(ivitas) | Car(vetiorum).

> "To the Emperor Caesar Marcus Cassianius Latinius Postumus Augustus Pius Felix, the republic of the *civitas* of the Carvetii *(set this up)*."

Note that the mason has misspelt the emperor's names. The expansion of *Car* as *Carvetii* (meaning stag-people) rests on the reading of no. 144, from Old Penrith, which refers to the *c. Carvetior*. Together these two inscriptions provide our only evidence for the existence and location of the *civitas Carvetiorum*, whose urban centre was most probably at Carlisle. This new *civitas* could have been created at some time in the mid- to later third century, perhaps when territory, hitherto military, became available for civilian development. For another milestone from the territory of this *civitas* see no. 168.

144 (137) A senator of the Carvetii   ? 4th. century AD

RIB 933. *Old Penrith, Cumbria* (Voreda). *Tombstone seen c. 1600 by Camden at Old Penrith. Now lost.*

> D(is) M(anibus) | Fl(avio) Martio sen(atori) | in c(ivitate) Carvetior(um) | questorio | vixit an(nos) XXXXV | Martiola filia et | heres ponen|[dum] curavit.

> "To the spirits of the departed (and) to Flavius Martius, a councillor in the *civitas* of the Carvetii, of quaestorian rank, who lived 45 years. Martiola his daughter and heiress had this set up."

The term *senator*, though mainly confined to the Roman senate, is occasionally used in the 4th. and 5th. centuries as an alternative name for city councillors. The Brougham milestone inscription (no. 143) enables us to expand the 'c' in line 3 as *civitas*. The quaestor was a magistrate with financial responsibilities.

145 (135) Catuvellauni repair Hadrian's Wall   Date unknown

RIB 1962. *Howgill (Hadrian's Wall milecastle 55). Building stone found in or before 1717, built into the wall of farm buildings.*

> Civitate Cat|uvellaun|orum Toss|[o]dio.

> "From the *civitas* of the Catuvellauni, Tossodio."

This undated (but broadly "late") inscription provides the sole specific reference to a *civitas* of the Catuvellauni; but see no. 28 (the Verulamium building inscription) for a possible case, and no. 204 for a woman described as *natione*

Catuallauna. For other civilian communities engaged in building repair work on the Wall, see no. 123.

146 (134) A vicus at Petuaria   AD 139–144

RIB 707. Brough-on-Humber (Petuaria). *Dedication slab found in 1937 near west wall of building I (of 1937). Now in Hull Museum.*

> Ob honor[em] | domus divi[nae] | imp(eratoris) Caes(aris) T(iti) Ael(i) H[adri]lani Antonini A[ug(usti)] Pii] | p(atris) p(atriae) co(n)s(ulis) III | et numinib(us) A[ug(usti)] | M(arcus) Ulp(ius) Ianuar[i]u[s] | aedilis vici Petu[ar(iensis)] | proscaen(ium) [...] | de suo [dedit].

> "In honour of the Divine House of the Emperor Caesar Titus Aelius Hadrianus Antoninus Augustus Pius, father of his country, three times consul, and to the Divine Powers of the emperor, Marcus Ulpius Ianuarius, councillor of the *vicus* of Petuaria, presented this new stage at his own expense."

This stone establishes the status of *Petuaria* as a *vicus* and one of very few places in Roman Britain known to have possessed a theatre. For the expansion *numinibus Aug(usti)* and not (as *RIB*) *numinibus Aug(ustorum)*, see Mann 1991, 173–4.

147 (138) T. Floridius Natalis, praepositus   AD 225–235

RIB 587. Ribchester (Bremetennacum). *Part of a dedication slab found in 1811 on the north bank of the river Ribble. Now at Ribchester Museum.*

> [...p]ro | [sa]l(ute) im[p(eratoris) Caes(aris) Al]ex[andri Aug(usti) N(ostri) et | Iul(iae) Mamaeae ma]t[r]is D(omini) N(ostri) et castr(orum) su[b cura] | Val(eri) Crescentis Fulviani leg(ati) eius pr(o) [pr(aetore)] | T(itus) Florid(ius) Natalis c(enturio) leg(ionis) praep(ositus) n(umeri) et regi(onis) | templum a solo ex responsu [dei re]lstituit et dedicavit d[e suo].

> "... for the welfare of the Emperor Caesar Alexander our Augustus and of Julia Mamaea the mother of our lord and of the camp under the charge of Valerius Crescens Fulvianus, governor, Titus Floridius Natalis, legionary centurion in charge of the unit and of the region, restored the temple from ground level as requested by the god, and dedicated (it) from his own resources."

The temple here referred to presumably lay outside the fort. The phrase *ex responsu* strongly suggests the cult of Jupiter Dolichenus which was very popular among the third-century soldiery and which reached its high-water mark in the reign of Severus Alexander. Natalis's special command over the region may be connected with its being used for veteran settlement: the Ravenna Cosmography (124) calls Ribchester *Bremetennacum Veteranorum*. For the *numerus* that he commanded see no. 148.

148 (139) Aelius Antoninus, praepositus   AD 238–244

RIB 583. Ribchester (Bremetennacum). *Shaft of pedestal found in 1578 at Ribchester; rediscovered in 1814. Now at Ribchester Museum.*

Deo san(cto) | [A]po(l)lini Mapono | [pr]o salute D(omini) N(ostri) | [et] n(umeri) eq(uitum) Sar|[m(atarum)] Bremetenn(acensium) | [G]ordiani | [A]el(ius) Antoni|nus c(enturio) leg(ionis) VI | Vic(tricis) domo | Melitenis | praep(ositus) n(umeri) et r(egionis) | [...].

"To the holy god Apollo Maponus, for the welfare of Our Lord *(the Emperor)* and of the Gordian's Own Sarmatian cavalry unit of Bremetennacum, Aelius Antoninus, centurion of the Sixth Legion Victrix, from Melitene, in charge of the unit and the region [...]."

The shaft is part of a monument. The right side has a relief of Apollo. On the back two female figures face one another, personifying (on the left) a young, unveiled and undraped *Regio Bremetennacensis* and (on the right) an older, veiled and draped *Britannia Inferior*, who hands an object to the left-hand figure.

Melitene, on the Euphrates, was the *base* of legion *XII Fulminata*. The *numerus* of Sarmatians has been thought to be descended from the 5,500 Sarmatians sent to Britain in 175 (Dio 71.16.2 = L11, 38). The use of the honorific *Gordiani* at the end of its name dates the inscription to the reign of the Emperor Gordian, since such titles were dropped on the death of the emperor concerned. For Apollo Maponus cf. no. 244. This is one of several examples of a unit being named after the place where it was based: cf. nos. 111, 235, 243.

149 (150) A case of vandalism   Date unknown

RIB 152. Bath (Aquae Sulis). Altar found in 1573 in lower part of Stall Street. Now in the Roman Baths Museum, Bath.

Locum reli|giosum per in|solentiam e|rutum | virtut(i) et n(umini) | Aug(usti) repurga|tum reddidit | C(aius) Severius | Emeritus c(enturio) | reg(ionarius).

"This holy place, wrecked by insolent people and cleansed afresh, Gaius Severius Emeritus, centurion in charge of the region, has restored to the Virtue and Divine Power of the Emperor."

A *centurio regionarius* was a district officer, seconded from his legion for duties, presumably connected with security, among the civilian population (cf. nos. 147, 148). The earliest example of the title *centurio regionarius* appears at Carlisle in the Trajanic period (*Tab. Vindol.* 2.122). Emeritus probably belonged to the Second Legion at Caerleon. His duties may conceivably have been connected with the imperial estate which has been postulated on the evidence of no. 134 from nearby Combe Down.

150 (140) A councillor of Lincoln   ?3rd. century AD

RIB 250. Lincoln (Lindum). Tombstone found in 1859 built into foundations of the west wall of the lower city. Now in the British Museum.

(a) D(is) M(anibus) | Volusia | Faustina | c(ivis) Lind(ensis) v(ixit) | ann(os) XXVI | m(ensem) I d(ies) XXVI | Aur(elius) Sene|cio dec(urio) ob | merita c(oniugi) p(osuit).

(b) D(is) M(anibus) | Cl(audia) Catiotu[os] | vixit a[n]|n(os) LX[...].

> "To the spirits of the departed: Volusia Faustina, a citizen of Lincoln, lived 26 years 1 month 26 days. Aurelius Senecio, decurion, set this up to his deserving wife."

> "To the spirits of the departed: Claudia Catiotuos, lived 60 (or more) years [...]."

Above the inscription are the busts of two women, wearing tunic and mantle; the figure to the left (? Volusia) wears a necklace. The hairstyles of both are consistent with the 3rd.-century date proposed for the inscription (Allason-Jones 1989, 135). The relationship of Claudia Catiotuos to the deceased is unknown: second wife or mother? Senecio's *nomen*, Aurelius, suggests that he descends from a family which acquired citizenship no earlier than the second half of the second century: he is not, therefore, a descendant of an original colonist. His wife could be. In this context (and that of nos. 151–152) a decurion is a member of the city council.

151 (141) A Gloucester councillor at Bath   Date unknown

RIB 161. *Bath (Aquae Sulis). Plinth of a tomb found in 1600 built into the medieval wall of Bath. Now lost.*

> [...] | dec(urio) coloniae Glev[ensis ...|...] vixit an(nos) LXXX VI[...].

> "[...] decurion of the colony of Glevum [...], lived 80 years, Vi[...]."

Glevum is Gloucester, which was established as a *colonia* at the time of Nerva (AD 96–97), on the evidence of the tombstone of a soldier named as *M. Ulpio Ner. Quinto Glevi* (*CIL* 6.3346). For the foundation of the colony see Hurst 1988.

152 (142) A councillor of York   3rd. century AD

RIB 674. *York (Eboracum). Stone coffin, with lid, found 1872 at Scarborough Railway Bridge. Now in the Yorkshire Museum.*

> D(is) M(anibus) | Fl[a]vi Bellatoris dec(urionis) col(oniae) Eboracens(is) | vixit annis XXVIIII mensib[us ...|...] III[...diebus ...] II[...]

> "To the spirits of the departed (and) of Flavius Bellator, decurion of the colony of York; he lived 29 years ... months ... days."

The skeleton of Bellator had on one finger a gold ring, set with a ruby. The gold ring was the badge of the equestrian aristocracy. The Julian Municipal Law (*CIL* 1.593 = Lewis and Reinhold 1966, I, 417–8) gives 30 as the normal minimum age for service as a magistrate; the Charter of Malaca gives 25 (*ILS* 6089 = Lewis and Reinhold 1966, II, 323–326). Unlike the other three colonies in Britain which were veteran settlements, York was a titular colony, the title having been bestowed on the pre-existing settlement which had grown up outside the legionary base.

153 (143) A British altar at Bordeaux   AD 237

JRS 11 (1921), 102. *Bordeaux (Burdigala). Altar found in 1921 at Bordeaux.*

Deae Tutel(a)e Boudig(ae) I M(arcus) Aur(elius) Lunaris se|vir Aug(ustalis) col(oniarum) Ebor(aci) et I Lind(i) prov(inciae) Brit(anniae) Inf(erioris) I aram quam vover(at) I ab Eboraci avect(us) I v(otum) s(olvit) l(ibens) m(erito) I Perpetuo et Corne(liano consulibus).

"To the goddess Tutela Boudig(a), Marcus Aurelius Lunaris, *sevir Augustalis* of the colonies of York and Lincoln in the province of lower Britannia *(set up)* the altar which he vowed when he set sail from York; he fulfilled his vow willingly and deservedly in the consulship of Perpetuus and Cornelianus."

The relief above the inscription shows, in the centre, the goddess with the attributes of Cybele; on the left, a bull and above the bull a tree (the sacred pine associated with the cult of Cybele?); far left is a priest wearing a Phrygian cap; to the right is an altar, and beyond the altar the dedicator. On one side of the altar a river god symbolises the Garonne, on which Bordeaux stands; on the other a boar symbolises York. The name *Boudig(a)* recalls that of the British queen, Boudica; alternatively the deity honoured may be intended to be *Bourdig(a)*, the tutelary deity of Bordeaux. A *sevir Augustalis* was a member of a board of six men who conducted emperor-worship at chartered towns such as the two colonies of York and Lincoln. The *seviri* were commonly freedmen.

This inscription provides the earliest dated reference to York as a colony, and useful evidence for the location of the boundary between upper and lower Britain.

The altar is made of millstone grit, from Yorkshire; it was thus conveyed from Britain, presumably with Lunaris, to be set up as an *ex voto* in thanks for a safe journey.

154 (144) M. Verecundius Diogenes   3rd. or 4th. century AD

RIB 678. *York* (Eboracum). *Stone coffin found in 1579 outside York. Lost before 1796.*

M(arcus) Verec(undius) Diogenes sevir col(oniae) I Ebor(acensis) idemq[ue] mor(i)t(ex) et cives Biturix I Cubus haec sibi vivus fecit.

"Marcus Verecundius Diogenes, *sevir* of the colony of York, seafarer and citizen of the Bituriges Cubi, set this up to himself in his lifetime."

For *sevir* see no. 153. The restoration *mor(i)t(ex)* is that of J. C. Mann, quoted in Birley (1966, 228) as against the earlier reading of *idem quinquennalis* given in *RIB*. A British trader described as *moritex* is known from Cologne (no. 217). Another possible reading is provided by Bogaers (quoted in Hassall 1978, 43) who suggests *sevir col. Ebor. itemq(ue) Mori(norum)*, pointing out that Tervanna (Therouanne in the Pas de Calais), chief town of the Morini, is called *colonia Morinorum* on an inscription from Nijmegen (*CIL* 12.8727). In this case Diogenes, like Lunaris, would be a *sevir* in two colonies. The Bituriges Cubi were located in central Gaul, centred on Bourges. The nature of his link with York may have been commercial, with wine as the most likely object of trade between the two cities. The quality of his coffin, and that which he provided for his wife (below, no. 155), suggest a degree of affluence, as does his assumption of duty as *sevir*. Like Lunaris he was probably a freedman.

155 (145) Diogenes' wife   3rd. or 4th. century AD

RIB 687. York (Eboracum). Stone coffin found in 1877, within a few metres of no. 152. Now in the Yorkshire Museum.

Iul(iae) Fortunat(a)e domo | Sardinia Verec(undio) Dio|geni fida coniuncta | marito.

"To Julia Fortunata, from Sardinia, a loyal wife to her husband, Diogenes."

The last two words may have been chosen from the end of a hexameter line: cf. Catullus 62.54. For Diogenes see no. 154.

156 (146) Provincia Britannia   Date unknown

RIB 5. London (Londinium). A slab found in 1850 near Cannon Street. Now lost.

Num(ini) C[aes(aris) Aug(usti)] | prov[incia] | Brita[nnia].

"To the Divine Power of the emperor, the province of Britain ..."

Caes. Aug. could refer to any emperor. The cult of the *numina* is a latish development, arising out of, but separate from, the official imperial cult (see Note on Religion, p. 18). The provincial council, which is presumably the corporate body intended here, was set up to maintain the official imperial cult. This council increased in importance because it developed rights of access to the emperor.

157 (-) The vicani of Carriden   Early to mid-Antonine

JRS 47 (1957), 229–230 no. 18. Carriden, West Lothian (Velunia or Veluniate). Altar, ploughed up in 1956, a short distance east of the site of Carriden fort. Now in the National Museums of Scotland, Edinburgh.

I(ovi) O(ptimo) M(aximo) | vikani consi[s]|tentes castel[lo] | Veluniate cu[ram] | agente Ael(io) Man|sueto v(otum) s(olverunt) l(aeti) l(ibentes) m(erito).

"To Jupiter Best and Greatest, the people living at the fort of Velunia, under the charge of Aelius Mansuetus, fulfilled their vow joyfully, freely and deservedly."

As well as pointing to the existence of an organised civilian community at Carriden, the easternmost fort on the short-lived Antonine frontier in Scotland, this inscription is of importance in fixing the location of the site of *Velunia*, thus showing that the ten place-names listed in the Ravenna Cosmography as lying on the Forth-Clyde isthmus run from east to west (Rivet and Smith 1979, 211, 490). The *vicus* in question here will have been subordinate to the authority of the military. *Vici* could also be subordinate to the authority of cities on whose territory they lay. The letter 'k' frequently replaces 'c' in later inscriptions (as also no. 158), and sometimes earlier ones (cf. no. 166).

158 (147) The vicani of Old Carlisle   AD 238–244

RIB 899. Old Carlisle, Cumbria (Maglona?). Part of an altar found in 1842 at Old Carlisle. Now in Carlisle Museum.

I(ovi) O(ptimo) M(aximo) et | V(u)lk(ano) pro sallute d(omini) n(ostri) M(arci) Anto(ni) | Gordiani P(ii) | F(elicis) Aug(usti) vik(ani) | Mag(lonenses) aram | a(ere) col(lato) a v(ikanis) d(edicaverunt).

"To Jupiter Best and Greatest and to Vulcan, for the welfare of our lord Marcus Antonius Gordian Pius Felix Augustus, the people of Maglona dedicated this altar from money contributed by the people."

The restoration *vik(ani) Mag(lonenses)* (in preference to the *vik(anorum) mag(istri)* given in *RIB*) arises from the reidentification of Old Carlisle as *Maglona* rather than *Olenacum*. For detail see Rivet and Smith 1979, 406–407, *Magis* and *Maglona*. The settlement at Old Carlisle grew up outside a fort and was subject to military authority. For a similar dedication to Vulcan by the inhabitants of a military *vicus* see no. 159 from Chesterholm. Vulcan, the god of smiths, was honoured in many places associated with industry.

159 (148) The vicani of Chesterholm   2nd. or 3rd. century AD

RIB 1700. *Chesterholm* (Vindolanda). *Altar found in 1914 west of the fort. Now in Chesters Museum.*

Pro Domu | Divina et Nulminibus Auglustorum Volclano sacrum | vicani Vindollandesses curam | agente [...] O[...]lv(otum) s(olverunt) l(ibentes) [m(erito)].

"For the Divine House and the Divine Powers of the emperors, the people of Vindolanda *(set up this)* sacred offering to Vulcan, willingly and deservedly fulfilling their vow under the charge of [...]."

The spelling Vindoland*esses* in place of Vindoland*enses* reflects spoken Latin (Mann 1971, 222); cf. the *venatores Banniesses* from Bewcastle (*RIB* 1905). For other dedications to the *Domus Divina* see nos. 137, 146. For *Numina Augustorum* see Note on Religion, p. 19.

160 (149) The curia of the Textoverdi   2nd. or 3rd. century AD

RIB 1695. *Beltingham, Northumberland. Altar found in 1835 in Beltingham churchyard. Now in the Museum of Antiquities, Newcastle upon Tyne.*

Deae | Sattadae | curia Texltoverdorum | v(otum) s(olvit) l(ibens) m(erito).

"To the goddess Sattada, the assembly of the Textoverdi fulfilled its vow willingly and deservedly."

The find-spot of this inscription, 3 km south-east of Chesterholm, suggests that the Textoverdi inhabited the area of the South Tyne. They are not otherwise known, nor is the deity to whom this altar is dedicated.

(c) GUILDS

161 (151) The guild of peregrini at Silchester   2nd. or 3rd. century AD

RIB 69. *Silchester* (Calleva). *Dedication slab found in 1907 in the shrine of a Romano-Celtic temple. Now in Reading Museum.*

[...]l(...) Attici | [...]apacis | [sine stipibus au]t collati|[onibus sibi com]missum | [a collegio peregri]nor[u]m | [c(onsistentium) C(allevae) donum d(e) s(uo)] d(edit) *or* d(ederunt).

"... of Atticus ... without their offerings or contributions, gave from his (or their) own resources, this gift entrusted to him (or them) by the guild of *peregrini* dwelling at Calleva."

The *peregrini* belonging to this guild at Silchester are probably immigrants, citizens of other cities who have come to Silchester most likely for commercial purposes. Alternatively, if the inscription predates the *constitutio Antoniniana* they may simply be people lacking in Roman citizenship. For two other practically identical texts cf. *RIB* 70, 71.

162 (153) Nonius Romanus statue base   AD 152

RIB 309. *Caerwent* (Venta Silurum). *Statue-base found in 1904 in house XI. Now in Newport Museum.*

[Deo] Marti Leno | [s]ive Ocelo Vellaun(o) et Num(ini) Aug(usti) | M(arcus) Nonius Romanus ob | immunitat(em) collegni | d(onum) d(e) s(uo) d(edit) | Glabrione et H[om]ulo co(n)s(ulibus) (a(nte) d(iem)) X K(alendas) Sept(embres).

"To the god Mars Lenus otherwise Ocelus Vellaunus and to the Divine Power of the Emperor, Marcus Nonius Romanus, in return for freedom from liability of the college, gave this gift from his own resources, ten days before the Kalends of September, in the consulate of Glabrio and Homulus *(i.e. 23 August, AD 152)*."

The relief on the statue base depicts a goose. Vellaunus is elsewhere identified with Mercury, one of whose familiars is a goose. A large temple of Mars Lenus is known at Trier, a centre of the cult (where he is known always as "Lenus Mars" rather than, as here, "Mars Lenus"); this may suggest that Nonius Romanus came from Trier. Note that 23 August is the date of the Roman feast of the Vulcanalia. The nature of the guild referred to is unknown. For *Numen Augusti* see Note on Religion, p. 19.

163 (154) Two guilds at Lincoln   Date unknown

(a) *RIB* 270. *Lincoln* (Lindum). *Inscribed plinth from monumental building; found in 1845 in High Street premises. Now lost.*

Vic(us) Hrapo Mercure(n)sium.

"The ... ward of the guild of Mercury."

(b) *RIB* 271. *Lincoln* (Lindum), *Moulded stone from a portico; found in 1785 on what is now called Lindum Road. Now lost.*

[A]polline(n)s[ium ?]

"... of the guild of Apollo."

Both of these inscriptions appear on building blocks, very probably from guild-rooms. The stones commemorate guilds of worshippers of Mercury and

Apollo. The *vicus* referred to in (a) is a ward within the colony, whose name is irrecoverable from the recorded reading HRAPO. (a) was found with coins of Domitian and Antoninus Pius.

164 (155) A Lincoln guild treasurer   AD 193–211

RIB 247. *Lincoln* (Lindum). *Altar found in 1884 on south side of the lower Roman city. Now in St Swithun's Church, Lincoln.*

> Parcis Dealbus et Nulminibus Aug(ustorum) I C(aius) Antistius I Frontinus I curator ter(tium) I ar(am) d(e) s(uo) d(edit) *or* d(edicavit).

> "To the goddesses of the Fates and to the Divine Powers of the Emperors, Gaius Antistius Frontinus, *curator* for a third time, gave (or dedicated) this altar at his own expense."

It is impossible to be certain of what Frontinus had charge; he may, as *RIB* suggests, be a guild-treasurer.

(d) ROADS

165 (157) Altar to the god who devised roads   AD 191

RIB 725. *Catterick* (Cataractonium). *Altar found in 1620 at Thornborough-on-Swale or Catterick Bridge. Now lost.*

> Deo qui vias I et semitas comlmentus est T(itus) Irldas, s(ingularis) c(onsularis), f(ecit) v(otum) l(aetens) l(ibens) m(erito) I Q(uintus) Varius Vitallis b(ene)f(iciarius) co(n)s(ularis) aram I sacram restiltuit I Aproniano et Braldua co(n)s(ulibus).

> "To the god who devised roads and paths, Titus Irdas, *singularis consularis* made a vow willingly, joyfully and deservedly. Quintus Varius Vitalis, *beneficiarius consularis* restored the sacred altar, when Apronianus and Bradua were consuls."

The *singulares consularis* were auxiliaries seconded to the provincial governor's bodyguard. For *beneficiarius consularis* see no. 130. On the roads leading to Catterick cf. no. 276 (*Tab. Vindol.* 2.343.21), which refers to their bad state of repair (nearly a century before the date of this inscription).

166 (160) Milestone on territory of Caerhun   AD 120–121

RIB 2265. *Near Llanfairfechan, Gwynedd. Milestone found in 1883 about 11 kilometres west of Caerhun fort, buried in a field. Now in the British Museum.*

> Imp(erator) Caes(ar) Trailanus Hadrianus I Aug(ustus), p(ontifex) m(aximus), tr(ibuniciae) p(otestatis) V I p(ater) p(atriae) co(n)s(ul) III I a Kanovio I m(ilia) p(assuum) VIII.

> "The Emperor Caesar Trajan Hadrian Augustus, high priest, in his 5th. year of tribunician power, father of his country, three times consul. From Kanovium, 8 miles."

This fine example stands 1.67 metres high. The distance is measured from Caerhun, the fort on whose territory it stands. It gives the correct form of the Roman name for Caerhun (Rivet and Smith 1979, 297). Like no. 141, it incorrectly credits Hadrian with the title *pater patriae*.

167 (158) A milestone from Buxton   Date unknown

RIB 2243. Buxton, Derbyshire, nearly 11 Roman miles south-west of Brough-on-Noe (Navio). *A milestone found in 1862 in Hardwick Square. Now in Buxton Museum.*

> ...]trib(unicia) pot(estate) co(n)s(uli) II | p(atri) p(atriae) a Navione | m(ilia) p(assuum) XI.

> "... with tribunician power, twice consul, father of his country, from Navio 11 miles."

The distance on this milestone is measured from the fort of Brough-on-Noe in whose territory it was set up. Milestones are also an important source of information on the dates of road building and repair, though in this case the crucial imperial name is missing.

168 (161) Hesket milestone   AD 307–337

RIB 2288. Hesket, Cumbria. Milestone found in 1776 on Roman road between Carlisle and Penrith. Now lost.

> Imp(eratori) C(aesari) | Fl(avio) Val(erio) | Cons|tanti|no P(io) F(elici) | Inv(icto) Aug(usto).

> "For the Emperor Caesar Flavius Valerius Constantinus Pius Felix Invictus Augustus."

This milestone may be assumed to lie on the territory of the *civitas Carvetiorum* (as the Brougham milestone, no. 143).

PART VII: SOLDIERS AND CIVILIANS

(a) LEGIONARIES

169 (162) A legate of the sixth legion

Late 2nd. century AD

RIB 658. *York* (Eboracum). *A dedication slab found in 1770 near Tanner Row, south-east of the Old Railway Station, York. Now in the Yorkshire Museum.*

> Deo sancto | Serapi | templum a sollo fecit | Cl(audius) Hieronyl mianus leg(atus) | leg(ionis) VI Victricis.

> "To the holy god Serapis, Claudius Hieronymianus, legate of the Sixth Legion Victrix, built this temple from ground level."

Hieronymianus may be identified with the senator mentioned in Ulpian, *Digest* 33.7.12.40, and with the governor of Cappadocia at the end of the second and beginning of the third century (Tertullian, *Ad Scapula* 3; Birley 1981, 263–64). The inscription was found in association with a building thought to be the temple in question and is one of very few pieces of evidence attesting the worship of this Egyptian deity in Britain.

170 (186) A camp prefect of legion XX

Early 3rd. century AD

RIB 490. *Chester* (Deva). *Fragments of a tombstone found in 1887 in the fortress north wall (east part). Now in the Grosvenor Museum.*

> D(is) M(anibus) | M(arcus) Aurelius Alexand(er) | praef(ectus) cast(rorum) leg(ionis) XX | [V(aleriae) V(ictricis)] nat(ione) Syrus Os[r(oenus) | vi]x(it) an(nos) LXXII[...|...]c[...]yces et S[...]

> "To the spirits of the departed, Marcus Aurelius Alexander, camp prefect of the twentieth legion Valeria Victrix, a native of Syria Os[roene], lived 72 years, [...]yces and S[... his heirs set this up]."

The names Marcus Aurelius indicate citizenship acquired no earlier than AD 161. Alexander was probably recruited at the time of Marcus' and Verus' Parthian war. This is the latest dated use of the title *praefectus castrorum* which was gradually superseded during the second century by *praefectus legionis*. The reading Syrus Os[roenus] is dubious; Syrus Co[mmagenus] is more probable. This area lay to the west of the Euphrates in northern Syria.

171 (163) Caecilius Avitus, *optio*

?3rd. century AD

RIB 492. *Chester* (Deva). *Tombstone found in 1891 in the fortress north wall. Now in the Grosvenor Museum.*

> D(is) M(anibus) | Caecilius Avitl us Emer(ita) Aug(usta) | optio leg(ionis) XX | V(aleriae) V(ictricis) st(i)p(endiorum) XV vix(it) | an(nos) XXXIIII | h(eres) f(aciendum) c(uravit).

"To the spirits of the departed, Caecilius Avitus, from Emerita Augusta, *optio* of the Twentieth Legion Valeria Victrix, of fifteen years' service, lived 34 years. His heir had this set up."

An *optio* served as second-in-command to a centurion. The bearded figure of the *optio* stands in a niche above the inscription. He is holding a tall knob-headed staff in his right hand, and the handle of a square case of writing tablets in his left. His head is bare and he wears over his tunic a heavy cloak (*sagum*), the ends of which cross and hang down in two tails. A sword with a large round pommel hangs at his right side. Emerita Augusta, modern Mérida, was a colony in Lusitania.

172 (187) Titinius Felix, *beneficiarius*   3rd. century AD

RIB 505. Chester (Deva). A tombstone found in 1887 in the fortress north wall (east part). Now in the Grosvenor Museum.

D(is) M(anibus) | Titinius Felix b(eneficiarius) | leg(ati) leg(ionis) XX V(aleriae) V(ictricis) mil(itavit) an(nos) | XXII (?) vix(it) an(nos) XLV | Iul(ia) Similina colniux et heres [...]

"To the spirits of the departed, Titinius Felix, *beneficiarius* of the legate of the Twentieth Legion Valeria Victrix, served 22 (?) years, lived 45 years; Iulia Similina his wife and heir [set this up]."

A date in the third century is indicated by the specific mention of the wife of this serving soldier, and also by the absence of a *praenomen*. On the left-hand margin of the inscription is a figure facing inwards, dressed in a cloak, tunic and Phrygian cap. On the right there was probably a corresponding figure. For other *beneficiarii* see nos. 15, 129–131, 165, 226, 245.

173 (189) Amandus the engineer   Early 3rd. century AD

RIB 2091. Birrens (Blatobulgium), Dumfriesshire. Statue of the goddess Brigantia, found in 1731 in the ruins of a building outside the fort at Birrens. Now in the National Museums of Scotland, Edinburgh.

Brigantiae s(acrum) Amandus | arc(h)itectus ex imperio imp(eratum fecit).

"Sacred to Brigantia: Amandus, engineer, by command fulfilled the order."

Architectus was a legionary grade, so presumably Amandus belonged to the Sixth Legion based at York. He has been identified with the *Val. Amandus discens (architectum)* (i.e. an apprentice *architectus*) of Legion I Minervia attested near Bonn in AD 209. This dedication to the territorial deity Brigantia suggests that the territory of the Brigantes extended at least as far north as Birrens. The winged figure of the goddess, carved in high relief and standing in a gabled niche, has a gorgon's head on her breast and wears a plumed helmet encircled by a turreted crown. In her right hand she holds a spear, in her left, a globe; to her left stands her shield, to her right an omphaloid stone. These attributes equate her with Minerva Victrix (see Joliffe 1941). It is said that when first discovered the statuette had traces of gilding.

174 (188) An armourer of legion XX   Probably 3rd. century AD

RIB 156. *Bath* (Aquae Sulis). *Tombstone found in 1708 near the Fosse Way. Now in the Roman Baths Museum.*

> Iulius Vitallis fabricie(n)slis leg(ionis) XX V(aleriae) V(ictricis) I stipendiorlum IX an(n)or(um) XXIIX natione Bellga, ex col(l)egio I fabric(i)e(nsium) elatuls h(ic) s(itus) e(st).

> "Iulius Vitalis, armourer of the Twentieth Legion Valeria Victrix, of 9 years' service, aged 29, by origin a Belga, with funeral at the cost of the guild of armourers. Here he lies."

Natione Belga very probably indicates an origin in the *civitas Belgarum* centred on Winchester, though the possibility of an origin in the province of Gallia Belgica cannot be totally excluded. The armourers of the legion had organised themselves into a guild, as was the case with a number of junior ranks and tradesmen within the army.

175 (180) A pilot of legion VI   ? Severan

RIB 653. *York* (Eboracum). *An altar found in Micklegate, opposite Holy Trinity Church, York. Now in the Yorkshire Museum, York.*

> Mat(ribus) Af(ris) Ita(lis) Ga(llis) I M(arcus) Minu(cius) Aude(ns) I mil(es) leg(ionis) VI Vic(tricis) I guber(nator) leg(ionis) VI I v(otum) s(olvit) l(aetus) l(ibens) m(erito).

> "To the African, Italian and Gallic Mother Goddesses, Marcus Minucius Audens, soldier of legion VI Victrix, pilot in legion VI, willingly, gladly and deservedly fulfilled his vow."

The pilot was ranked next below the captain in a Roman warship. Audens is the only legionary pilot known. His presence at York points to the importance of access to the sea for supplying a legionary base. The dedication to African, Italian and Gallic Mother Goddesses may be an indicator of the mixed origins of the men then serving at York, very probably in the wake of the Severan campaigns. (For a discussion of men from Africa serving in Legion VI, cf. Swan 1992).

176 (181) An eques of legion IX   1st. century AD

RIB 254. *Lincoln* (Lindum). *Tombstone found in about 1800, about a kilometre south of the south gate of the extended* colonia. *Now lost; sketch in the Society of Antiquaries.*

> Q(uinti) Corneli I Q(uinti) f(ilii) Cla(udia tribu) eq(uitis) I le(gionis) VIIII [c(enturia)] Cassi I Martialis an(norum) I XL stip(endiorum) XIX I h(ic) s(itus) e(st).

> "(In memory of) Quintus Cornelius, son of Quintus, of the Claudian voting tribe, cavalryman in legion VIIII from the century of Cassius Martialis, aged 40 years, served 19 years, lies buried here."

Legionary cavalrymen, unlike auxiliaries, were not organised in separate troops (*turmae*) but were carried on the books of the centuries. For the dating of this stone see no. 17.

177 (165) C. Murrius Modestus (legio II Adiutrix)   AD 71–*c*.87

RIB 157. *Bath* (Aquae Sulis). *Rectangular tombstone found (with no. 182) before 1590 on the Fosse Way, about 1600 metres north-east of the baths. Now lost.*

C(aius) Murrius | C(ai) f(ilius) Arniensis | Foro Iuli Mo|destus mil(es) | [l]eg(ionis) II Ad(iutricis) P(iae) F(idelis) | [c(enturia)] Iuli Secundi | ann(orum) XXV stip(endiorum) [...] | h(ic) [s(itus) e(st)].

"Gaius Murrius Modestus, son of Gaius, of the Arniensian voting tribe, from Forum Iulii, soldier of the Second Legion Adiutrix Pia Fidelis, from the century of Iulius Secundus, aged 25 years, served ... years, here he lies."

The legion, based at Lincoln when it first arrived in Britain in AD 71, is thought to have been the first unit stationed at Chester, when the fortress was constructed in the late 70s (cf. no. 27). It remained there until its withdrawal from Britain in about 87. Forum Iulii is most probably the site of that name at Fréjus, in Provence, though there is another Forum Iulii at Cividale del Friuli in northeast Italy.

178 (166) C. Iuventius Capito (legio II Adiutrix)   *c.* AD 77–*c* 87

RIB 476. *Chester* (Deva). *A tombstone found in 1891 in the fortress north wall (west part). Now in the Grosvenor Museum.*

C(aius) Iuventius | C(ai filius) Cla(udia tribu) Capito | Apro mil(es) leg(ionis) II | Ad(iutricis) P(iae) F(idelis) c(enturia) Iuli Cle|mentis ann(orum) XL | stip(endiorum) [X]VII.

"Gaius Iuventius Capito, son of Gaius, of the Claudian voting tribe, from Aprus, soldier of the Second Legion Adiutrix Pia Fidelis, from the century of Iulius Clemens, aged 40 years, served 17 years."

Aprus (or Apri) is a Claudian colony in southern Thrace (western Turkey). This is one of three tombstones (the others are *RIB* 475 and 477) from Chester recording soldiers from this city serving in II Adiutrix.

179 (167) Q. Valerius Fronto (legio II Adiutrix)   *c.* AD 77–*c.* 87

RIB 479. *Chester* (Deva). *A tombstone found in 1891 in the fortress north wall (west part). Now in the Grosvenor Museum.*

Q(uintus) Valeri|us Q(uinti) f(ilius) Cla(udia tribu) | Fronto Cele|(i)a miles leg(ionis) | II Ad(iutricis) P(iae) F(idelis) an|norum L | stipendiorum | XXV[...]

"Quintus Valerius Fronto, son of Quintus, of the Claudian voting tribe, from Celeia, soldier of the Second Legion Adiutrix Pia Fidelis, aged 50 years, served 25 (+) years."

Celeia (modern Celje in Slovenia) was a city (a *municipium*) in the south-east part of Noricum. The numerals giving Fronto's years of service are damaged, but were probably between 25 and 29 years: there certainly were cases, particularly in the first century, where soldiers served more than the normal term of 25 years. Since II Adiutrix was not raised until AD 69, Fronto must have been transferred into it from another unit.

180 (168) Gabinius Felix (legio II Augusta)   AD 211–222

RIB 488. *Chester* (Deva). *A tombstone found in 1891 in the fortress north wall (west part). Now in the Grosvenor Museum.*

> D(is) M(anibus) s(acrum) I Gabinius Fellix miles Ileg(ionis) II Aug(ustae) Ant(oninianae) I [vix]sit an(n)is I XXXX h(eres) p(onendum) c(uravit).

> "Sacred to the spirits of the departed, Gabinius Felix soldier of the second legion Augusta Antoniniana, lived 40 years; his heir had this set up."

The title *Antoniniana* dates the text to AD 211–222. This stone was incorporated in the north wall when it was reconstructed. *II Augusta* was stationed at Caerleon; it can only be conjectured why Gabinius was visiting Chester. The formulae DMS and HPC do not recur at Chester. For the use of *vixsit* in place of *vixit* see Mann 1971, 221.

181 (164) T. Flaminius (legio XIV Gemina)   Before AD 61

RIB 292. *Wroxeter* (Viroconium). *Base of a sculptured tombstone, found in 1861 in the Roman cemetery on the east side of Wroxeter. Now in Rowley's House Museum, Shrewsbury.*

> [T(itus) F]laminius T(iti filius) Pol(lia tribu) Fa[v(entia) I an]norum XXXXV stip(endiorum) XXII mil(es) leg(ionis) I [XII]II Gem(inae) militavi a(t)q(ue) nunc hic s[u]m. *(followed by advice on leading a good life)*

> "[Titus] Flaminius, son of Titus, of the Pollian voting tribe, from Faventia, aged 45 years, of 22 years' service, a soldier of the Fourteenth Legion Gemina; I have done my service and now am here."

The absence of a *cognomen* suggests an early date, as does the omission of the legion's titles *Martia Victrix* which it was awarded on the occasion of the suppression of the Boudican rebellion in AD 61 (cf. no. 19). Faventia, now Faenza, is in Gallia Cisalpina.

182 (169) M. Valerius Latinus (legio XX)   1st. century AD

RIB 158. *Bath* (Aquae Sulis). *Tombstone found with no. 177. Now lost.*

> Dis Manibus I M(arcus) Valerius M(arci) I fil(ius) Latinus c(ivis) Eq(uester) I mil(es) leg(ionis) XX an(norum) I XXXV stipen(diorum) XX I h(ic) s(itus) e(st).

> "To the spirits of the departed, Marcus Valerius Latinus son of Marcus, citizen of Equestris, soldier of the twentieth legion, aged 35 years, of 20 years' service, lies buried here."

Latinus came from *Colonia Iulia Equestris* (Nyon, on Lake Geneva in Switzerland), a colony founded by Caesar for the veterans of *legio X Equestris*. Stylistically, the stone should date no later than the early second century and, given the absence of the titles *Valeria Victrix*, is likely to be pre-61.

183 (170) P. Rustius Crescens (legio XX Valeria Victrix)

? late 1st.–early 2nd. century AD

RIB 503. Chester (Deva). A tombstone found in 1887 in the north wall (east part). Now in the Grosvenor Museum.

> D(is) M(anibus) P(ublio) Rustio I Fabia (tribu) Crescen(ti) Brix(ia) I mil(iti) leg(ionis) XX V(aleriae) V(ictricis) I an(norum) XXX stip(endiorum) X I Groma heres I fac(iendum) cur(avit).

> "To the spirits of the departed and to Publius Rustius Crescens of the Fabian voting tribe, from Brixia, soldier of legion XX Valeria Victrix, aged 30 years, served for 10 years; Groma, his heir, had this made."

Of the figure above the inscription, only the left foot and a trace of the right remain. Brixia is now Brescia in northern Italy. Very few Italians served in the legions after the time of Hadrian.

184 (173) Vivius Marcianus (legio II Augusta)   Probably 3rd. century AD

RIB 17. London (Londinium). Tombstone found in 1669 in St. Martin's Church, Ludgate Hill. Now in the Ashmolean Museum, Oxford.

> D(is) M(anibus) I Vivio Marcilano c(enturioni) leg(ionis) II I Aug(ustae) Ianuaria I Martina coniunx I pientissima posulit memoriam.

> "To the spirits of the departed and to Vibius Marcianus, centurion of legion II Augusta; Ianuaria Martina his most devoted wife set up this memorial."

Below the inscription stands the figure of the centurion in a niche. He holds a scroll in his left hand, perhaps indicating an administrative role. Like nos. 185 and 186, Marcianus has been seconded to the staff of the governor in London. Collingwood (1928, 173) correctly identified the elaborate leaf-stop after the name as a blundered centurial sign. Thus the reason for the date given by *RIB* – the permission to marry given by Severus to all serving soldiers – is invalid, since at no time did a centurion require such permission. A third-century date would, however, appear probable from the style of the inscription.

185 (171) Flavius Agricola (legio VI Victrix)   Probably 3rd. century AD

RIB 11. London (Londinium). Tomb found in 1787 in Goodman's fields, the Minories, east of the Roman city wall. Now at the Society of Antiquaries, Burlington House, London.

> D(is) M(anibus) I Fl(avius) Agricola mil(es) I leg(ionis) VI Vict(ricis) v(ixit) an(nos) I XLII d(ies) X Albia I Faustina coniugi I inconparabili I f(acien-dum) c(uravit).

"To the spirits of the departed, Flavius Agricola, soldier of legion VI Victrix, lived 42 years 10 days; Albia Faustina had this made for her peerless husband."

The practice of allowing a soldier to marry during his term of service was first allowed by Septimius Severus (193–211). This fact, together with the lack of *praenomen*, indicates a date for the inscription no earlier than the third century. A. Birley suggests that he may be a descendant of a man who was enfranchised when Julius Agricola was governor of Britain, taking the *nomen* of the then imperial family (Flavius) and giving the governor's *cognomen* to his son to pass on to his heirs (Birley 1979, 85).

186 (172) Julius Valens (legio XX Valeria Victrix) Date unknown

RIB 13. London (Londinium). *Tombstone found in 1776 in Church Lane, Whitechapel. Now lost.*

D(is) M(anibus) I Iul(ius) Valens I mil(es) leg(ionis) XX V(aleriae) V(ictricis) I an(norum) XL h(ic) s(itus) e(st) I c(uram) a(gente) Flavio I Attio her(ede).

"To the spirits of the departed, Julius Valens, soldier of legion XX Valeria Victrix, aged 40 years, lies here; his heir Flavius Attius having the matter in charge."

Valens had probably been seconded to the governor's staff.

187 (175) The century of Iulius Rufus Hadrianic

RIB 1356. *Between Benwell* (Condercum) *and Rudchester* (Vindovala) *on Hadrian's Wall. The stone was found in 1804 probably near Denton Hall. Now in Denton Hall stable.*

C(enturia) Iuli I Rufi

"The century of Iulius Rufus *(built this)*."

Iulius Rufus is mentioned on two further inscriptions, *RIB* 1357 and 1386. This stone is assumed to relate to the original construction of the Wall.

188 (174) A cohort of legion II Augusta Antonine?

RIB 1343. Benwell (Condercum). *Building stone found before 1873 in Benwell fort. Now in Denton Hall stable.*

leg(ionis) II cloh(ors) IIII

"The fourth cohort of legion II *(built this)*."

This inscription is one of a group from the Benwell area which are more ornate than the usual simple building stones. They may not be Hadrianic at all, but may relate to a later rebuild. (See Hooley and Breeze 1968, esp. 104–5, discussing Stevens 1966). There is some evidence that Benwell fort remained in occupation when the frontier was moved forward to the Antonine Wall (*RIB* 1330).

189 (176) A cohort of legion VI Victrix   Antonine

RIB 1388. *Between Benwell* (Condercum) *and Rudchester* (Vindovala). *Building stone found in 1751 on the line of the Wall, probably near Heddon-on-the-Wall. Now lost.*

Leg(ionis) VI [V]i|c(tricis) P(iae) F(idelis) re[f]lecit coh(ors) X.

"The tenth cohort of legion VI Victrix Pia Fidelis rebuilt this."

This stone is very similar to *RIB* 1389 (no. 64), found at the same place, which has a consular date of AD 158.

(b)   AUXILIARIES

190 (192) A successful boar hunt   Later 2nd. or 3rd. century AD

RIB 1041. *Bollihope Common, south of Stanhope, in Weardale, Co. Durham. An altar found in 1747. Its exact find-spot is unknown. Now in Stanhope Church.*

Primary text:

[Numinibus August]orum | et [...

Secondary text:

Silvano Invicto sacr(um) | C(aius) Tetius Veturius Micia|nus pr[(a)e]f(ectus) alae Sebosian|nae ob aprum eximiae | formae captum quem | multi ante-cesso|res eius praedari | non potuerunt v(oto) s(uscepto) l(ibens) p(osuit).

Primary text:

"To the Divine Powers of the Emperors and ..."

Secondary text:

"To the Unconquered Silvanus, Gaius Tetius Veturius Micianus, prefect of the *ala Sebosiana*, on fulfilment of his vow willingly set this up for taking a wild boar of remarkable fineness which many of his predecessors had been unable to bag."

The fort closest to the find-spot of this inscription, Binchester, was occupied in the 3rd. century by the *ala Vettonum*; the *ala Gallorum Sebosiana* was then stationed at Lancaster. Neither the garrison of Binchester nor the location of the *ala Sebosiana* is known in the later 2nd. century. For *numina Augustorum* see Note on Religion, p. 19.

191 (-) Ammonius, auxiliary centurion   Flavian

RIB 2213. *Ardoch, Perthshire. Tombstone found in, or before, 1672, reused in the so-called* praetorium *(actually a medieval chapel). Now in the Hunterian Museum, Glasgow.*

Dis Manibus | Ammonius Da|mionis (filius) c(enturio) coh(ortis) | I Hispanorum | stipendiorum | XXVII heredes | f(aciendum) c(uraverunt).

"To the spirits of the departed: Ammonius (son of) Damio, centurion of the First Cohort of Spaniards, of 27 years' service *(lies here)*. His heirs had this made."

The fact that *Dis Manibus* is written out in full, that the soldier's name appears in the nominative and that he served more than the standard 25-year term, means that this tombstone must date to the Flavian rather than the Antonine occupation of Scotland. Hence this soldier almost certainly took part in Agricola's campaigns.

192 (41n.) Death at Ambleside fort   3rd. or 4th. century AD

JRS 53 (1963), 160 no. 4. Ambleside (Galava). A double tombstone found in 1962 about 90 metres east of the fort. It had been reused as part of a modern drain.

D(is) B(onis) M(anibus) | Fla(vius) Fuscinus eme(ritus) | ex ordi(nato) visi(t) an(n)is LV ‖ D(is) B(onis) M(anibus) | Fla(vius) Romanus act(arius) | vixit anni(s) XXXV | in cas(tello) inte(rfectus) ab hosti(bus).

"To the good spirits of the departed, Flavius Fuscinus, retired from the centurionate, lived 55 years. To the good spirits of the departed, Flavius Romanus, record clerk, lived for 35 years, killed in the fort by the enemy."

The expansion of the "B" as "*Bonis*" is speculative as it is unparalleled on a tombstone. The circumstances of Romanus's death are unknown; the stone is not dated but is very unlikely to be earlier than the third century AD. For the spelling *visit* for *vixit*, see Mann 1971, 223.

193 (-) A doctor at Housesteads   3rd. century AD

RIB 1618. Housesteads (Vercovicium). Tombstone found in, or before, 1813. Now in the Museum of Antiquities, Newcastle upon Tyne.

D(is) M(anibus) | Anicio | Ingenuo | medico | ord(inario) coh(ortis) | I Tungr(orum) | vix(it) an(nos) XXV.

"To the spirits of the departed (and) to Anicius Ingenuus, *medicus ordinarius* of the First Tungrian Cohort: he lived 25 years."

Medicus ordinarius is most probably a doctor with the rank equivalent to that of a centurion.

194 (-) An auxiliary standard-bearer   Flavian

RIB 1172. Hexham, Northumberland. Tombstone found in 1881 in the foundations of a porch at Hexham Abbey and thought to have been transported there from Corbridge.

Dis Manibus Flavinus | eq(ues) alae Petr(ianae) signifer | tur(ma) Candidi an(norum) XXV | stip(endiorum) VII h(ic) s(itus est).

"To the spirits of the departed, Flavinus, cavalryman in the *ala Petriana*, standard-bearer in the troop of Candidus, aged 25 years, of 7 years' service, lies buried here."

Above the inscription is a relief showing a cavalryman carrying a standard which bears a human portrait (an *imago?*), and riding down a naked barbarian. The unit appears without the honorary title *c(ivium) R(omanorum)* (attesting a block grant of Roman citizenship) which it had gained by AD 98. It was later doubled in size to become the one *ala milliaria* stationed in Britain.

195 (-) Nectovelius   Antonine ?

RIB 2142. Mumrills, Stirlingshire. Tombstone found in 1834 near the fort. Now in the National Museums of Scotland, Edinburgh.

> Dis M(anibus) Nectovelius f(ilius) I Vindicis an(norum) IXXX I stip(endio-rum) VIIII natlionis Brigans I militavit in I coh(orte) II Thr(acum).

> "To the spirits of the departed, Nectovelius, son of Vindex, aged 29 years, of 9 years' service, a Brigantian, served in the Second Cohort of Thracians."

The lettering retains traces of red paint. This stone provides evidence for local recruitment to the *auxilia* in Britain. For other examples see Dobson and Mann 1973.

(c) THE FLEET

196 (179) L. Aufidius Pantera, fleet prefect   Mid- to late 130s AD

RIB 66. Lympne (Lemanis). Altar found in 1850 in the east gate of the Roman fort. Now in the British Museum.

> [N]eptu[no] I aram I L(ucius) Aufidius I Pantera I praefect(us) I clas(sis) Brit(annicae).

> "To Neptune, Lucius Aufidius Pantera, prefect of the British fleet, *(set up this)* altar."

Pantera's command of the British fleet is approximately dated by a diploma of AD 133 (*CIL* 16.76) on which he is named as commander of a milliary *ala*, a post which he will have held shortly before his fleet command. The discovery of this second-century inscription reused in the late Roman fort at Lympne contributes to the evidence that there was an earlier site in the vicinity (cf. Reece 1989, 155). For another prefect of the British fleet see above, no. 46 (Maenius Agrippa): for a detachment of the fleet on Hadrian's Wall, no. 37.

(d) NUMERI

197 (177) The Raeti Gaesati at Great Chesters   3rd. century AD

RIB 1724. Great Chesters (Aesica). Altar found in 1908 in the bath building south-east of Great Chesters fort. Now in the Museum of Antiquities, Newcastle upon Tyne.

D[(e)ae F]or[t]u(nae) | vexs(illatio) G(aesatorum) R(a)eto(rum) | quorum
cur|am agit Tabelllius Victor | c(enturio).

"To the goddess Fortune, a detachment of the Raetian javelin-men, under
the command of Tabellius Victor, centurion *(set this up)*."

The Raeti Gaesati were an irregular unit, a *numerus*, originally raised in
Switzerland (see above, no. 84). On *numeri* in general see Southern 1989. For
another dedication to Fortuna from a bathhouse see no. 49.

198 (178) The Raeti at Jedburgh   3rd. century AD

*RIB 2117. Cappuck, Roxburgh, 6 kilometres east of Jedburgh on the line of Dere
Street. Altar, first noticed 1853, forming the lintel over the entrance to the north-
west turret of Jedburgh Abbey. Now in the Abbey; cast in the Museum of
Antiquities, Newcastle-upon-Tyne.*

I(ovi) O(ptimo) M(aximo) ve[x]|il(l)atio R(a)eto|rum Gaesat(orum) |
q(uorum) c(uram) a(git) Iul(ius) | Sever(inus) trib(unus).

"To Jupiter Best and Greatest, a detachment of Raetian javelin-men under
the command of Iulius Severinus, tribune, *(set this up)*."

This inscription (together with *RIB* 2118, a text of *cohors I Fida Vardullorum*)
is assumed to have been carried to Jedburgh Abbey from Cappuck, the nearest
known Roman fort. The Raeti Gaesati were based at Risingham, together with
the *cohors I Vangionum* (see no. 84), a milliary unit of which Severinus was
presumably the tribune. Severinus is attested at Risingham on *RIB* 1212, an
altar dedicated to Fortuna Redux on completion of the bathhouse.

(e)   VETERANS AND THEIR FAMILIES

199 (182) A veteran of legion II Augusta   2nd. or 3rd. century AD

*RIB 363. Caerleon (Isca). Tombstone found about 1815 at Great Bulmore, 2 kilo-
metres north-east of Caerleon fortress. Now in Caerleon Museum.*

[D(is) M(anibus)] | Iul(ius) Valens vet(eranus) | leg(ionis) II Aug(ustae) vixit
| annis C Iul(ia) | Secundina coniunx | et Iul(ius) Martinus filius | f(acien-
dum) c(uraverunt).

"To the spirits of the departed, Iulius Valens, veteran of legion II Augusta,
lived 100 years; Iulia Secundina, his wife, and Iulius Martinus, his son,
had this set up."

This inscription was found, together with seven others (including *RIB* 373,
the memorial to Valens' wife, no. 200), a coin of Trajan and other remains,
suggesting that they may have formed part of a communal tomb.

200 (183) A veteran's wife   2nd. or 3rd. century AD

*RIB 373 Caerleon (Isca). Tombstone found in 1815, at Great Bulmore, as no 199.
Now in Caerleon Museum.*

D(is) M(anibus) et I memoriae I Iuliae SecundiInae matri piIissim(a)e vixit anInis LXXV G(aius) IuI(ius) I Martinus fil(ius) I f(aciendum) c(uravit).

"To the spirits of the departed and the memory of Iulia Secundina, (his) devoted mother, who lived 75 years; Gaius Iulius Martinus (her) son had this set up."

The mother and son of this inscription are identical with the wife and son of no. 199.

201 (184) Flavius Natalis, veteran   2nd. or 3rd. century AD

RIB 358. Caerleon (Isca). Part of a tombstone found in 1909 about 900 metres west of Caerleon fortress. Now in Caerleon Museum.

D(is) [M(anibus)] I T(itus) FI(avius) Nata[l]is I veteran[u]s I vixit an(nos) LXV curatum I per FI(avium) Ingenuinum et FI(avium) I Flavinum fil(ios) et FI(aviam) I Veldiccam coniu[gem].

"To the spirits of the departed, Titus Flavius Natalis, veteran, lived 65 years. This was set up by Flavius Ingenuinus and Flavius Flavinus, his sons, and Flavia Veldicca, his wife."

Since Natalis was presumably a legionary, though he makes no mention of his unit, the stone will be post-Flavian in date, an ancestor rather than the veteran himself having been awarded citizenship under one of the Flavian emperors. For another veteran (presumably an auxiliary) who does not mention his unit see no. 230.

202 (185) Died on active service in Germany   3rd. century AD

RIB 369. Caerleon (Isca). A tombstone found about 1849 approximately 900 metres west of Caerleon fortress. Now in Caerleon Museum.

D(is) M(anibus) I Tadia Vallaun[i]us vixit I ann(os) LXV et Tadius Exuper(a)tus I filius vixit ann(os) XXXVII defun(c)Itus expeditione Germanica I Tadia Exuperata filia I ma[t]ri et fratri piiss(i)ma I secus tumulum I patris posuit.

"To the spirits of the departed, Tadia Vallaunius lived 65 years and Tadius Exuperatus, her son, lived 37 years and died on the German expedition. Tadia Exuperata, most devoted daughter, set this up to her mother and brother beside her father's tomb."

The German expedition cannot be identified with certainty. Ritterling suggested the German campaign of Caracalla. In the gable, in between the letters D and M, are a crescent and two rosettes. The lettering has traces of its original red paint. Vallaunius is a Celtic feminine.

(f)   CIVILIANS

203 (190) Barates from Palmyra   3rd. century AD

RIB 1171. Corbridge (Coria?). Tombstone found in 1911 reused as a paving-stone. Now in Corbridge Museum.

[D(is)] M(anibus) I [Ba]rathes Pallmorenus vexil(l)a(rius) I vixit an(n)os LXVIII.

"To the spirits of the departed, Barates of Palmyra, trader in ensigns, lived 68 years."

The identification with Barates in no. 204 is near certain. The man was not a soldier; no army unit is mentioned, so he was not a military standard-bearer (another meaning of *vexillarius*). He may, alternatively, have been the standard-bearer of a trade guild. This tombstone is of poor quality, in stark contrast to the fine memorial which he set up to his wife (no. 204).

204 (191) Barates' wife   3rd. century AD

RIB 1065. *South Shields* (Arbeia). *A tombstone found in 1878 south of Bath Street, to the south-west of the fort of South Shields. Now in South Shields Museum.* (Fig. 7).

Fig. 7

D(is) M(anibus) Regina liberta et coniuge I Barates Palmyrenus natione I Catuallauna an(norum) XXX.

"To the spirits of the departed (and) to Regina (his) freedwoman and wife, a Catuvellaunian, aged 30, Barates of Palmyra *(set this up)*."

Beneath the Latin text is another in Palmyrene script:
"Regina, the freedwoman of Barates, alas."

In a gabled niche above the inscription is the seated figure of Regina wearing a long-sleeved robe over her tunic, reaching to her feet. Round her neck is a necklace of cable pattern, and on her wrists similar bracelets. On her lap she holds a distaff and spindle, while at her left side is her work-basket with balls of wool. With her right hand she holds open her unlocked jewellery box.

205 (193) A Roman knight   Date unknown

RIB 202. *Colchester* (Camulodunum). *Tombstone found in 1910 in grounds of Colchester Grammar School. Now in Colchester Museum.*

...]o[...] Macri[...I...]us eq(ues) R(omanus), vix(it) I [an(nos)] XX Val(eria) Fron[t]ina coniuux I et Flor(ius) Cogitaltus et Flor(ius) Fidellis fecerunt.

"...Macri...us, Roman knight, lived 20 years; Valeria Frontina, his wife, and Florius Cogitatus and Florius Fidelis set this up."

This is the sole explicit mention of an *eques Romanus*, a member of the lesser aristocracy, apparently originating in Britain. The name Macri[...] may suggest a connection with the two Macrinii Vindices, prominent generals of the later second century, for whom an origin at Colchester is possible (Birley 1979, 116–17).

Note spelling *coniuux* for *coniunx*.

206 (152) The Tammonii family   ?2nd. century AD

(a) *RIB* 67. *Silchester* (Calleva Atrebatum). *Dedication slab found in 1744 in the forum at Silchester. Now lost.*

> Deo Her[culi] I Saegon[...] I T(itus) Tammon[ius] I Saeni Tammon[i fil(ius)] I Vitalis I ob hono[rem I...].

> "To the god Hercules Saegon[...], Titus Tammon(i)us Vitalis, son of Saen(i)us Tammonius, *(set this up)* in honour of [...]"

(b) *RIB* 87. *Silchester* (Calleva Atrebatum). *Tombstone found in or before 1577 at Silchester. Now at the Museum of Archaeology, Cambridge.*

> Memoriae I Fl(aviae) VictoriInae T(itus) Tam(monius) I Victor I coniunx I posuit.

> "In memory of Flavia Victorina. Titus Tammonius Victor, her husband, set this up."

The stone of which (a) was made is described as "black marble" and the letters are well-cut. The Tammoni(i) appear to have been a family of local worthies. Titus Tammonius Vitalis is a Roman citizen who, instead of adopting the *nomen* of the emperor under whom he was enfranchised, has adopted a Romanised form of his Celtic family name.

207 (196) Alfidius Olussa from Athens   1st. or early 2nd. century AD

RIB 9. *London* (Londinium). *Tombstone found in 1852 on Tower Hill. Now in the British Museum.*

> A(ulus) Alfid(ius) Pomp(tina tribu) I Olussa ex tesItamento her(es) I pos(uit) annor(um) LXX I nat(us) Atheni(s) I h(ic) s(itus) est.

> "Aulus Alfidius Olussa, of the voting tribe Pomptina, set up by his heir in accordance with his will, aged 70, born in Athens; here he lies."

The phrase *nat. Atheni.* appears to be an addition, but is probably contemporary – an inadvertent omission by the stone-cutter?

208 (195) Flavius Helius the Greek   Date unknown

RIB 251. *Lincoln* (Lindum). *A tombstone found in 1785 south of the Roman north wall, west of the north gateway. Now in Lincoln Museum.*

> D(is) M(anibus) I Fl(avius) Helius natiIone Gr(a)ecus viIxit annos XXXX I Fl(avia) Ingenua coIniugi posuit.

> "To the spirits of the departed, Flavius Helius, a Greek, lived 40 years. Flavia Ingenua set this up to her husband."

Flavius Helius may perhaps have been a trader.

209 (194) A woman of the Mediomatrici   1st. or 2nd. century AD

RIB 163. *Bath* (Aquae Sulis). *Tombstone found in 1803 in the borough walls. Now in the Roman Baths Museum.*

... | Rusoniae Avent[i]|nae c(ivi) Mediomatr(icae) | annor(um) LVIII h(ic) s(ita) e(st) | L(ucius) Ulpius Sestius | h(eres) f(aciendum) c(uravit).

"To Rusonia Aventina, a citizen of the Mediomatrici, aged 58 years; here she lies: Lucius Ulpius Sestius, her heir, had this set up."

The Mediomatrici were centred on Metz in northern France, in the province of Gallia Belgica.

210 (197) The tombstone of Philus   1st. or 2nd. century AD

RIB 110. *Cirencester* (Corinium Dobunnorum). *Tombstone found in 1836 at Watermoor. Now in Gloucester City Museum.*

Philus Ca|ssavi fili(us) | civis Sequ(anus) | ann(orum) XXXXV | h(ic) s(itus) e(st).

"Philus, son of Cassavus, a Sequanian, aged 45 years; here he lies."

A hooded and cloaked man stands in a niche formed by two fluted pilasters and a pediment with leaf rosettes flanking the gable. Haverfield (1918) suggested that Philus might be a merchant as he has died so far from his native land. The *Sequani* were centred on Besançon (*Vesontio*) in the upper Saône valley, eastern France. The slender letters of the inscription and the formula HSE may suggest a relatively early date; military tombstones found near to this one belong to the first century.

211 (198) Lossio Veda the Caledonian   *c.* AD 222–235

RIB 191. *Colchester* (Camulodunum). *Bronze ansate plate found in 1891 on the south side of Colchester. Now in the British Museum.*

Deo Marti Medocio Camp|esium et Victori(a)e Alexan|dri Pii Felicis Augusti nos(tr)i | donum Lossio Veda de suo | posuit, nepos Vepogeni Caledo.

"To the god Mars Medocius of the Campeses and to the Victory of our emperor Alexander Pius Felix, Lossio Veda, descendant of Vepogenus, a Caledonian, set up this gift from his own resources."

The god Mars was the one most frequently associated with the Celtic deities, in this case (given the accompanying dedication to the emperor's Victory) presumably in his guise as a war god. Medocius is unparalleled as is Campesium; Haverfield suggested that *Campestrium* may have been intended. The Campestres were Mother Goddesses particularly concerned with the exercise grounds of the cavalry (cf. *RIB* 2121). Lossio Veda and Vepogenus appear to be Celtic names. Birley (1979, 128) suggests that since Veda gives, not his filiation, but the names of the person whose *nepos* he was, he was Pictish – with matriarchal descent, Vepogenus would be his mother's brother. Veda's status and the reason for his sojourn in Colchester are open to discussion. He has been seen variously as a merchant, a mercenary in Roman service, a noble hostage and a friendly chief.

212 (199) A stonemason   Date unknown

RIB 149. *Bath* (Aquae Sulis). *Dedication stone found about 1880 near the Great Bath. Now in the Roman Baths Museum.*

> Priscus | Touti f(ilius) | lapidariu[s] | cives Car[nu]|tenus Su[li] | deae v(otum) [s(olvit) l(ibens) m(erito)].

> "Priscus, son of Tout(i)us, stonemason, a Carnutenian, to the goddess Sulis willingly and deservedly fulfilled his vow."

The *civitas* of the Carnutes was centred on *Autricum*, modern-day Chartres. Priscus is one of two stone-workers attested at Bath. The other, Sulinus (no. 248), origin unstated but, on the evidence of his name, possibly local, is a sculptor.

213 (200) A coppersmith   Date unknown

RIB 194. *Colchester* (Camulodunum). *Bronze plate, with letters made with a blunt punch. Found in 1946 outside the walled area of the city, in the playing fields of Colchester Grammar School, near the remains of a Roman building. Now in Colchester Museum.*

> Deo Silvano | Callirio d(onum) | Cintusmus | aerarius | v(otum) s(olvit) l(ibens) m(erito).

> "To the god Silvanus Callirius, Cintusmus the coppersmith willingly and deservedly fulfilled as a gift his vow."

The plaque was found in a temple precinct, which strongly suggests that the temple was dedicated to Silvanus. An alternative understanding of the text is *deo Silvano | Calliriod(aco)* ... Close by, in a votive pit, was found a second dedication to Silvanus by Hermes (*RIB* 195; Hull 1958, 239–40). Most of the two dozen dedications to Silvanus are by soldiers, but these two are by civilians. Another coppersmith, Celatus, is attested as the maker of the Foss Dyke Mars (*RIB* 274: below, no. 223).

214 (201) A goldsmith's servant   Date unknown

RIB 712. *Malton* (Derventio), *Yorkshire. Building stone found in 1814 at Norton, the civil settlement south of Malton, near New Malton. Now in the Yorkshire Museum, York.*

> Feliciter sit | Genio Loci | servule utere | felix tabern|am aurefi|cinam.

> "Good luck to the Genius of this place. Young slave, may fortune be yours in using this goldsmith's shop."

One other inscription attests gold working in Britain (*RIB* 2.2. 2413, a gold handle from Ecclefechan, near Birrens). Smiths were at work in Cirencester, Southwark and Verulamium, and evidence for refining has been found on the site of the later Flavian governor's palace in London (Marsden 1980, 96–97).

215 (-) A trader at York   AD 221

Britannia 8 (1977), 430, no. 18 + Hassall 1978, 46. *York (Eboracum). Upper three-quarters of the right-hand portion of a gritstone dedication slab found in 1976 at Clementhorpe, reused in a medieval lime kiln. Now in the Yorkshire Museum.*

[Neptuno] et Genio Loci | [et Numinib(us) Au]g(ustorum) L(ucius) Viducius | [Viduci f(ilius) Pla]cidus domo | [civitate] Veliocas[s]ium | [prov(inciae) Lugd(unensis) n]egotiator | [Britann(icianus) ar]cum et ianuam | [pro se et suis de]d[it] Grato et | [Seleuco co(n)s(ulibus)]

"To Neptune and the Genius of the place and the Spirits of the Emperors, Lucius Viducius Placidus, the son of Viducius, from the Veliocasses in the province of Lugdunensis, trader with Britain, presented the arch and gate on behalf of himself and his descendants in the consulship of Gratus and Seleucus."

The entire left half of the text is missing. Detail is restored with the help of another dedication made by Placidus, to the goddess Nehalennia, at Colijnsplaat, a harbour site near the mouth of the Scheldt (see no. 216). Here he lacks the *tria nomina* of the Roman citizen; he was perhaps enfranchised as a result of the *Constitutio Antoniniana* in AD 212. The Veliocasses lived in the area around Rouen. The above restoration is that of Hassall 1978 which differs from Tomlin in *Britannia*, who restores: line 1, *[I(ovi) O(ptimo) M(aximo) D(olicheno)]*; lines 5–6, *[sevir n]egotiator | [cret(arius) ...*

216 (-) A trader in pottery   later 2nd.–3rd. century AD

ILS 4751. *Domburg, Holland. Altar found in 1647 near the mouth of the East Scheldt estuary. Now in the Rijksmuseum van Oudheden, Leiden.*

Deae N[e]halenniae | ob merces recte conser|vatas M(arcus) Secund(inius ?) Silvanus | negotiator cretarius | Britannicianus | v(otum) s(olvit) l(ibens) m(erito).

"To the goddess Nehalennia, on account of goods duly kept safe, Marcus Secund(inius ?) Silvanus, trader in pottery with Britain, fulfilled his vow willingly and deservedly."

Example from one of two remarkable collections of altars, the vast majority dedicated to the goddess Nehalennia, set up by traders at shrines at Domburg (as this) and Colijnsplaat, which lay, in Roman times, on either side of the Scheldt estuary, presumably at or near harbour sites. 32 dedications are known from Domburg, 125 from Colijnsplaat. Silvanus made a second dedication to Nehalennia at Colijnsplaat (*AE* 1973, 370).

217 (-) A trader with Britain   later 2nd.–3rd. century AD

CIL 13.8164a = *ILS* 7522. *Cologne (Colonia Claudia Ara Agrippinensium). Dedication slab of black marble found at St Pantaleon. Now in the Römisch-Germanisches Museum, Köln.*

Apollini | C(aius) Aurelius C(ai) l(ibertus) | Verus negotiator | Britannicianus | moritex d(ono) d(edit) | l(oco) d(ato) d(ecreto) d(ecuri-onum).

"To Apollo, Gaius Aurelius Verus, freedman of Gaius, trader with Britain, seafarer, gave as a gift, the site being given by decree of the decurions."

This inscription provides a parallel for the use of the term *moritex* in no. 154. Verus may have been trading in fine pottery or glass or perhaps salt, as was the case with two other traders from Cologne (see Hassall 1978, 43).

PART VIII: RELIGIOUS CULTS

(a) THE ROMAN DEITIES

Jupiter Optimus Maximusque, Jupiter Best and Greatest, normally abbreviated to IOM, is by far the most invoked of the official gods of Rome. Auxiliary units appear to have set up annual dedications to him, the clearest evidence coming from Maryport, where three or four altars dedicated under the same prefect have been found: cf. nos. 44, 45 and 219. Here the cult of the *Numen Augusti* is linked with him: see the Note on Religion, p. 19.

Other gods of Rome mentioned in earlier sections are Apollo, no. 163; Diana Regina, no. 59; Fortuna, nos. 49, 77 and 197; Mars (identified with Celtic gods), no. 162; Mercury, no. 163; Minerva, no. 137; Neptune, nos. 137 and 196; Neptune and Ocean, no. 34; Ocean and Tethys, no. 126; Parcae, no. 164; Silvanus, no. 190; Victoria, nos. 87 and 211. Note also the cult of the Genius, Genius Domini et Signorum, no. 111; Genius Loci, nos. 214 and 239.

218 (43) To Jupiter Best and Greatest at Maryport   Hadrianic

RIB 815. Maryport, Cumbria (Alauna). Altar found in 1870 outside the fort at Maryport. Now in the Senhouse Museum, Maryport.

> I(ovi) O(ptimo) M(aximo) | et Num(ini) | Aug(usti) coh(ors) | I Hisp(anorum) | pos(uit).

> "To Jupiter, Best and Greatest, and to the Divine Power of the Emperor, the First Cohort of Spaniards set this up."

219 (202) Another altar to IOM at Maryport   2nd. half of 2nd. century AD

RIB 830. Maryport, Cumbria (Alauna). Altar found in 1870 near the fort. Now in the Senhouse Museum, Maryport.

> I(ovi) O(ptimo) M(aximo) | coh(ors) I Baetasiorum | c(ivium) R(omanorum) cui praelest T(itus) Attius | Tutor praef(ectus) | v(otum) s(olvit) l(ibens) l(aetus) m(erito)

> "To Jupiter, Best and Greatest, the First Cohort of Baetasians, Roman citizens, which is commanded by Titus Attius Tutor, prefect, willingly, gladly and deservedly fulfilled its vow."

For Tutor's later career see *CIL* 3.5331 (*ILS* 2734). The unit also dedicated altars to Mars Militaris and Victoria Augusta while he was prefect, *RIB* 837 and 842.

220 (203) To IOM at Moresby   Date unknown

RIB 797. Moresby, Cumbria (Gabrosentum?). A base found about 1878 outside the fort. Now in Carlisle Museum.

> I(ovi) O(ptimo) M(aximo) | coh(ors) II T(h)ra(cum) | eq(uitata) c(ui) p(raeest) Mamilus N(e)pos pralef(ectus).

"To Jupiter, Best and Greatest, the Second Cohort of Thracians, part cavalry, under the command of its prefect Mamius Nepos, *(set this up)*."

For other dedications to IOM by units or commanding officers see nos. 112 and 198; nos. 131 and 245 are by *beneficiarii consularis*; no. 135 by a governor; no. 158 by *vicani*; no. 239 by legionaries.

221 (204) A promise to Jupiter and Vulcan   Date unknown

RIB 215. Stony Stratford, Buckinghamshire. A piece of silver plate, found in 1789 with other silver articles in an urn on the line of Watling Street. Now in the British Museum.

Deo I Iovi et Volca(no) I Vassinus I cum velli|nt me con|sacratum I conservare I promisi dena|rios sex pro vo|to soluto pec(uniam) d(edi).

"To the god Jupiter and Volcanus I, Vassinus, promised six denarii when they might be pleased to bring me, their votary, safe home; and on the fulfilment of my vow I have paid the money."

The letters are small, since the plate is less than 8 centimetres square, but neatly executed. Jupiter and Vulcan are worshipped together by an individual. They appear together also on no. 158; Vulcan appears alone on no. 159; both are by *vicani*.

222 (205) The birthday of Augustus   23 September AD 244

RIB 327. Caerleon (Isca). Fragments from an inscribed pilaster or door jamb, found in 1800 on the site of the offices of the headquarters building in the fortress. All are now lost except for one fragment which is in the Caerleon Museum.

N(uminibus) I Aug(ustorum) I Genio I leg(ionis) I II Aug(ustae) I in hono(rem) [aquilae ? ...] I ... I ... I ... I ... I p(rimus) p(ilus) I d(ono) d(edit) I d(e)d(icatum) I VIIII I Kal(endas) Octob(res) I P[e]r[e]gr(ino) e[t Ae]m[i]l(iano) I co(n)s(ulibus) I cur(ante) I Urso I actar(io) I [l]e[g(ionis) I e]ius|[dem ...].

"To the Divine Powers of the Emperor and the Genius of the Second Legion Augusta, in honour of the Eagle, the senior centurion gave this gift; dedicated on 23 September in the consulship of Peregrinus and Aemilianus, under the charge of Ursus, *actarius* of the same legion."

23 September was the birthday of Augustus, which the legion celebrated as its own birthday. On *numina Augustorum*, and the various ways in which honouring the emperors was included in official and non-official worship of the gods, see the Note on Religion, p. 18–19.

223 (206) The Foss Dike Mars   Late 2nd. or 3rd. century AD

RIB 274. The Foss Dike, Lincolnshire. Two panels of a bronze statuette of Mars, found about 1774 on the Foss Dike (the canal which connects Lincoln with the Trent). Now in the British Museum.

(a) Deo Mar(ti) et I Nu(mini)b(us) Aug(ustorum) Col|asuni Bruccil|us et Caratius de I suo donarunt I

(b) ad sester(tios) n(ummos) c(entum) | Celatus aerarlius fecit et aeralmenti lib(ram) donavlit factam (denariis) III.

"To the god Mars and the Divine Powers of the Emperors the Colasuni, Bruccius and Caratius, presented this at their own expense at a cost of 100 sesterces; Celatus the coppersmith fashioned it and gave a pound of bronze made at the cost of 3 denarii."

The engraving, which is on two panels of the base of the statuette (standing 27 centimetres high) is well executed (see *RIB* I, Plate VI).

Mars was popular in his own right, not only in his military but his agricultural aspects; he is frequently identified with other gods – see below, nos. 228–237, and no. 162.

224 (207) Anencletus *provincialis*   Late 1st.–early 2nd. century AD

RIB 21. *London* (Londinium). *A statue-base found in 1806 near the London Coffee House, Ludgate Hill. Now in the Museum of London.*

D(is) M(anibus) | Cl(audiae) Martilnae an(norum) XIX | Anencleltus | provinc(ialis) | coniugi | pientissimae | h(ic) s(ita) e(st).

"To the spirits of the departed (and) to Claudia Martina, aged 19; Anencletus, slave of the province, *(set this up)* to his most devoted wife; here she lies."

The "provincial cult" honoured past emperors who had been deified. It was maintained by the provincial council, which, on the strength of this inscription and no. 156, is thought to have met at or near London. It had its own staff, including slaves, who were termed "slaves of the province".

225 (208) To the god Romulus   Date unknown

RIB 132. *Custom Scrubs, Bisley, Gloucestershire. A gabled relief found in 1799 built into a summer-house at Watercombe House. Now in the Gloucester City Museum.*

Deo Rom[u]lo | Gulioepius | donavit | Iuventinus | fecit.

"To the god Romulus: Gulioepius presented this, Juventinus made it."

Illustrated in *RIB*. The inscription is above the figure of the war-clad Romulus, who has a crested helmet with side-plumes and cheek-pieces, and also a large protective apron. He holds spear and shield, rather clumsily carved, and on his right is an altar with offerings. It was found with *RIB* 131 which is a similar relief, dedicated to Mars Olludius.

226 (211) To the god Silvanus   Date unknown

RIB 1085. *Lanchester, Co. Durham* (Longovicium). *A pedestal found before 1807 at Lanchester. Now in the Museum of Antiquities, Newcastle upon Tyne.*

Deo | Silvano | Marc(us) Didius | Provincialis | b(ene)f(iciarius) co(n)s(ularis) | v(otum) s(olvit) l(ibens) m(erito).

"To the god Silvanus, Marcus Didius Provincialis, *beneficiarius* (on the staff) of the governor, willingly and deservedly fulfilled his vow."

For *beneficiarii* see nos. 129–131. For other dedications to Silvanus, see nos. 190, 213 and 258.

227 (212) Corellia Optata   Date unknown

RIB 684. *York* (Eboracum). *Part of a tombstone, found in 1861 at The Mount, York. Now in the Yorkshire Museum.*

> [D(is)] M(anibus) | Corellia Optata an(norum) XIII: |
> Secreti Manes qui regna | Acherusia Ditis
> incoli|tis, quos parva petunt post | lumina vit(a)e
> exiguus cinis | et simulacrum corpo(r)is um|bra:
> insontis gnat(a)e geni|tor spe captus iniqua |
> supremum hunc nat(a)e | miserandus defleo finem. |

> Q(uintus) Core(llius) Fortis pat(er) f(aciendum) c(uravit).

> "To the spirits of the departed: Corellia Optata, aged 13.
> You mysterious spirits of the departed: who dwell
> in Pluto's Acherusian realms, who are sought by
> the paltry ashes and by the shade the phantom
> of the body, after the brief light of life: I, the
> father of an innocent daughter, a pitiable victim
> of unfair hope, lament this, her final end.

> Quintus Corellius Fortis, her father, had this set up."

A large glass vessel, sealed with lead and containing the ashes of the girl, was found near the tombstone. This is of interest because it reflects Roman philosophy about death, although it does not name a god. Lines 3–11 are hexameter verses. No. 181 also included verses as part of the epitaph.

(b)   CELTIC AND GERMANIC DEITIES

228 (221) Barkway Mars Alator   Date unknown

RIB 218. *Barkway, Herts. A fine silver plaque, found in 1744 during the digging of a chalkpit in Rookery Wood near Barkway. Now in the British Museum.*

> D(eo) Marti Alatori | Dum(...) Censorinus | Gemelli fil(ius) | v(otum)
> s(olvit) l(ibens) m(erito).

> "To the god Mars Alator Dum(...) Censorinus, son of Gemellus, willingly and deservedly fulfilled his vow."

Illustrated in *RIB*. This and no. 237 formed part of a small but valuable cache. They had probably been looted from a shrine on the line of Ermine Street. This one is a votive plaque 10 cm x 18 cm high, with the inscription surmounted by Mars, standing in his shrine and looking to his right. The whole is surrounded by a leaf-pattern. It was probably attached to wood.

Celtic gods and goddesses are diverse and elusive; where it suits the worshipper, he may identify them with Roman counterparts. Mars appealed most strongly to the Celts, and he appears conjoined with a wide range of local deities: note nos. 162 and 211 in addition to those in this section, nos. 228, 231–35, 237. Celtic gods from earlier sections include Anociticus no. 69, Boudiga no. 153, Sattada no. 160, and Hercules Saegon no. 206a.

229 (-) To Mars Belatucadrus   Late 2nd. or 3rd. century AD

RIB 918. *Old Penrith, Cumbria* (Voreda). *Altar found about 1783 apparently within the fort at Old Penrith. Now in the British Museum.*

> Deo | Marti | Belatucad|ro et Numi|nib(us) Aug(ustorum) | Iulius Au|gustalis | actor Iul(i) Lu|pi pr(a)ef(ecti).

> "To Mars Belatucadrus and to the Divine Powers of the Emperors, Julius Augustalis, *actor* of Julius Lupus, the prefect, *(set this up)*."

Belatucadrus appears also in a number of inscriptions from Brougham, Cumbria, without reference to Mars, *RIB* 772–777.

230 (217) To Belatucadrus at Old Carlisle   Late 2nd. or 3rd. century AD

RIB 887. *Old Carlisle, Cumbria* (Maglona?). *Altar found c. 1868 at Greenhill, about 1600 metres south-west of the fort at Old Carlisle. It is built into the garden wall of Greenhill House, Wigton.*

> Deo | Belatucal|dro sancto | Aur(elius) Tasulus | vet(eranus) v(otum) s(olvit) l(ibens) [m(erito)].

> "To the holy god Belatucadrus, Aurelius Tasulus, veteran, willingly and deservedly fulfilled his vow."

The veteran does not mention his unit. For the suggestion that the Roman name of Old Carlisle was Maglona, see Rivet and Smith 1979, 407; the key inscription is no. 158.

231 (220) To Mars Corotiacus   Date unknown

RIB 213. *Martlesham, Suffolk. Bronze shield-shaped base of a statuette with rounded recesses; inscribed round rim. Now in the British Museum.*

> Deo Marti | Corotiaco | Simplicia | pro se v(otum) p(osuit) l(ibens) m(erito):

> *(beneath base)* Glaucus fecit.

> "To Mars Corotiacus, Simplicia for herself willingly and deservedly set up this offering." "Glaucus made it."

All that remains of the statuette is a headless foeman and traces of hooves.

232 (218) To Mars Loucetius and Nemetona   Date unknown

RIB 140. *Bath* (Aquae Sulis). *An altar found in Stall Street, Bath, in 1753. Now in the Roman Baths Museum.*

Peregrinus | Secundi fil(ius) | civis Trever | Loucetio | Marti et | Nemetona | v(otum) s(olvit) l(ibens) m(erito).

"Peregrinus, son of Secundus, a Trever, to Loucetius Mars and Nemetona willingly and deservedly fulfilled his vow."

The height of lettering and the spacing are both uneven, suggesting inferior workmanship. NEMETONA should grammatically be NEMETONAE. Mars Loucetius and Nemetona were Celtic deities sometimes worshipped together: an example occurs on the west bank of the Rhine (*CIL* 13.6131 = *ILS* 4586).

233 (219) To Mars Rigisamus   Date unknown

RIB 187. *West Coker, Somerset. A bronze plate found on the site of the villa at West Coker in 1862. Now in the Yeovil Museum.*

Deo Marti | Rigisamo | Iventius | Sabinus | v(otum) s(olvit) l(aetus) l(ibens) m(erito).

"To Mars Rigisamus, Iventius Sabinus gladly, willingly and deservedly fulfilled his vow."

This plate, which has punched letters and a central hole for attaching it to a wooden base, may well be associated with a bronze statuette of Mars found elsewhere on the site. Mars Rigisamus comes from Aquitania. Iventius is a by-form of Iuventius.

234 (223) To Mars Thincsus   Probably third century AD

RIB 1593. *Housesteads* (Vercovicium). *Tall square pillar, probably the left-hand jamb of the doorway to the shrine. Found in 1883 at the foot of the north slope of Chapel Hill, Housesteads. Now in Chesters Museum.*

Deo | Marti | Thincso | et Duabus | Alaisiagis | Bed(a)e et Fi|mmilen(a)e | et N(umini) Aug(usti) Ger|m(ani) cives Tu|ihanti | v(otum) s(olverunt) l(ibentes) m(erito).

"To the god Mars Thincsus and the two Alaisiagae, Beda and Fimmilena, and to the Divine Power of the Emperor, the Germans, being citizens of the Tuihanti, willingly and deservedly fulfilled their vow."

The Tuihanti may have come from the district of Twenthe, which is in the province of Overijssel, Holland. The pillar has a female figure, presumably a goddess, carved on its right side, and nothing on its left. With it was found no. 235 and a sculptured arcuate lintel, having in its central panel a figure of Mars with sword, shield, and spear, and at his right hand a goose. The Alaisiagae, portrayed naked, cross-legged and as male, each extend towards Mars what appears to be a palm branch, and carry a wreath in their other hand (*CSIR* I.6, no. 159, plate 44). These German deities are brought from the lower Rhine area. Note the linkage of this and nos. 235–236 with the *Numen Augusti*, on which see the Note on Religion, p. 19.

235 (224) To Mars Thincsus   *c.* AD 222–235

RIB 1594. Housesteads (Vercovicium). Altar found in 1883 with no. 234 (q.v.) and a sculptured arcuate lintel. Now in Chesters Museum.

Deo | Marti et duabus | Alaisiagis et N(umini) Aug(usti) | Ger(mani) cives Tuihanti | cunei Frisiorum | Ver(covicianorum) Se(ve)r(iani) Alexand|riani votum | solverunt | libent[es] | m(erito).

"To the god Mars and the two Alaisiagae and to the Divine Power of the Emperor, the Germans being citizens of the Tuihanti of the unit of Frisians of Vercovicium, *Severiana Alexandriana*, willingly and deservedly fulfilled their vow."

On the left side are carved a knife and an axe, on the right a *patera* and a jug. For the Tuihanti see no. 234.

236 (225) To the Alaisiagae   3rd. century AD

RIB 1576. Housesteads (Vercovicium). Altar found in 1920 on the Chapel Hill, Housesteads. Now in Housesteads Museum.

Deabus | Alaisia|gis Bau|dihillie | et Friaga|bi et N(umini) Aug(usti) | n(umerus) Hnau|difridi | v(otum) s(olvit) l(ibens) m(erito).

"To the goddesses the Alaisiagae, Baudihillia and Friagabis, and to the Divine Power of the Emperor, the unit of Hnaudifridus gladly and deservedly fulfilled its vow."

237 (222) Barkway Mars Toutatis   Date unknown

RIB 219. Barkway, Herts. A silver votive plaque found with no. 228. Now in the British Museum.

Marti | Toutati | Ti(berius) Claudius Primus | Attii liber(tus) | v(otum) s(olvit) l(ibens) m(erito).

"To Mars Toutatis, Tiberius Claudius Primus, freedman of Attius, willingly and deservedly fulfilled his vow."

Toutatis (or -es) is well-known in north-east Gaul. This plaque has no nail-holes. The inscription is punched in dots in an ansate panel.

238 (237) To the goddess Brigantia   Date unknown

RIB 1053. South Shields (Arbeia). Altar found in 1895 near the fort at South Shields. Now in Arbeia Fort Museum, South Shields.

Deae Bri|gantiae | sacrum | Congenn(i)c|cus v(otum) s(olvit) l(ibens) m(erito).

"Sacred to the goddess Brigantia; Congenniccus willingly and deservedly fulfilled his vow."

On the back is carved a bird; on the right side a *patera*; on the left a jug. For other dedications to Brigantia see nos. 82, 173 and 263. She is presumably the goddess of the Brigantes, and is identified with Victory (82), Minerva Victrix (173) and with Iuno Caelestis, the consort of Jupiter Dolichenus (263). The dedications all come from the territory ascribed to the Brigantes, if no. 173 is evidence for Birrens being in Brigantian territory.

239 (228) To IOM, Cocidius and the Genius Loci   Date unknown

RIB 1583. *Housesteads* (Vercovicium). *Altar found in 1898 in the Mithraeum, south of Housesteads fort. Now in Chesters Museum.*

> I(ovi) O(ptimo) M(aximo) l et deo Cocidio l Genioq(ue) Hui(u)s l Loci mil(ites) leg(ionis) l II Aug(ustae) agentes l in praesidio l v(otum) s(olverunt) l(ibentes) m(erito).

> "To Jupiter, Best and Greatest, and to the god Cocidius, and to the Genius of this place, the soldiers of the Second Legion Augusta on garrison-duty willingly and deservedly fulfilled their vow."

For Cocidius, a local god of the north-west of England, with worship centred on Bewcastle (*Fanum Cocidi*), see also nos. 240–241. For worship of the Genius Loci, the tutelary deity of a place, cf. no. 214.

240 (232) Altar to Cocidius   3rd. century AD

RIB 988. *Bewcastle,Cumbria* (Fanum Cocidi). *Altar found c. 1792 in the bed of the Kirk Beck at Bewcastle. Now in Carlisle Museum.*

> Sancto Colcidio Aurunc(eius) l Felicesselmus tribun(us) l ex evocato l v(otum) s(olvit) l(ibens) m(erito).

> "To holy Cocidius, Aurunceius Felicessemus, tribune, promoted from *evocatus*, willingly and deservedly fulfilled his vow."

Fanum Cocidi means "the shrine of Cocidius". For the identification of Bewcastle as Fanum Cocidi see Rivet and Smith 1979, 363. An *evocatus* was a soldier of the praetorian guard who had been retained in the army after completion of his sixteen years' service. Some *evocati* were promoted to a higher rank: *ex* does not necessarily imply that the promotion here was direct from *evocatus* to tribune.

241 (233) Altar to Cocidius   3rd. or early 4th. century AD

RIB 989. *Bewcastle, Cumbria* (Fanum Cocidi). *Altar found in 1898 built into the foundations of Bewcastle church. Now in Carlisle Museum.*

> Deo sancto Cocidio l Q(uintus) Peltrasi[u]s l Maximus trib(unus) l ex cornic-ulario l praef(ectorum) pr[a]etorio elm(inentissimorum) v(irorum) v(otum) s(olvit) l(ibens) m(erito).

> "To the holy god Cocidius, Quintus Peltrasius Maximus, tribune, promoted from *cornicularius* to their Eminences, the Praetorian Prefects, willingly and deservedly fulfilled his vow."

For the identification of Bewcastle as Fanum Cocidi see no. 240. As in no. 240, *ex* does not necessarily imply a direct promotion to tribune.

242 (235) Dedication to Coventina   Probably 3rd. century AD

RIB 1534. Carrawburgh (Brocolitia). *Dedication found in 1876 in Coventina's Well, west of Carrawburgh fort. Now in Chesters Museum.*

> Deae | Covventinae | T(itus) D(...) Cosconialnus pr(aefectus) coh(ortis) | I Bat(avorum) l(ibens) m(erito).

> "To the goddess Covventina, Titus D(...) Cosconianus prefect of the First Cohort of Batavians, willingly and deservedly (*fulfilled his vow*)."

The inscription is set beneath a relief of the goddess reclining with a branch in her right hand. The First Cohort of Batavians is well attested at Carrawburgh in the third century AD (the earliest instance, *RIB* 1544, being dated AD 213–217) and is still there in the *Notitia Dignitatum*. For the sculpture see *CSIR* I.6, 150 Pl. 42.

243 (234) To the goddess Garmangabis   AD 238–244

RIB 1074. Lanchester (Longovicium). *Altar found in 1893 near Lanchester fort. Now in the south porch, Lanchester church.*

> Deae Garlmangabil et N(umini) Gor[di]lani Aug(usti) n(ostri) pr[o] | sal(ute) vex(illationis) Suebolrum Lon(govicianorum) Gor(dianae) (vexillarii) voltum solverunt m(erito).

> "To the goddess Garmangabis and to the Divine Power of our Emperor Gordian for the welfare of the detachment of Suebians of Longovicium, *Gordiana*, the soldiers deservedly fulfilled their vow."

On the left side is carved a knife and a jug; on the right a *patera* and a disk. Cf. nos. 109–110, inscriptions from Lanchester also set up under Gordian III. For irregular units in forts in the third century cf. nos. 111, 197–198, 235–236.

244 (227) To Apollo Maponus   2nd.–early 3rd. century AD

RIB 1120. Corbridge (Coria?). *Altar found c. 1866 beside Hexham Abbey. Now in the south transept, Hexham Abbey.*

> Apollini | Mapono | Q(uintus) Terentius | Q(uinti) f(ilius) Ouf(entina tribu) | Firmus Saen(a) | praef(ectus) castr(orum) | leg(ionis) VI V(ictricis) P(iae) F(idelis) | d(edit) d(edicavit).

> "To Apollo Maponus, Quintus Terentius Firmus, son of Quintus, of the Oufentine voting-tribe, from Saena, prefect of the camp of the Sixth Legion Victrix Pia Fidelis, gave and dedicated this."

Saena is Sena Julia, in Etruria. For Apollo Maponus cf. no. 148. The title *praefectus castrorum legionis* is gradually replaced by *praefectus legionis*, and the last-known example of the fuller title is early third century (*CIL* 13.8014, AD 201; *RIB* 490 should be later, but cannot be precisely dated).

245 (226) To Jupiter and the Matres Ollototae   Date unknown

RIB 1030. Binchester (Vinovia). *Altar found in 1891 about 70 metres south of Binchester fort. Now in the Museum of Antiquities, Newcastle upon Tyne.*

I(ovi) O(ptimo) M(aximo) | et Matrib|us Olloto|tis sive Tra|nsmarinis|
Pomponius | Donatus | b(ene)f(iciarius) co(n)s(ularis) pro | salute sua | et
suorum | v(otum) s(olvit) l(ibens) a(nimo).

"To Jupiter, Best and Greatest, and to the Mother Goddesses Ollototae,
or Overseas, Pomponius Donatus, *beneficiarius* of the governor, for the
welfare of himself and his household willingly fulfilled his vow."

For *beneficiarius consularis* cf. nos. 129–131, 226. For other dedications to
Mother Goddesses cf. nos. 130, 175, 246–249.

246 (238) A promise to the Mother Goddesses   Date unknown

RIB 2059. *Bowness-on-Solway* (Maia). *A dedication-slab found c. 1790 at
Bowness. Now in Carlisle Museum.*

[Matribus deabus aed]em | [Ant]onianus dedico |
[se]d date ut fetura quaestus | suppleat votis fidem |
aureis sacrabo carmen | mox viritim litteris.

[To the Mother Goddesses] I, [Ant]onianus, dedicate this shrine. But grant
that the increase of my venture may confirm my prayers, and soon I will
hallow this poem with golden letters one by one."

Lines 3–4 and 5–6 in the original are catalectic trochaic tetrameters. The
proposed restorations in lines 1–2 fit the same metric pattern. The probable
inspiration was Virgil, *Eclogues* 7.35–36 (to Priapus):

nunc te marmoreum pro tempore fecimus; at tu
si *fetura* gregem *suppleverit*, *aureus* esto.

The Mother Goddess triad is frequently found in Britain and the Rhineland
– cf. nos. 130, 175 and 245.

247 (239) To the Matres Suleviae at Colchester   Date unknown

RIB 192. *Colchester* (Camulodunum). *Dedication stone found in 1881 just west
of west wall. Now in Colchester Museum.*

Matribus | Sulevis | Similis Atti f(ilius) | ci(vis) Cant(iacus) | v(otum) l(ibens)
s(olvit).

"To the Mother Goddesses Suleviae, Similis, son of Attius, a citizen of the
Cantiaci, willingly fulfilled his vow."

The *civitas* of the Cantiaci was centred around Canterbury. The Suleviae seem
to originate in Gaul.

248 (240) To the Suleviae at Bath   ?2nd. century AD

RIB 151. *Bath* (Aquae Sulis). *Statue-base found in 1753 in Stall Street. Now in
the Roman Baths Museum.*

Sulevis | Sulinus | scultor | Bruceti f(ilius) | sacrum f(ecit) l(ibens) m(erito).

"To the Suleviae, Sulinus, a sculptor, son of Brucetus, gladly and deservedly made this offering."

Cf. no. 212, who is a *lapidarius* at Bath.

249 (241) To the Suleviae at Cirencester   ?2nd. century AD

RIB 105. *Cirencester* (Corinium). *Altar found in 1899 in the north-west part of the town. Now in the Corinium Museum.*

Sule(v)is | Sulinus | Bruceti (filius) | v(otum) s(olvit) l(ibens) m(erito).

"To the Suleviae, Sulinus, son of Brucetus, willingly and deservedly fulfilled his vow."

Two reliefs of the three *matres* and other sculptures were found with this altar. The site may possibly have been the workshop of Sulinus, who was a sculptor, no. 248, but is more likely to have been a local shrine of the Matres Suleviae, as Haverfield proposed.

250 (229) To Sulis Minerva   Late 2nd. or 3rd. century AD

RIB 146. *Bath* (Aquae Sulis). *An altar found in 1809 in the cistern of the Cross Bath. Now in the Roman Baths Museum.*

Deae Sulli Min(ervae) et Nulmin(ibus) Aug(ustorum) C(aius) | Curiatius | Saturninus | c(enturio) leg(ionis) II Aug(ustae) | pro se sulisque | v(otum) s(olvit) l(ibens) m(erito).

"To the goddess Sulis Minerva and to the Divine Powers of the Emperors, Gaius Curiatius Saturninus, centurion of the Second Legion Augusta, willingly and deservedly fulfilled his vow for himself and his kindred."

The altar is plain, but stylishly engraved.

251 (230) To the goddess Sulis   2nd. or 3rd. century AD

RIB 143. *Bath* (Aquae Sulis). *An altar found in 1790 on the site of the Pump Room. Now in the Roman Baths Museum.*

[D]eae Suli | pro salute et | incolumita[l[te] Mar(ci) Aufid[i] | [M]aximi c(enturionis) leg(ionis) | VI Vic(tricis) | [A]ufidius Eultuches leb(ertus) | v(otum) s(olvit) l(ibens) m(erito).

"To the goddess Sulis for the welfare and safety of Marcus Aufidius Maximus, centurion of the Sixth Legion Victrix, Aufidius Eutuches, his freedman, willingly and deservedly fulfilled his vow."

The Sixth Legion was transferred to Britain in or about AD 122. For Sulis cf. no. 212. Note LEB(ERTVS) for LIB(ERTVS).

The important temple and sacred spring complex at Bath has produced a number of notable inscriptions and sculpture, the majority of which are made from the high-quality local stone, Bath oolite.

252 (231) A priest of the goddess Sulis   2nd. or 3rd. century AD

RIB 155. Bath (Aquae Sulis). Altar-shaped tombstone found near the Baths. Now in Roman Baths Museum.

> D(is) M(anibus) I C(aius) Calpurnius I [R]eceptus sacerIdos Deae Sullis vix(it) an(nos) LXXV I Calpurnia Trifolsa l[i]bert(a) coniunx I f(aciendum) c(uravit).

> "To the spirits of the departed: Gaius Calpurnius Receptus, priest of the goddess Sulis, lived 75 years; Calpurnia Trifosa his freedwoman and wife had this set up."

253 (-) A *haruspex* of the goddess Sulis   Date unknown

JRS 56 (1966), 217 no. 1. Bath (Aquae Sulis). Base found below a cellar floor beneath the Pump Room. Now in Roman Baths Museum.

> Deae Suli I L(ucius) Marcius Memor I harusp(ex) I d(ono) d(edit).

> "To the goddess Sulis, Lucius Marcius Memor, *haruspex*, gave and dedicated *(this)*."

HAR was carved originally, and centred on the line. VSP were added later. This is the first mention of HARVSPEX ("soothsayer") in Britain. This official, often of high standing in the town, interpreted omens and inspected sacrificial victims.

254 (242) To the God(desse?)s Vitires   Date unknown

RIB 1047. Chester-le-Street (Concangium). Altar found in 1849 on the north side of Chester-le-Street fort. Now in the Museum of Antiquities, Newcastle upon Tyne.

> Daeab[u]ls Vitirlibus I Vitalis I [v(otum)] s(olvit) l(ibens) m(erito).

> "To the goddesses Vitires, Vitalis willingly and deservedly fulfilled his vow."

The name of this god or gods appears in a number of forms, singular and plural, masculine and feminine. It seems as suggested by Birley 1979, 107 that the worshippers have difficulty in representing the god's name in the Latin alphabet. This is a poor person's deity, and the altars are small and clumsily inscribed. Of over 50 altars known, in many instances the name of the dedicator is not given or is illegible, and only two of the 30 or so named worshippers record a military rank. See further the discussion in Birley 1979, 107f.

255 (243) To Veteris   3rd. or 4th. century AD

RIB 1795. Carvoran (Magnis), Northumberland. Altar found c. 1757 near Thirlwall Castle. Now in the Museum of Antiquities, Newcastle upon Tyne.

> Deo sanct[o] I Veteri I Iul(ius) Pastor I imag(inifer) coh(ortis) II I Delma(tarum) v(otum) s(olvit) l(ibens) m(erito).

> "To the holy god Veteris, Julius Pastor, *imaginifer* of the Second Cohort of Dalmatians, willingly and deservedly fulfilled his vow."

The *imaginifer* carried on a standard the *imago*, the portrait of the emperor.

256 (244) To Hueteris   Date unknown

RIB 1602. *Housesteads* (Vercovicium). *Altar found in 1910 in the north-west or north-east angle tower at Housesteads. Now in Chesters Museum.*

Deo | Hueteri | Superstes [et] | Regulu[s] | v(otum) s(olverunt) l(ibentes) [m(erito)].

"To the god Hueteris, Superstes [and] Regulus willingly and deservedly fulfilled their vow."

RIB 1603 has DEO HVITRI as a further variation.

257 (245) A grammatical impossibility   Date unknown

RIB 1604. *Housesteads* (Vercovicium). *Altar found in 1898 in block VI in Housesteads fort. Now in Chesters Museum.*

Deo | veteriblus votulm.

DEO is singular, VETERIBVS plural. The intention is clearly to make a vow to this god or gods.

258 (209) Altar to Vinotonus Silvanus   ?Early 3rd. century AD

RIB 732. *Bowes, Yorkshire* (Lavatrae). *Altar of millstone grit, found in 1936 in a rectangular shrine near the Eller Beck. Now in the Bowes Museum, Barnard Castle.*

[Deo] | Vinotono | Silvano Iul(ius) | Secundus c(enturio) | coh(ortis) I Thrac(um) | v(otum) s(olvit) l(aetus) l(ibens) m(erito).

"To the god Vinotonus Silvanus, Julius Secundus, centurion of the First Cohort of Thracians, gladly, willingly and deservedly fulfilled his vow."

This and the next inscription were found in separate shrines on the Pennine moors. They commemorate successful hunting expeditions. Silvanus was the god of the country wilds and of hunting (see also nos. 190 and 213). Vinotonus was a stream-god whom the centurion identified with Silvanus. The First Cohort of Thracians was stationed at Bowes under Severus.

259 (210) Altar to Vinotonus   ?Early third century AD

RIB 733. *Bowes* (Lavatrae). *An altar of sandstone, found in 1946 in a circular shrine near the Eller Beck. Now on loan in the Bowes Museum, Barnard Castle.*

Deo Vinlotono | L(ucius) Caesius | Frontinus prlaef(ectus) coh(ortis) I Thrac(um) | domo Parma | v(otum) s(olvit) l(aetus) l(ibens) m(erito).

"To the god Vinotonus, Lucius Caesius Frontinus, prefect of the First Cohort of Thracians, from Parma, gladly, willingly, and deservedly fulfilled his vow."

Parma is in North Italy. The careful and elegant lettering of this altar contrasts with the firm, unadorned style of the previous one. The First Cohort of Thracians was stationed at Bowes under Severus.

(c) EASTERN DEITIES

260 (-) To Asklepios, Hygeia and Panakeia   Date unknown

JRS 59 (1969), 235 no. 3. Chester (Deva). Altar, found in 1968 on the Old Market site, possibly the praetorium. Now in the Grosvenor Museum, Chester.

πανυπειρόχα|ς ἀνθρώπων | σωτῆρας ἐν ἀθα|νάτοισιν Ἀσκληπιὸν ἠ|πιόχειρα Ὑγεί|ην Πανάκει|αν εἰητρὸς | [Ἀ]ντί[ο]χος | ...

"The doctor Antiochos *(honoured)* the saviours of men pre-eminent among the immortals, Asklepios of healing hand, Hygeia *(and)* Panakeia ..."

Doctors, often Greek themselves, naturally honoured the Greek gods of medicine and healing. *RIB* 1028, also by a doctor, honours Aesculapius and Salus, in a Latin inscription.

261 (215) Pulcher to Astarte   Date unknown

RIB 1124. Corbridge (Coria?). Altar found c. 1754. Now in Carlisle Museum.

Ἀστ[άρ]της | βωμόν μ᾿ | ἐσορᾶς· | Ποῦλχέρ μ᾿ | ἀνέθηκεν.

"You see me, an altar of Astarte; Pulcher set me up."

Pulcher was a *peregrinus*, lacking the *tria nomina* of a citizen. The altar probably came from the same shrine as *RIB* 1129, which was found at Corbridge in the seventeenth century. This is also a hexameter verse in Greek (now in the British Museum):

Ἡρακλεῖ | Τυρίω(ι) | Διοδώρα | ἀρχιέρεια.

"To Heracles of Tyre Diodora the priestess *(set this up)*."

These inscriptions are similar and form a pair. They indicate the presence at Corbridge of an exotic cult of Heracles (Hercules) and Astarte, worshipped (with Zeus) as a triad at Tyre from very early times. For other localised foreign cults cf. Dea Syria (Carvoran), no. 67; and Mars Thincsus and the Alaisiagae (Housesteads), nos. 234–236. Note also Serapis, no. 169, an Egyptian deity with a temple at York built by a legionary legate; and no. 66, a dedication to Sol Invictus by a detachment of the Sixth Legion.

262 (-) To Isis   3rd. century AD

Britannia 7 (1976), 378–379, no. 2. London (Londinium). Altar, found in Upper Thames Street, reused in the Roman riverside wall.

In h(onorem) d(omus) d(ivinae) | M(arcus) Martian |<n>ius Pulch|er v(ir) c(larissimus) leg(atus) | Aug(ustorum) pro | praet(ore) templ(u)m | Isidis C[...] | TIS vetustate | collabsum | restitui prae|cepit.

"In honour of the Divine House, Marcus Martianius Pulcher, of senatorial rank, governor of the emperors, ordered the temple of Isis *(some unintelligible word or words)* which had collapsed through old age to be restored."

V E may be the reading rather than V C, but produces problems. A *v(ir) e(gregius)* would be an equestrian, who cannot be a *legatus Augusti pro praetore*. A possible explanation would be that the stonecutter left out V A, *v(ice) a(gens)*, "acting", after V E, and the inscription should run *v. e. v. a. leg(ati)* etc., "of equestrian rank, acting governor of the emperors".

The reference to a temple of Isis immediately recalls the famous graffito on a flagon, LONDINI AD FANVM ISIDIS, "At London at (or near) the temple of Isis". It is probably derived from a burial in Southwark or the City. The flagon would normally be dated before *c.* AD 75, a very early date for the appearance of Isis worship in London. Isis is of course an Egyptian goddess, but her worship spread beyond Egypt; cf. the vivid description of her cult in Apuleius, *The Golden Ass*, where she delivers the hero from his transformation into an ass, and takes to herself the names of many classical goddesses. This is an extreme example of recognition of the same god under different names.

263 (237 n.) To Dolichenus   2nd. or 3rd. century AD

RIB 1131. Corbridge (Coria?). Altar, found in 1910 as a kerb-stone to the latest road-level south of Site XI. Now in Corbridge Museum.

> Iovi Aeterno | Dolicheno | et Caelesti | Brigantiae | et Saluti | C(aius) Iulius Ap|olinaris | c(enturio) leg(ionis) VI iuss(u) dei.

> "To eternal Jupiter of Doliche and to Caelestis Brigantia and to Salus, Gaius Julius Apolinaris, centurion of the Sixth Legion, at the command of the god (*set this up*)."

On the left side of the altar is a crowned Genius, with right hand held above an altar, and left hand supporting a cornucopia; on the right side a winged cupid with a sickle in its right hand and a bunch of grapes in its left; on either side of the capital is a head in a medallion.

Dolichenus was a sky-god whose worship centred on Doliche, in the Roman province of Syria. The cult enjoyed some popularity in the Roman army – cf. no. 101. The centurion of the Sixth links with worship of Dolichenus that of Brigantia, identified with Dolichenus's consort Juno Caelestis, and of the Roman god Salus.

264 (214) To Mithras   3rd. century AD

RIB 1545. Carrawburgh (Brocolitia). Altar found in 1949 in the Carrawburgh Mithraeum. Now in the Museum of Antiquities, Newcastle upon Tyne. (Fig. 8).

> D(eo) In(victo) M(ithrae) s(acrum) | Aul(us) Cluentius | Habitus, pra(e)f(ectus) | coh(ortis) I | Batavorum | domu Ulti|n(i)a Colon(ia) Sept(imia) Aur(elia) L(arino) | v(otum) s(olvit) l(ibens) m(erito).

> "Sacred to the Invincible god Mithras; Aulus Cluentius Habitus, prefect of the First Cohort of Batavians, of the Ultinian voting-tribe, from Colonia Septimia Aurelia Larinum, willingly and deservedly fulfilled his vow."

This is one of three altars all dedicated by prefects of the First Batavian Cohort. The top is flat and roughly chiselled to carry some feature which may

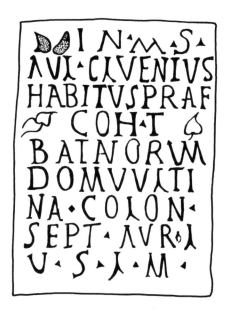

Fig. 8

have been a statue or a container for fire or water; on the face of the capital is a frieze of three eggs. The dedicator presumably belonged to the family of Aulus Cluentius Habitus, defended by Cicero in 66 BC, or was descended from a freed slave of that family, as the *nomen* CLVENTIVS is rare, and Cicero's client also came from Larinum.

Among the other *mithraea* known in Britain is one in London. Here in 1954 was found a collection of sculpture including a fine marble Mithraic relief. This carried the dedication VLPI|VS | SILVA|NVS | EMERI|TVS LEG | II AVG | VOTVM | SOLVIT | FAC|TVS | ARAV|SIONE – "Ulpius Silvanus, discharged from the Second Legion Augusta, initiated at Orange, has paid his vow" (*RIB* 3).

(d) CURSES

265 (-) A curse from Bath   4th. century AD

Britannia 13 (1982), 404–5, no. 7. *Bath (Aquae Sulis). Irregular rectangle cut from a leaden alloyed sheet, found in 1979 in the votive deposit recovered from the hot spring and Roman reservoir excavated beneath the floor of the King's Bath.* (Fig. 9).

> (a) *(after restoring normal letter order)*
> seu gen(tili)s seu C|
> h(r)istianus quaecumque utrum vir|
> [u]trum mulier utrum puer utrum puella |
> utrum s[er]vus utrum liber mihi Annian|o
> ma<n>tutene de bursa mea s(e)x argente[o]s |
> furaverit tu d[o]mina dea ab ipso perexi[g]|
> e[.eo]s si mihi per [f]raudem aliquam in DEP |
> REG[.]STVM dederit nec sic ipsi dona sed ut sangu|
> inem suum EPVTES qui mihi hoc inrogaverit.

"Whether pagan or Christian, whosoever, whether man or woman, whether boy or girl, whether slave or free, has stolen from me, Annianus, in the morning (?), six silver coins from my purse, you, lady Goddess, are to exact [them] from him. If through some deceit he has given me ..., and do not give thus to him, but [...] his blood who has invoked this upon me."

(b) *(18 personal names appear on other side)*

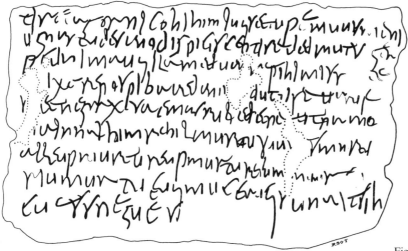

Fig. 9

Lead was the traditional material for "curse tablets", though at Bath most of them are alloys. The individual letters were written left to right, but with the sequence of letters reversed from beginning to end of (a) and in each line of (b), giving privacy to what is rather a prayer demanding justice than a magical curse. Of the 18 names ten are "Roman", including two of Greek etymology, and eight are "Celtic".

This is the first occurrence of the word CHRISTIANVS in the epigraphy of Roman Britain. Christianity is ignored otherwise by British curse tablets, except for the Eccles curse, *Britannia* 17 (1986), 431 no. 2, which may imply it.

The goddess addressed is Sulis Minerva: cf. nos. 212; 250–253. The complete collection of curses from Bath, together with a general discussion of "curse tablets", is published in Tomlin 1988. This curse appears as no. 98, with a few variations in the reading and interpretation: notably MA<N>TVTENE becomes "son of Matutina (?)" rather than "in the morning (?)" and (R)EPVTES is suggested for EPVTES, "reckon as (?) his blood". For the sacred spring see Cunliffe 1985.

266 (213) The Caerleon curse   Date unknown

RIB 323. *Caerleon (Isca). A lead plate found in 1927 in the arena of the amphitheatre. Now in Caerleon Museum.*

Dom(i)na Nelmesis do ti|bi palleum | et galliculas | qui tulit non | redimat ni | vita Sanguinei | sui.

> "Lady Nemesis, I give thee a cloak and a pair of boots; let him who wore them not redeem them except with the life of his blood-red charger."

The writing is disjointed and barely legible, so that different interpretations are possible. The interpretation in *RIB* is that of Egger. Another possible translation (reading SANGVINE SVO: there is little certainty about these two words) is: "let him who took them (TVLIT for ABSTVLIT) not pay for his crime except with his own blood." This would imply that the author has had articles of clothing stolen and that he is putting a curse on the thief. The cloak and boots are promised to the goddess if she returns them; or perhaps "handed over" to her temporarily so that she may curse the illicit wearer.

Other curses found in amphitheatres (e.g. at Carthage and Carnuntum) express ill-will towards particular performers. An altar to Nemesis was found in 1966 at the Chester amphitheatre: *JRS* 57 (1967), 203 no. 5. Nemesis is the goddess of justice who punishes human pride and arrogance; she might bring hope to worthy but less successful gladiators.

267 (236) Silvianus to Nodens   Date unknown

RIB 306. Lydney Park, Gloucestershire. A lead plate found in 1817. Now in the site museum at Lydney Park.

Primary text:

Devo | Nodenti Silvianus | anilum perdedit | demediam partem | donavit Nodenti | inter quibus nomen | Seniciani nollis | petmittas sanita|tem donec perfera(t) | usque templum [No]dentis.

Secondary text: Rediviva.

"To the god Nodens: Silvianus has lost his ring and given half its value to Nodens. Among those who are called Senicianus do not allow health until he brings it to the temple of Nodens."

"*(This curse)* comes into force again."

Devo, anilum, perdedit, demediam, nollis and *petmittas* might more correctly have been spelt *Deo, anulum, perdidit, dimidiam, nolis* and *permittas*. Nodens was a complex Celtic god, associated with healing, hunting, the sea and lost property (see Lewis 1966, 88–92). Some time must have elapsed before Silvianus, still without his ring, felt that he had to renew his curse and added the single word REDIVIVA above the original inscription. A gold ring inscribed with the name SENICIANE (vocative of Senicianus) was found at Silchester in 1953, *RIB* 2.3.2422.14. The situation is complicated by the formula following the name, VIVAS I<I>N DE(O), "May you live in God", which suggests that this Senicianus was a Christian; but the ring also possesses an earlier dedication to Venus which suggests a previous owner. Tomlin's caution in his comments on *RIB* 2.3.2422.14 over the identification of the two Seniciani seems justified.

268 (-) A curse from Uley   Between 2nd. and 4th. century AD

Britannia 19 (1988), 485–487 no. 2. Uley, Gloucestershire. Found in 1978 at the temple of Mercury on West Hill. Rounded oblong cut from sheet lead. Now in the British Museum.

Reconstructed text:

Biccus dat Mⁱercurio quidquid ǀ pe(r)d(id)it si vir si mⁱascel ne meiat *(trans-posed)* ǀ ne cacet ne loquaⁱtur ne dormiat ǀ n[e] vigilet nec s[a]l[l]utem nec salⁱnitatem neⁱss[i] in templo ǀ Mercurii perⁱtulerit ne co(n)ⁱscientiam de ǀ perferat ness[i] ǀ me intercedenⁱte.

"Biccus gives Mercury whatever he has lost *(that the thief)*, whether man or male *(sic)*, may not urinate nor defecate nor speak nor sleep nor stay awake nor [have] well-being or health, unless he bring (it) in the temple of Mercury; not gain consciousness *(sic)* of (it) unless with my intervention."

It is possible that NE TACEAT "may not be silent" has fallen out after NE LOQVATVR "may not speak". SI VIR SI MASCEL, "whether man or male" is a confusion of *si vir si femina*, "whether man or woman", with *si mascel si femina*, with the same meaning. *nessi = nisi*.

This is one of a collection of 140 lead tablets (86 inscribed), found during excavation of the temple complex. They were distributed through all levels from the 2nd. century onwards, with a concentration in late 4th. century destruction deposits and in unstratified/ploughsoil contexts. An interim report on the collection is published in Woodward and Leach 1993, 113–130, where this appears as no. 4.

(e) CHRISTIANITY

269 (-) Church plate   ?4th. century AD

RIB 2.2.2414.2. *Chesterton* (Durobrivae), *Cambridgeshire. Part of a silver cup or bowl. Found in 1975 within the Roman town. Now in the British Museum.*

(a) *in single-stroke capitals around the rim:*

Sanctum altare tuum Dⁱomine subnixus honoro.

"Prostrating myself, Lord, I honour your sacred sanctuary."

(b) *in the same lettering, on the outside of the base:*

Publianus. *Probably the subject of* (a).

A Chi-Rho between A and Ω comes before SANCTVM, a second separates D from OMINE. The text forms a hexameter. This cup or bowl is part of a collection of items of precious metal (often referred to as the Water Newton hoard) which appears to consist of church plate. The collection comprises one gold object (a roundel) and 27 of silver (9 vessels, 17 plaques and some fragments of silver sheet).

270 (215n.) A Christian tombstone?   4th. century AD

RIB 955. *Carlisle* (Luguvalium). *Tombstone found in 1892 in the Roman cemetery on Gallows Hill, Carlisle. The lower part has been broken off. Now in Carlisle Museum.*

D(is) M(anibus) ǀ Fla(viu)s Antigon(u)s Papias ǀ civis Gr(a)ecus vixit annos ǀ plus minus LX quem ad ǀ modum accom(m)odatam ǀ fatis animam revocavit ǀ Septimia Do[…].

"To the spirits of the departed: Flavius Antigonus Papias, a citizen of Greece, lived sixty years, more or less, and gave back to the Fates his soul lent for that period of time. Septimia Do[...] *(set this up)*."

RIB rates this as "probably Christian". PLVS MINVS is said to be "characteristically Christian", implying an indifference to the length of time spent in this life; *animam reddere* is used on Christian tombstones elsewhere, and REVOCAVIT in the sense of "restored" can be paralleled. There is as yet no certain example of a Christian tombstone from Roman Britain; this is perhaps the most promising candidate.

271 (-) A mysterious word-square   ?2nd. century AD

RIB 2.4.2447.20. Cirencester (Corinium). A fragment of red wallplaster, on which is incised a palindromic word-square. Found in 1868 at Victoria Road, Cirencester. Now in Corinium Museum, Cirencester.

ROTAS
OPERA
TENET
AREPO
SATOR

"Arepo the Sower holds the wheels carefully."

AREPO is a personal name otherwise unattested, required to make the word-square possible. Examples of this word-square are widely distributed in the Roman Empire, including Pompeii (dated to before AD 79) and Dura Europos (third century AD). It can be read forwards, backwards, upwards and downwards to give the same words. The letters can be rearranged to form PATER NOSTER, "Our Father", twice over by using the central N twice, the remaining letters, two As and two Os, being understood to stand for the Greek letters Alpha and Omega, titles of Christ in *Revelation* 1.8. TENET also forms a cross. This apparent Christian connection is more difficult to sustain now that recent examples from Budapest (early second-century) and Manchester (late second-century) seem too early for a credible Christian association. (For the Manchester example see *Britannia* 10 (1979), 353, no. 34). There is also one, perhaps in a first-century context at Conimbriga, Portugal. The conclusion in the *RIB* commentary on this, on which the comments above are based, is that the word-square was certainly adopted by Christians in post-Constantinian times; in earlier centuries Christians used it, but others did so also. Its origins go back to the first century and are obscure.

PART IX: WRITING TABLETS

272 (-) A stilus-tablet   ?1st. or 2nd. century AD

RIB 2.4.2443.2. *London* (Londinium). *Wooden stilus-tablet, recessed on one face, found in or near the Walbrook, in or before 1934. Now in the British Museum.*

On the plain (outside) face, a branded circular stamp:
Proc(uratores) Aug(usti) dederunt | Brit(anniae) | prov(inciae).

"The imperial procurators of the province of Britain issued (this)."

On the recessed (inside) face there are traces of about five lines of lettering. The original message would have been written with a stilus on wax filling the recess, the traces being left by the stilus penetrating to the wood beneath. The branded stamp authenticates the document. There was the procurator of the province and various procurators concerned with different aspects of the emperor's affairs; it is not clear who is acting together here. Tile-stamps have been interpreted as referring to *p(rocuratores) p(rovinciae) Bri(tanniae) Lon(dinio?)*, "procurators of the province of Britain at London", see *Britannia* 16 (1985), 193–196. These are collected and discussed in *RIB* 2.5.2485. Cf. no. 24 above, the tombstone of Iulius Classicianus, for a provincial procurator in London by the 60s AD, and no. 134 above for an imperial freedman acting as assistant to "procurators" at Combe Down.

273 (-) A military strength report   Last decade of 1st. century AD

Tab. Vindol. 2.154. Chesterholm (Vindolanda). A diptych found in the ditch of the pre-Hadrianic fort of Period 1: it is probable that the tablets found here in fact belong to Period 2.

xv K(alendas) Iunias n(umerus) p(urus) [co](hortis)	
i Tungrorum cui pra(e)est Iulius Verecundus	
praef(ectus) dcclii in is (centuriones)	vi
ex eis absentes	
singulares leg(ati)	xlvi
officio Ferocis	
Coris	cccxxxvii
	in is (centuriones) ii
Londinio	(centurio) [i]
(fragmentary lines 10–16 not reproduced)	
summa absentes	cccclvi
	in is (centuriones) v
reliqui praesentes	cclxxxxvi
	in is (centurio) i
ex eis	
aegri	xv
volnerati	vi
lippientes	[x]

summa eor[um]	xxxi
reliqui valent[es	cc]lxv
	in [is (centurio) i]

"18 May, net number of the First Cohort of Tungrians, of which the
commander is Iulius Verecundus the prefect,   752

including centurions 6,	
of whom there are absent:	
guards of the governor	46
at the office of Ferox	
at Coria	337
including centurions (?)2	
at London centurion	1
(lines 10–16 not translated here, though numbers legible)	
total absentees	456
including centurions 5	
remainder present	296
including centurion 1	
from these:	
sick	15
wounded	6
suffering from inflammation of the eyes	10
total of these	31
remainder, fit for active service	265
including centurion 1	"

This is one of a handful of records of the actual strength of units, apart
from a relatively large number of late date, all referring to the same unit, from
Dura Europos. It is the only one found so far in Britain, and the only one
anywhere which is not written on papyrus, as it belongs to the enormous
number of ink writing-tablets produced by Vindolanda. It is unique in being
the actual strength of a *cohors milliaria peditata*, the infantry unit nominally
one thousand strong, in this case the Cohors I Tungrorum, known from the
evidence of other tablets to be at Vindolanda at this time. Oddly it has only
six centurions, appropriate for the smaller size unit, the *cohors quingenaria
peditata*, not the ten appropriate to the larger unit. This suggests perhaps that
the unit is in process of enlargement. A total of 752 would fit the larger unit,
800, ten centuries of 80 men, being its most probable theoretical strength.
Many men are absent: 46 are detached as guards of the provincial governor;
no fewer than 337 are at Coria, which as noted above, no. 51, is thought to
be Corbridge on the strength of this and other Vindolanda documents. Of the
296 men present, 31 are unfit for duty, which is not a remarkable percentage
for military units, *pace* Bowman and Thomas 1994, 98, who think it is. There
is no need to think of the wounded as wounded in battle; accidental injuries
are common enough. The number away from the fort shows how real was the
problem Trajan saw (Pliny, *Letters*, 10.22): *curandum, ne milites a signis absint*,
"Care must be taken that the soldiers be not away from their units" (standards, literally), and how insoluble it was.

274 (-) British cavalry   *c.* AD 97–*c.* 102/3

Tab. Vindol. 2.164. Chesterholm (Vindolanda). *A diptych found in Room IV, Period 3?*

> … nenu [.]n Brittones | nimium multi equites | gladis non utuntur equi|tes nec residunt | Brittunculi ut iaculos | mittant

> "… the Britons are unprotected by armour (?). There are very many cavalry. The cavalry do not use swords nor do the wretched Britons mount in order to throw javelins."

This is apparently "a military memorandum of some kind describing the fighting characteristics and qualities of the native Britons with particular reference to cavalry" (Bowman and Thomas 1994, 106). It may be understood to refer to hostile Britons, or to the suitability for recruitment of native Britons. There is no certain reference to native British cavalry fighting against the Roman army. Bowman and Thomas 1994, 107 cite Tacitus *Agricola* 36 as evidence, but this clearly refers to the Roman cavalry. Formation of Britons into a Roman cavalry regiment seems assured by the existence of an *ala I Britannica*, but Kennedy, 1977 argued that this title only indicated that the regiment had been stationed in Britain. This text is the first definite evidence that Britons fought as cavalry, whether against or for Rome. If it does refer to the quality of native recruits, NIMIVM must be translated with its primary meaning of "too many". This would then mean that too many Britons wanted to be taken on as cavalry, as opposed to infantry (cavalry were better-paid) but they were unsuitable for the reasons stated. BRITTVNCVLI, "wretched Britons", is noteworthy as a term of contempt.

275 (-) A soldier's letter   *c.* AD 97–102/3

Tab. Vindol. 2.310, as published in Bowman and Thomas 1994, 289–294. Chesterholm (Vindolanda). *A diptych found in Room VIA, Period 3.*

> i
> Chrauttius Veldeio suo fratri | contubernali antiquo pluri|mam salutem. et rogo te Veldei frater miror | quod mihi tot tempus nihil | rescripsti a parentibus nos|tris si quid audieris aut | Quot.m in quo numero | sit et illum a me salutabis | <s> *(letter s crossed out by the scribe)* verbis meis et Virilem | veterinarium rogabis | illum ut forficem

> ii
> quam mihi promissit pretio | mittas per aliquem de nostris | et rogo te frater Virilis | salutes a me Thuttenam | sororem Velbuteium | rescribas nobis cum | se habeat *vacat* | opt(o) sis felicissimus | vale

> *Back:* Londini | Veldedeio | equisioni co(n)s(ularis) | a Chrauttio | fratre

> "Chrauttius to Veldeius his brother and old messmate, very many greetings. And I ask you, brother Veldeius – I am surprised that you have written nothing back to me for such a long time – whether you have heard anything from our elders, or about … in which unit he is; and greet him from me in my words and Virilis the veterinary doctor. Ask him (*Virilis*)

whether you may send through one of my friends the pair of shears which he promised me in exchange for money. And I ask you, brother Virilis, to greet from me our sister Thuttena. Write back to us how Velbuteius is (?). (*2nd. hand?*) It is my wish that you enjoy the best of fortune. Farewell. (*Back, 1st. hand*) (Deliver) at London. To Veldedeius, *equisio* of the governor, from his brother Chrauttius."

VELDEDEIVS seems to be the correct form of the name of the addressee, as VELDEDII occurs on a leather off-cut from Vindolanda, discovered on the floor of a room near to the find-spot of this tablet and identified as belonging to horse equipment, appropriate for an *equisio*.

It is the general view that FRATER here, "brother" is simply a term of affection, not of relationship, cf. no. 276, as a true brother would hardly be addressed as an "old messmate". A further difficulty is that Chrauttius seems to be Germanic and Veldedeius seems to be Celtic. This of course means that "parents" also cannot be literal, and that "sister" is simply a term of affection, as in no. 277. An alternative view that could perhaps be considered is that the relationships were real: if the two brothers had served together for some time, which is not unparalleled, "old messmate" might be used almost playfully. The names of the two brothers would then reflect some oddity in a mixed frontier population. "Parents" could then be taken literally; "sister" remains ambiguous.

Thuttena, whatever her relationship to Chrauttius, is one of the few women referred to, other than officers' wives, in connection with the Roman army. Another possible example is in *Tab. Vindol.* 2. 181, *contubernalis Tagamatis*, which it is suggested refers to the unofficial "wife" of a soldier. Bowman and Thomas (1994, 290) argue that LONDINI, a locative, must imply that the letter had been sent to Veldedeius in London, and had simply been received in London and brought to Vindolanda. An *equisio*, apparently the same as a *strator*, was a groom, but in later contexts *stratores* have the job of inspecting horses bought for the army. Veldedeius could either be accompanying the governor or engaged in official business. Alternatively he could have been detached for service in London as the governor's *equisio*, and had now returned to his unit at Vindolanda, carrying with him this old letter.

276 (-) Concerning supplies   ?c. AD 104–120

Tab. Vindol. 2.343. Chesterholm (Vindolanda). Room XIV, Period 4. Two complete diptychs.

i

Octavius Candido fratri suo | salutem | a Marino nervi pondo centum | explicabo e quo tu de hac | re scripseras ne mentionem | mihi fecit aliquotiens tibi | scripseram spicas me emisse | prope m(odios) quinque milia proplter quod (denarii) mihi necessari sunt | nisi mittis mi aliquit (denariorum)

ii

minime quingentos futurum | est ut quod arre dedi perdam | (denarios) circa trecentos et erubeslcam ita rogo quam primum aliquit | (denariorum) mi mitte coria que scribis | esse Cataractonio scribe | dentur mi et karrum

de quo I scribis et quit sit cum eo karro I mi scribe iam illec petissem I nissi
iumenta non curavi vexsare I dum viae male sunt vide cum Tertio I de
(denariis) viii s(emisse) quos a Fatale accepit I non illos mi *vacat* accepto
tulit

iii

scito mae explesse <exple> *(surplus letters crossed out by the scribe)* coria
I clxx et bracis excussi habeo I m(odios) cxix fac (denarios) mi mittas ut
possiIm spicam habere in excussoIrio iam autem si quit habui I perexcussi
contuberInalis Fronti amici hic fuerat I desiderabat coria ei adIsignarem et
ita (denarios) daturI<ur>us erat dixi ei coria inItra K(alendas) Martias
daturum Idibus

iv

Ianuariis constituerat se venturIum nec intervenit nec curavit I accipere cum
haberet coria si I pecuniam daret dabam ei FrontiInium Iulium audio
magno liceIre pro coriatione quem hic I comparavit (denarios) quinos I
saluta Spectatum I ... I -rium Firmum I epistulas a Gleucone accepi
val(e)

Back: Vindol

"Octavius to his brother Candidus, greetings. The hundred pounds of sinew
from Marinus – I will settle up. From the time when you wrote about this
matter, he has not even mentioned it to me. I have several times written
to you that I have bought about five thousand *modii* of ears of grain, on
account of which I need cash. Unless you send me some cash, at least five
hundred *denarii*, the result will be that I shall lose what I have laid out as
a deposit, about three hundred *denarii*, and I shall be embarrassed. So, I
ask you, send me some cash as soon as possible. The hides which you write
are at Catterick – write that they be given to me, and the wagon about
which you write. And write to me what is with that wagon. I would have
already been to collect them except that I did not care to injure the animals
while the roads are bad. See with Tertius about the eight and a half *denarii*
which he received from Fatalis. He has not credited them to my account.
Know that I have completed the 170 hides and I have 119 *modii* of threshed
bracis. Make sure that you send me cash so that I may have ears of grain
on the threshing-floor. Moreover, I have already finished threshing all that
I had. A messmate of our friend Frontius has been here. He was wanting
me to allocate (?) him hides, and that being so, was ready to give cash. I
told him I would give him the hides by 1 March. He decided that he would
come on 13 January. He did not turn up nor did he take any trouble to
obtain them since he had hides. If he had given the cash, I would have
given him them. I hear that Frontinius Iulius has for sale at a high price
the leather ware (?) which he bought here for five *denarii* apiece. Greet
Spectatus and ... and Firmus. I have received letters from Gleuco. Farewell.
(Back) (Deliver) at Vindolanda."

The ink was still wet when this was folded. It has been written in two columns
but beginning with the right-hand one, suggesting that the writer was left-
handed. Spectatus and Firmus seem to be military personnel, being known from

Tab. Vindol. 2.180. Firmus had been responsible for issuing supplies to legionaries, and it has been suggested that some or all of the people referred to may be legionary centurions. A number of identifications have been suggested for Candidus, who also seems to be military, including a Candidus on *Tab. Vindol.* 2.180, 181. The tablet comes from the rooms at the end of the barrack, which should be the centurion's quarters. Bowman and Thomas (1994, 322) think some or all of the people might be *optiones*, as concerned with supplies. Who Octavius himself was is uncertain, whether civilian or military. The sums of money and quantity of goods involved are considerable. It is difficult to be sure what is going on here, in view of the uncertainties about the people involved, and our lack of knowledge on how the army was supplied. It is certainly the procuring of supplies on a large scale, presumably for the army's needs, and quite possibly from a civilian contractor, with some fascinating details. There is archaeological evidence from Catterick for a leather production centre, cf. Burnham and Wacher 1990, 111–117.

277 (-) Invitation to a birthday party   *c.* AD 97–102/3

Tab. Vindol. 2.291. *Chesterholm* (Vindolanda). *Room VIA, Period 3.*

i
Cl(audia) Severa Lepidinae [suae | sa]l[u]tem | iii Idus Septembr[e]s soror ad diem | sollemnem natalem meum rogo | libenter facias ut venias | ad nos iucundiorem mihi

ii
[diem] interventu tuo factura si| [.].[*c.3*]s *vacat*
Cerial[em t]uum saluta Aelius meus .[|
et filiolus salutant *vacat*
vacat sperabo te soror | vale soror anima | mea ita valeam | karissima et have

Back: Sulpiciae Lepidinae
Cerialis
a S[e]vera.

"Claudia Severa to her Lepidina greetings. On 11 September, sister, for the day of the celebration of my birthday, I give you a warm invitation to make sure that you come to me, to make the day more enjoyable for me by your arrival, if you are present (?). Give my greetings to your Cerialis. My Aelius and my little son send him (?) their greetings.
(*2nd.hand*) I shall expect you, sister. Farewell, sister, my dearest soul, as I hope to prosper, and hail. (*Back, 1st. hand*) To Sulpicia Lepidina, wife of Cerialis, from Severa."

Claudia Severa is the wife of Aelius Brocchus. He was a commanding officer, perhaps stationed at Briga, the location of which is not known. She has added a note in her own hand to the birthday invitation, the earliest known example of writing in Latin by a woman. Sulpicia Lepidina is the wife of Flavius Cerialis, prefect of the Ninth Cohort of Batavians at Vindolanda.

INDEX 1: NAMES OF PERSONS MENTIONED IN THE TEXTS

Listed by *nomen* (or *cognomen* if *nomen* unknown)

Members of imperial family in capitals under the name by which they are commonly known: e.g. HADRIAN (not P.AELIUS HADRIANUS)

Aelius: 277
L. AELIUS: 49
Aelius Antoninus: 148
P. Aelius Erasinus: 102
Aelius Mansuetus: 157
Aemilius Aemilianus: 84
Aemilius Crispinus: 112
Aemilius Salvianus: 83
Aessicunia: 265
Agricola: 88
Alauna: 265
Albanus: 9
Albia Faustina: 185
L. Alfenus Senecio: 79, 80, 81, 83, 85, 86, 87
A. Alfidius Olussa: 207
Amandus: 173
Ammonius: 191
Anencletus: 224
Anicius Ingenuus: 193
P. Anicius Maximus: 16
Anicius Saturninus: 132
Annianus: 265
Fl. Antigonus Papias: 270
Antiochus: 260
C. Antistius Frontinus: 164
L. Antistius Lupus Verianus: 45
Antonianus: 246
ANTONINUS PIUS: 46, 51, 52, 53, 54, 55, 56, 57, 58, 60, 61, 62, 63, 68, 146
Antonius Lucretianus: 130
C. Arrius Domitianus: 59
Atticus: 161
T. Attius Tutor: 219
M. Aufidius Maximus: 251
L. Aufidius Pantera: 196
M. Aurelius Alexander: 170
Aurelius Arpagius: 119
T. Aurelius Aurelianus: 82
Aurelius Iulianus: 85
M. Aurelius Lunaris: 153
Aurelius Macrinus: 133
M. Aurelius Quirinus: 109, 110
M. Aurelius Salvius: 104
Aurelius Senecio: 150
Aurelius Tasulus: 230
C. Aurelius Verus: 217
Aurunceius Felicessemus: 240
Avitianus: 265

Barat(h)es: 203, 204
Biccus: 268
Breucus: 33

Caecilius Avitus: 171
Caecilius Lucanus: 68
L. Caesius Frontinus: 259
Calliopis: 265
Sex. Calpurnius Agricola: 65, 66, 67
C. Calpurnius Receptus: 252
Calventius Celer: 27
Candidina: 265
Candidus: 194
Candidus: 276
Capitonius [...]scus: 62
CARACALLA: 75, 76, 78, 79, 80, 81, 83, 85, 86, 89, 90, 93, 94, 95, 97, 98, 99, 100, 134
CARAUSIUS: 115, 116, 117
Cassavus: 210
Cassius Martialis: 176
Cassius Sabinianus: 111
Celatus: 223
Celerianus: 265
[...] Celsus: 128
Censorinus: 228
Cerialis: 277
Cesennius Senecio: 96
C. Cesennius Zonysius: 96:
Chrauttius: 275
Cintusmus: 213
Claudia Catiotu[os]: 150
Claudia Martina: 224
Claudia Severa: 277
Claudia Prima: 7
CLAUDIUS: 14, 20, 21, 22, 23
Ti. Claudius Cogidubnus: 137
Ti. Claudius Cyras: 21
Ti. Claudius Hermas: 21
Claudius Hieronymianus: 169
Ti. Claudius Paulinus: 102, 139
Ti. Claudius Primus: 237
Ti. Claudius Seleucus: 7
Ti. Claudius Tirintius: 12
Claudius Xenephon: 106
CLODIUS ALBINUS: 74
A. Cluentius Habitus: 264
Colasuni, The: 223
Commius: 1, 4

INDEX 2: ARMY UNITS

INDEX 3: GODS AND GODDESSES

INDEX 4: LATIN TITLES

INDEX 5: BUILDINGS AND MONUMENTS

INDEX 6: GEOGRAPHICAL NAMES

INDEX 7: FIND-SPOTS OF INSCRIPTIONS

(The numbers and letters in brackets indicate the coordinates on the
map on the last page)

GLOSSARY

actarius

Senior soldier on the staff of an officer commanding a unit, with responsibility for keeping records.

actor

Person who acts on someone's behalf, agent or steward.

ala

Basic meaning "wing". Applied under the Republic to allied infantry or cavalry, who normally fought on the wings (flanks). Under the Empire it designates an auxiliary cavalry regiment.

ansatus
(Eng. *ansate*)

With a triangular projection with base outwards at either end of a panel.

beneficiarius

Senior soldier serving on the staff of an officer commanding a unit, or, in the case of a legion, serving on the staffs of other officers down to tribune.

catafractata

Epithet indicating that a cavalry regiment was heavily armoured.

cohors

An auxiliary infantry regiment, or a subdivision of a legion.

cohors equitata

A unit of infantry with a cavalry element attached to it.

cornicularius

Senior soldier in charge of the writing-office of a governor, legionary or auxiliary commander, of the prefect of the camp of a legion, or of the prefects of the guard.

equo publico

An equestrian sometimes mentions this grant of a "public horse", which seems to mean that the man concerned had taken part in the annual ride-past of the equestrians in Rome, the *transvectio*, a relic of the equestrians' original role as the cavalry of Rome.

hospes

Can mean host or guest; used in connection with the emperor it presumably implies the first, and a close friendship.

legatus Augusti pro praetore

The official title of the governor of an imperial province, as he is simply delegated that particular responsibility by the emperor as proconsul. He himself may be an ex-praetor or an ex-consul, depending on the importance of the province: the title is the same in either case.

milliaria

This, meaning literally a thousand strong, is applied to *alae* and *cohortes* which are of a larger size than the standard-size units, which are *quingenaria*.

numerus

This means basically a unit which is neither an *ala*, *cohors* nor a legion.

Pia Fidelis

These epithets, "Pious and Loyal", generally refer to some past display of loyalty by the unit which earned it the right to these titles in perpetuity.

pontifex maximus

"Chief priest", a dignity held exclusively by the emperors from Augustus onwards, and numbered among their official titles.

praeses

An informal name for governor which becomes the formal title in the later empire.

quingenaria

This, meaning literally five hundred strong, is used to distinguish the smaller size of auxiliary cohorts and *alae*.

BIBLIOGRAPHY

Allason-Jones, L. 1989: *Women in Roman Britain*. London.

Birley, A. R. 1979: *The People of Roman Britain*. London.

Birley, A. R. 1981: *The Fasti of Roman Britain*. Oxford.

Birley, A. R. 1988: *Septimius Severus: the African Emperor*. London.

Birley, E. B. 1983: A Roman altar from Old Kilpatrick and interim commanders of auxiliary units, *Latomus* 42, 73–83.

Birley, E. B. 1961: *Roman Britain and the Roman Army*. Kendal.

Birley, E. B. 1966: Review and discussion of R. G. Collingwood and R. P. Wright, *The Roman Inscriptions of Britain I: Inscriptions on Stone, Journal of Roman Studies* 56, 226–31.

Bogaers, J. E. 1979: King Cogidubnus: another reading of *RIB* 91, *Britannia* 10, 243–54.

Bowman, A. K. and Thomas, J. D. 1983: *Vindolanda: the Latin Writing Tablets*. Britannia Monograph No. 4. London.

Bowman, A. K. and Thomas, J. D. 1991: A military strength report from Vindolanda, *JRS* 81, 62–73.

Bowman, A. K. and Thomas, J. D. 1994: *The Vindolanda Writing-Tablets (Tabulae Vindolandenses II)*. London.

Bowman, A. K., Thomas, J. D. and Adams, J. N. 1990: Two letters from Vindolanda, *Britannia* 21, 35–52.

Breeze, D. J. and Dobson, B. 1969–70: The development of the mural frontier in Britain from Hadrian to Caracalla, *Proc. Soc. Antiq. Scot.* 102, 109–21.

Breeze, D. and Dobson, B. 1987: *Hadrian's Wall*. Harmondsworth.

Burnham, B. C. and Wacher, J. 1990: *The Small Towns of Roman Britain*. London.

Casey, P. J. 1979: Magnus Maximus in Britain: a reappraisal, in P. J. Casey (ed.), *The End of Roman Britain*. British Archaeological Reports 71, London, 66–79.

Casey, P. J., Davies, J. L. and Evans, J. 1993: *Excavations at Segontium (Caernarfon) Roman Fort, 1975–1979*. CBA Research Report 90. London.

Collingwood, R. G. 1928: Inscriptions of Roman London, in RCAHM, *An Inventory of the Historical Monuments in London. Vol. III. Roman London*, Appendix II, 170–77.

Collingwood, R. G. and Richmond, I. A. 1969: *The Archaeology of Roman Britain*. London.

Cunliffe, B. 1985: *The Temple of Sulis Minerva at Bath. Vol. 1. The Site*. Oxford University Committee for Archaeology, Monograph No. 7.

Dobson, B. 1972: Legionary centurion or equestrian officer? A comparison of pay and prospects, *Ancient Society* 3, 194–207.

Dobson, B. 1978: *Die Primipilares. Entwicklung und Bedeutung Laufbahnen und Persönlichkeiten eines römischen Offiziersranges*. Cologne.

Dobson, B. and Mann, J. C. 1973: The Roman Army in Britain and Britons in the Roman Army, *Britannia* 4, 191–205.

Donaldson, G. H. 1988: Signalling communications and the Roman Imperial Army, *Britannia* 19, 349–56.

Donaldson, G. H. 1990: A reinterpretation of *RIB* 1912 from Birdoswald, *Britannia* 21, 207–14.

Frere, S. S. 1987: *Britannia: a History of Roman Britain*. 3rd edition. London.

Hanson, W. and Maxwell, G. 1983: *Rome's North West Frontier: the Antonine Wall*. Edinburgh.

Harris, E. and Harris, J. R. 1965: *The Oriental cults in Roman Britain*. Leiden.

Hassall, M. 1978: Britain and the Rhine provinces: epigraphic evidence for Roman trade, in J. du Plat Taylor and H. Cleere (eds), *Roman Shipping and Trade: Britain and the Rhine Provinces*. CBA Research Report 24, 41–48.

Haverfield, F. 1918: Roman Cirencester, *Archaeologia* 19, 1917–18, 161–200.

Haynes, I. P. 1993: The romanization of religion in the *auxilia* of the Roman imperial army from Augustus to Septimius Severus, *Britannia* 24, 141–58.

Hooley, J. and Breeze, D. J. 1968: The building of Hadrian's Wall: a reconsideration, *Archaeologia Aeliana* 4th series 46, 97–114.

Hull, M. R. 1958: *Roman Colchester*. Report of the Research Committee of the Society of Antiquaries of London. London.

Hurst, H. 1988: Gloucester *(Glevum)*, in G. Webster (ed.), *Fortress into City: the consolidation of Roman Britain, First Century AD*. London, 48–73.

Jarrett, M. G. 1976: *Maryport, Cumbria: A Roman fort and its Garrison*. Kendal.

Jarrett, M. G. 1976b: An unnecessary war, *Britannia* 7, 145–51.

Jarrett, M. G. 1978: The case of the redundant official, *Britannia* 8, 289–92.

Jarrett, M. G. and Mann, J. C. 1970: *Britain from Agricola to Gallienus, Bonner Jahrbücher* 170, 178–210.

Joliffe, N. 1941: Dea Brigantia, *Archaeol. J.* 98, 36–61.

Kennedy, D. 1977: The ala I and cohors I Britannica, *Britannia* 8, 249–55.

Keppie, L. J. F. 1979: *Roman Distance Slabs from the Antonine Wall: a brief guide*. Glasgow.

Keppie, L. J. F. 1991: *Understanding Roman Inscriptions*. London.

Keppie, L. J. F. 1995: The IXth Legion in Britain, in R. Brewer (ed.), *Roman fortresses and their legions. Essays in honour of George Boon*. Cardiff.

Lewis, M. J. T. 1966: *Temples in Roman Britain*. Cambridge.

Lewis, N. and Reinhold, M. 1966: *Roman Civilization: Sourcebook I: The Republic; II: The Empire*. Harper and Row, New York.

Mann, J. C. 1969: *The Northern Frontier in Britain from Hadrian to Honorius: Literary and Epigraphic Sources*. Privately printed.

Mann, J. C. 1971: Spoken Latin in Britain as evidenced in inscriptions, *Britannia* 2, 218–24.

Mann, J. C. 1977: The Reculver inscription – a note, in D. E. Johnson (ed.), *The Saxon Shore*, CBA Research Report 18, London, 15.

Mann, J. C. 1991: Numinibus Aug. *Britannia* 22, 173–77.

Marsden, P. 1980: *Roman London*. London.

Marsh, G. 1979: Nineteenth and twentieth century antiquities dealers and Arretine ware from London, *Trans. London and Middlesex Archaeol. Soc.* 30, 125–129.

Maxfield, V. A. 1981: *The Military Decorations of the Roman Army*. London.

Maxfield, V. A. (ed.) 1989: *The Saxon Shore: a Handbook*. Exeter Studies in History No. 25. Exeter.

Painter, K. 1977: *The Water Newton Early Christian Silver*. London.

Reece, R. 1989: Lympne, in V. A. Maxfield (ed.), *The Saxon Shore: a Handbook*. Exeter Studies in History No 25. Exeter.

Rivet, A. L. F. and Smith, C. 1979: *The Place-Names of Roman Britain*. London.

Robertson, A. S. 1980: The bridges on Severan coins of AD 208 and 209, in W. S. Hanson and L. J. F. Keppie (eds), *Roman Frontier Studies* 1979. Oxford, 131–40.

Roxan, M. M. 1990: *RIB* 2401: the Diplomata, in *RIB* II. 1, 1–2.

Salway, P. 1981: *Roman Britain*. Oxford.

Southern P. 1989: The Numeri of the Roman Imperial Army, *Britannia* 20, 81–140.

Stevens, C. E. 1937: Gildas and the civitates of Britain, *English Historical Review* 52, 193–203.

Stevens, C. E. 1941: Gildas Sapiens, *English Historical Review* 56, 353–73.

Stevens, C. E. 1966: *The Building of Hadrian's Wall*. Kendal. (Reprint of an article first published in *Archaeologia Aeliana* 4th series 1948, 10–49).

Swan, V. 1992: Legio VI and its men: African legionaries in Britain, *Journal of Roman Pottery Studies* 5, 1–34.

Syme, R. 1958: *Tacitus*. Oxford.

Todd, M. 1981: *Roman Britain 55BC–AD400*.

Tomlin, R. S. O. 1983: Non Coritani sed Corieltauvi, *Antiq. J.* 63, 352–3.

Tomlin, R. S. O. 1988: The curse tablets, in B. Cunliffe (ed.), *The Temple of Sulis Minerva at Bath*. Oxford. Vol. 2, 59–277.

Tomlin, R. S. O. 1992: The twentieth legion at Wroxeter and Carlisle in the first century: the epigraphic evidence, *Britannia* 23, 141–58.

Tomlin, R. S. O. 1993: Roman towns and Roman inscriptions of Britain, 1939–89, in S. J. Greep (ed.), *Roman Towns: the Wheeler Inheritance. A review of 50 years' research*. CBA Research Report 93, 134–46.

Wenham, L. P. 1939: Notes on the garrisoning of Maryport, *Trans. Cumberland and Westmorland Antiq. and Archaeol. Soc.* 39, 19–30.

Whittick, G. Clement 1982: Roman Lead-Mining on Mendip and in North Wales, *Britannia* 13, 113–23.

Woodward, A. and Leach, P. 1993: *The Uley Shrines. Excavation of a ritual complex on West Hill, Uley, Gloucestershire*: 1977–9. English Heritage Archaeological Report No. 17. London.

Wright, R. P. 1974: Carpow and Caracalla, *Britannia* 5, 289–92.

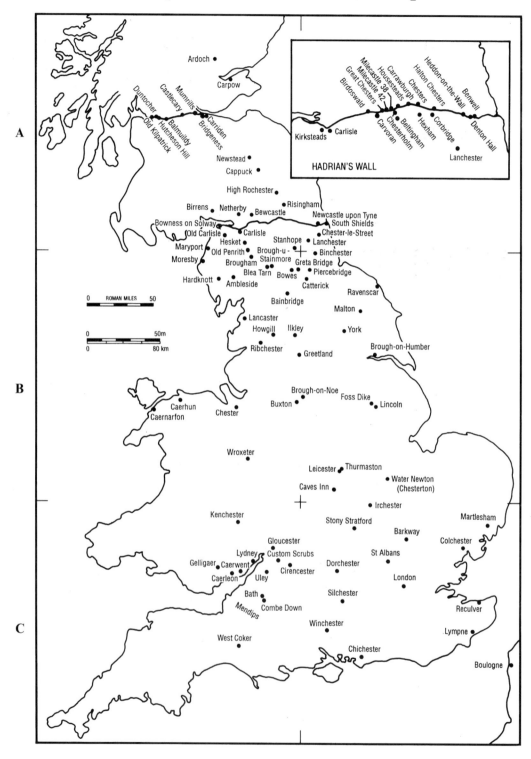

1

2

Ardoch

Carpow

Duntocher
Old Kilpatrick
Castlecary
Balmuildy
Hutcheson Hill
Mumrills
Carriden
Bridgeness

A

Newstead

Cappuck

High Rochester

Birrens Netherby Bewcastle Risingham

Bowness on Solway Newcastle upon Tyne
Old Carlisle Carlisle South Shields
Maryport Hesket Stanhope Chester-le-Street
Moresby Old Penrith Brough-u- Lanchester
Brougham Stainmore Binchester
Hardknott Blea Tarn Bowes Greta Bridge
Ambleside Piercebridge
Catterick

Ravenscar

Bainbridge Malton

ROMAN MILES 0 50

Lancaster
Howgill Ilkley York
0 50m
0 80 km
Ribchester Brough-on-Humber

Greetland

B

Brough-on-Noe Foss Dike
Caerhun Buxton Lincoln
Caernarfon Chester

Wroxeter

Leicester Thurmaston
Water Newton
Caves Inn (Chesterton)

Irchester
Kenchester Martlesham

Stony Stratford Barkway Colchester

Gloucester Custom Scrubs St Albans
Lydney
Gelligaer Caerwent Cirencester Dorchester
Caerleon Uley London
Bath Silchester
Mendips Combe Down Reculver

Winchester
C Lympne
West Coker
Chichester
Boulogne

Inset: HADRIAN'S WALL

Birdoswald
Great Chesters
Milecastle 42
Milecastle 38
Housesteads
Carrawburgh
Chesters
Halton Chesters
Heddon-on-the-Wall
Benwell

Kirksteads Carlisle Carvoran Chesterholm Bellingham Hexham Corbridge Denton Hall

Lanchester

HADRIAN'S WALL